WILL I EVER FIND LOVE AGAIN?

*One Man's Journey through grief
and loneliness to new hope*

DR. ARNOLD L. STAUFFER

Will I Ever Find Love Again?
One Man's Journey through grief and loneliness to new hope
by Dr. Arnold L. Stauffer

Printed in the United States of America

ISBN 9781628713091

www.xulonpress.com

Comments

From Facebook Support Group Members
who followed Arnold's journaling

James D. Janzen: A privilege to be invited and to join this group and be part of what the Lord wants to do. Arnold, it is hard to express the powerful impact of your open sharing on my life. Thank you again and again. I read all your posts and am learning so much. Thank you for blessing me in your pain. Your insights minister to me.

Louise Holwerda: Thank you so very much for this blog, Arnold. I have cried with you, our family has prayed for you. You have also really helped me grieve my dad's passing away when I was 20 (nineteen years ago). I did not grieve properly – didn't know how, and the memories and hurt were stuffed away. I now cry most every day, in a healthy way, for a relationship snatched away too early, and have resurrected long put away pictures, and am now openly living with his memory and celebrating his life and working through the sadness. God be praised!

Makiko: Arnold, what I appreciate about this site is that you are real and you don't sugarcoat what's happening. It helps me understand the reality of what's going on. Thank you for being willing to share with us. We continue to keep you close in our hearts and lift you two up in our prayers. I am sorry for your pain.

Joyce: You are a gifted writer in articulating your thoughts and emotions so well. It is cathartic for you, and helpful to others who have gone, or are going through similar circumstances. You give us a lot to think about. **Lyle**: You are adding beauty and grace to a fearsome journey. **Irene**: You should write a book! **Jan**: What a joy to read your heart! You are so gifted and it means so much to me. Thank you for sharing your heart. **Amanda**: You are an amazingly talented writer Uncle Arnold. It's so refreshing to see such an honest expression of grief and hope. **April**: Arnold, write a book, you are an amazing writer! **Glenna**: So lovely, Arnold! Your love and commitment to Betty has been a great example. **Colleen**: Arnold, how happy we are for your new found love. I will be one of the first to buy your book.

Suzan: Hey Unc, can't wait to see what else you teach us. Your book will be truly inspiring and full of times to laugh, cry and end up on bended knee for all God has done for you. We will be inspired, blessed and encouraged by each word you write.

Ann: We marvel at your tenacious faith as you trust our loving Father to do what he thinks is the best. You have given all us a lesson in realizing how we should treasure our spouses while we have them. The journaling of your grieving is amazing, putting into words what many feel but are unable to express so well. You refresh and bless others.

Dr. Martin Reedyk: Arnold: I have so appreciated your transparency and seeing your Christ like grieving. I have been very inspired.

Will I Ever Find Love Again?
One Man's Journey through grief
and loneliness to new hope

Written/Edited by Arnold L. Stauffer, D.Miss.

I remember my afflictions and my wandering. . .
I well remember them,
and my soul is downcast within me.
Yet this I call to my mind,
and therefore I have hope:
Because of the Lord's great love we are not consumed,
for his compassions never fail.
They are new every morning;
great is your faithfulness.
I say to myself, "The Lord is my portion;
therefore I will wait for him."
The Lord is good to those whose hope is in him,
to the one who seeks him;
it is good to wait quietly
for the salvation of the Lord.

. . . .

For men are not cast off
by the Lord forever.
Though he brings grief, he will show compassion,
so great is his unfailing love.
For he does not willingly bring affliction
or grief to the children of men.

Lamentations 3:19-26; 31-33 NIV

Weeping may remain for a night,
but rejoicing comes in the morning.
Psalm 30:5

I will sing of your strength,
in the morning I will sing of your love;
for you are my fortress,
my refuge in times of trouble.
Psalm 59:16

To my son, Todd
and
my daughter, Tara
whom your Mother loved so much,
as do I

And to the members of my Facebook Support Group,
who helped me turn page after page of sorrow, grief and sadness
into hope, victory and joy

Contents

Preface

This is not your usual story, or genre. It is not a novel. Perhaps you might call it a documentary of sorts, but written by the participants. Someone called it part blog. This heart of this book records the journal of the devastating evil of cancer that brought dying and death, followed by grief, loneliness, and aloneness. But this story ends well, the result of much care, prayer and counsel from the supporting, believing community and the discovery of new hope.

You will see a thread throughout the story – the touch of God's hand, found in his repeated fingerprints from beginning to the end. You will discover the story's essence in the community of believers who invested their time and energy in comforting, caring and counseling the main characters throughout. You will meet two of the main characters in the introduction: Arnold and Betty.

Told in four parts, the first consists of excerpts from a journal written by Betty as she describes her first battle – with breast cancer. You will go with her to clinic visits, operations, radiation, and experience her fear of its return. And you will observe how she repeatedly turned to her Lord for sustenance and relief from this fear.

The second part reproduces the Facebook Support Group dialogue between Arnold and a group of relatives and close friends. It was established originally to keep these folks updated regarding Betty's planned operation for a cyst on her pancreas. Then following many clinic visits came the doctor's devastating news, that she has inoperable pancreatic/liver cancer. Arnold reports daily for months to this caring group that eventually grew to 153. He daily journalled the month at home while looking after Betty, and for the next month when he lived with her in the palliative care unit in the local hospital. Then the third part describes the aftermath of the dying and death and how he dealt with the absence of his Love of 48 years. Finally, out of the anger and questions of grief and loneliness came his plaintive cry, "Will I ever find love again?"

Out of Arnold's heart and mind poured a series of difficult emotionally laden questions and heart rending complaints. He struggled with grief, anger, and wondered where God was. Why did he not honour his word to heal? How come such a lovely lady had to suffer so much? In his loneliness and aloneness after Betty left, he struggled with the sense of dishonoring her when he wondered if he should marry again. Each of these matters he worked through on his computer and passed them on to "The Group". Then he looked for responses from the members to calm his soul and mind, who always enabled him to turn the page to the next matter.

In part four you will read the wonderful finale of this tale, the thrilling ChristianMingle story of Internet love, Facebook and Skype courting and then the start of a new life.

Part two illustrates the power of community. The responses from the members of the Facebook Support group surprised Arnold. At his heaviest times he daily wrote several pages, and then checked in three or four times each day to read these responses. Always they were helpful, comforting and encouraging. Often the people who posted on Facebook simply promised their prayers, and sometimes that was all there was to say.

At the end Arnold states to the group, "But the benefit has been mostly mine. Every day I shared with you my struggles and issues with the most difficult series of events in my life. To write my feelings every day was a deeply meaningful therapy that helped me process each new phase and to turn the page to the next one. As my painful thoughts surfaced on the computer screen they translated from one language to another, from abstract difficult-to-understand thoughts, to concrete statements that now I could better deal with. . . .This journaling and your responses saved me – helped me to move along instead of wallowing in my disappointment, sorrow, loneliness and grief. Sometimes I hesitated to post some thoughts because they were so deep and so personal. But always I decided to do so because I wanted to tell you the whole story, not just parts."

These counselors helped him survive a difficult experience over several months. His posted "essays" that grappled with sometimes very personal issues helped and encouraged his counselors. He wondered why and concluded that few people have had the opportunity to walk alongside a person whose loving spouse had reluctantly left in death. His grieving process helped other grievers along their path to wholeness.

Dozens of those who he helped in his journaling encouraged the publishing of this story.

Here it is, with the hope from Arnold and his counselors that you also will be blessed. And perhaps be helped to find the courage to travel your own difficult path, whatever deep valley you may be passing through.

1

Introduction: Arnold and Betty Meet

R ita Holloway and her pre-teen daughter, Betty, walked across the Gull Lake Bible Camp yard toward the dining hall. Suddenly she stopped and pointed to the children's sand box and said to her daughter, "See that little girl with the long ringlets in her hair – she has seven brothers!"

This was Betty's introduction to the Stauffer Family. Later, as a teenager, she got to know one of these brothers, Virgil, at the summer camp and one year they exchanged a couple of "love" letters after camp. However, nothing long term developed in this relationship – a very brief teenage romance.

Betty and I crossed paths several times over the following years, at Camp Meeting or summer kids' camp, but did not get interested in each other till Bible College. Like many college students I occasionally thought of looking for a marriage partner, and certainly would have liked to have a girlfriend. So I started looking and Betty often came to my attention. I was a teaser and discovered I could make her laugh. She responded by passing on to me most of her care packages from home – goodies like cookies and fudge made by her Mom who I quickly discovered was a great cook.

Other students began to notice our rather casual interest in each other and several decided that a relationship for us was made in heaven. So they set about to get us together. As a result we ended up on the same committees and were the official photographers for three years for the student yearbook.

I was not too happy about getting "pushed" together; I had this macho attitude that made me want to engage in my own conquests, not have others decide for me. However, I found out when Betty's musical practices were and often visited her there while she was supposed to be practicing. It was kind of neat because we were alone for a few minutes of chit chat. Getting alone on campus was difficult; too many people everywhere.

At the end of our first year we had a couple of dates, one going to the city for an event with two other couples. Over the summer we exchanged several letters, just newsy epistles about what we were doing and thinking. Not really love letters. By the end of the summer I started getting some misgivings about getting any more serious in this relationship, so I broke it off before we got back to college in September.

Our story repeated the next year: pushed together, a couple of dates at the end of the school year, and writing over the summer, then I callously cut it off before school started in the fall. I just was not ready to settle down, yet.

At the end of the third year, I started to "smell the coffee," as Betty later described what happened. A ton of love dropped down from above and seriously enveloped me. I don't know a better way to explain what happened as I fell madly in love with Betty. She may have attracted this passionate response in me by starting to date the most popular sought-after guy at the school, Walt.

We were both on a weekend long choir trip. Whenever we stopped on the road or at a church, I had this inordinately powerful desire to be near her, just to be in her presence. This just happened. I was suddenly consumed with this passion for Betty, and as surprised by this development as was Betty.

As we traveled on the bus toward the college that Sunday evening, I struggled with what to do about this totally new experience. I knew I was in love, deeply and irreversibly taken over by this oldest passion in the history of the human race. What to do about it? As I pondered this matter I realized that I would have to do something about Walt. And the other matter, I had unceremoniously dropped Betty two summers in a row. Would she take another chance on me when she had a crack at Walt? Didn't seem likely.

When we got back to the boys' dorm I sat on my bed for a few minutes working up enough courage to go down to the other end of the hall to talk to Walt. Finally, I walked into his room, sat on the bed opposite him and tried to get the words out. "Walt, I am interested in Betty and wondering if it would be okay with you if I asked her out." I was treading softly here because I did not know how serious his relationship was with Betty.

Walt knew about my on-off relationship with Betty and asked, "Well. . .are you serious this time?" Hesitating only a moment, I replied, "I've never been more serious about anything in my life!" Walt the gentleman, said, "Arnold, if that is the way you really feel, then go ahead. We really do not have a very serious relationship. We're just friends."

Man o man! What a relief. I thanked Walt and danced back to my room. Immediately I began to plan my next move in this strategic endeavor to win back the heart of this lady I'd spurned twice and now deeply yearned to reverse this position. What does a College Guy do next? Well. . .same as a high school fellow. You go find the gal's best friend and check out the lay of the land.

I found Hannah, Betty's friend and Breakfast Cook partner, and asked her if she thought Betty would go out with me. She hesitated far too long, I thought, but promised to find out and let me know. She asked Betty if she would go out with me and the rather forceful reply was, "You gotta be kidding! There is no way I am going to hurt Walt!" Hannah asked, "Do you really think he would be hurt?" After thinking about this she realized that Walt probably would not be hurt. He and Betty had agreed that they were "just friends". Hannah told Betty, then, that Walt had already given me permission to ask her out. But Betty did not want to be hurt by me again.

However, by the next morning, after searching her heart, Betty realized she still had feelings for me and said, "Okay." Phase Two: A Success.

The next day, Monday, I asked Betty to go with me to Wednesday Dress-up Supper. Each Wednesday we all put on our best threads and could sit with a date for this special meal. We would meet upstairs in the waiting room and then go down to the basement dining room for the meal. No one suspected that Betty and I were a "date" as male and female were mixed at the tables anyway.

After supper Betty and I had some work to do on a huge chart, which we spread out on the dining room floor. Just her and me. Wow! A perfect set up. After working an hour I was taking a break, sitting on a table. I asked her to come and we chatted for a bit. Finally, I had built up enough courage to tell her I loved her. Surprised, she asked, "Are you sure, this time?" I assured her that I had never been more sure of anything. I then asked her if she would come out to my folks the next day to help me put together a project for one of my courses. They lived just five miles out of town on the farm where I had grown up.

She came, and we worked in the living room till mid-night. We were both exhausted. I snuggled over to her on the chesterfield, took her hand, and asked her to marry me. After a brief hesitation, a wonderful smile communicated her response, along with, "Yes, Arnold, I will!"

I had already checked with the local jeweler for engagement rings. He had just what I knew she would like – a solitary diamond for $180. I didn't have any money so I sold the double pedestal mahogany desk I'd made in Grade 12 Shop class to the guy across the hall for $35. An old car to my kid brother for $15, along with a box of tools. Somehow I was able to scrape together another $10 to make an even $60, the one-third down payment the jeweler required. Friday I picked up the ring.

Friday evening we went with my folks to Red Deer for a birthday party for one of my kid brothers. Riding in the back of an old red Ford panel truck, sitting on an ancient wooden bench, we at least got to snuggle a bit and hold hands. I warned Betty that my older brother, Curly, would be there. When he saw her he would say quite pointedly, with a grin of course, "Betty, this is a family get-together, you have no right to be here!" I suggested that then she should simply take off her glove and push her ringed finger into his face. He said it as I predicted and she did. Perhaps the only time in his life, Curly was dumbfounded and totally speechless. With all this commotion in the entry way, everyone present soon found out that Betty and Arnold were engaged. This stole the attention away from the real purpose of the party but it certainly was great fun. But the excitement had only begun.

We swore everyone to secrecy till Monday. At 6:30 am I stopped by the College kitchen where Betty and Hannah were cooking Breakfast. We told Hannah we were engaged and she went into orbit, ran upstairs to the Girl's Dorm on the third floor, where twenty or so female students were attempting to wake up and prepare for another day. She shouted, "Betty's engaged! Betty's engaged!" A first-year student, who had no knowledge of Betty's and my history, stuck her head out her door and asked, "Who to?"

Then at 7:00 am Betty and I stopped by the President's office, stepped up to his desk and announced our engagement. He jaw dropped and all he could say was, "Well. . .well. . . .well!"

Monday, Betty phoned her Mom and asked, "Mom, can you get ready for a wedding this Fall?" After a moment of silence on the other end, Betty heard, "Well. . .isn't this all of a sudden?" Walt had just visited the last week end, and this was the first time Mom knew she was having anything to do with him. "Mom, it's not who you think. Arnold and I are getting married!" Her Mom responded with great relief as I had been to the farm several times and seemed to have won over the hearts of her whole family. I'd had great fun playing with Betty's young brothers and sister, helped out with chores as well as laid tile on the kitchen floor. So the wedding was on.

We were madly in love, and this was exam week. An emotional high does not make writing exams any easier. We survived the week, finding as much time as possible to be together, and eventually discovered that we both did okay on all our courses.

That summer we ran head-on into a tough decision. Betty had applied for Nurse's training. A few weeks after we both graduated from College and were planning an October wedding, she received her acceptance into the program. Married women were not allowed into it, neither could they be married during the three-year program. This was something she had badly wanted and now had to decide between me and becoming a Registered Nurse.

When she presented this problem to me I rather naively said, okay. If she wanted to take this program I would wait the three years. She pondered and prayed about this for only a week and opted for me. She had a pretty good idea that I would not be around in three years, so decided to not take the chance. We tied the knot October 5, 1963 and were married for 48 years and two and a half months.

We had two children, a son and a daughter. Our son, Todd, and his wife, Lisa, gave us three lovely granddaughters. Tara married David Zimmerman and they gifted us with four wonderful grandchildren, two girls and two boys.

Both our children were adopted. We experienced four miscarriages, including one son born at seven and a half months, who lived for an hour and a half. After ten years of marriage we decided to adopt. Both our son and daughter arrived nine months after we applied through the Province of Alberta adoption services.

It was an exciting moment when we travelled to Edmonton to pick up our red-headed son. Betty held him first. I had wondered what my feelings would be. Could I really accept him as my son? It happened instantaneously. The moment Betty handed him to me he was my wonderful, adorable, much loved child.

A year went by and we decided Todd should have a little sister. One of the advantages of adoption, you have choices. Whether you want a boy or girl, when you want delivery, what colour hair, and so on. On the adoption application was a line for any Special Requests. I wrote, "Todd has red hair and it would be nice for him to have a red-headed sister." One of the welfare agents had red hair, which in those days was not so popular as it is today. She discovered this lovely new baby blessed with red hair. She requested from her supervisor the privilege of placing this little one. She flipped through the files and found our Special Request. We got our very special strawberry blond daughter.

Over the years we had lots of fun with our two carrot tops! In the grocery store it seemed half the people we met stopped to admire them as they sat together in the shopping cart. One lady exclaimed, "I've tried to get that color out of a bottle for thirty years!"

Often they wondered where they got their red hair. Humorously, I would sometimes say, "From their step Grandmother." Half the time the person would accept that. Betty had a step Mother and seven step siblings with red hair. No genes involved here! However, sometimes a person would press us, and we would tell them they were adopted. Usually this comment caused them some embarrassment. But the adoption was not at all a problem for us to talk about. We discussed with both of them about their physical heritage from the beginning. We wanted no surprises later in life. When they were both in high school we discussed the possibility of them searching for their birth parents. Our purpose was to take any tension out of such a possibility. They were not the least bit interested. Tara exclaimed somewhat passionately, "Why would we want to do that?"

In 1993 we moved to Three Hills, Alberta, where I was to become the Associate Dean of Prairie Bible College and Graduate School. My job was to head up the Distance Education Department. The same year we moved we sold our restaurant business. Todd left home for work and Tara spent the next year attending Bible College in Calgary.

Every family could tell a thousand stories about raising children. I am tempted to site a few here but this is not what this book is about.

Betty was a wonderfully devoted Mother. She doted on her children and did not go to work until they both had started school. At two and a half months Todd was diagnosed with cystic fibrosis. For a month she drove an hour every day to spend the day with him in the Calgary Children's Hospital. Then daily, for years, she gave him physical therapy several times a day. So tender hearted, she found it difficult to discipline them, so that responsibility became mine.

When they both left home at the same time she experienced the empty nest syndrome for several months. I jokingly said that for me it was only twenty minutes. Suddenly I had realized that I no longer had to eat spaghetti, pizza, and lasagna, or macaroni and cheese every week. Now I could help choose the menu for dinner!

My job at Prairie lasted for fourteen and a half years. Betty began work in Three Hills at the Red Rooster convenience store where she started at 4:30 AM to do the baking and open up. Later she worked as receiver and clerk in the Prairie Book Room until she retired.

In the meantime, I engaged my hobby of creating woodart from barnboard. And Betty became famous for her multi-grain bread, muffins, and sticky buns.

21

Part One

Our Introduction to Cancer

2

Betty's First Cancer Attack

"Arnold, why don't you start selling your wood art at the Farmers' Market?" For a moment I thought about this suggestion from Betty, and then replied, "Okay. I will if you come along with your bread and buns."

Since we married in 1963 Betty baked our bread and buns. She was told so many times, "Betty, you should be selling these buns. They are the best I have eaten anywhere!" Family expected several dozen of her dinner buns to arrive at our campouts and Christmas get-togethers. Her buns, stuffed with roast beef or turkey, or slathered with butter and honey – something to cross the ocean for! Grandkids would leave their veggies and turkey and eat one or two of them, if they could get away with it, with nothing on them.

So we made a pact. We would team up to market our wares. Ten years earlier I tore down a granary that my Dad had built 65 years before. The weather over that period had produced a wonderful bright grey finish on the siding which I salvaged and began re-making it into shelves, cupboards, boxes and trunks. My seven siblings all wanted a piece of Dad's granary. They'd all probably shoveled grain or chop in it many times (well, maybe not Lil). Then the nephews and nieces heard about the granary project and wanted a barnboard souvenir from Grampa's farm.

When I had finally satisfied all of these requests, the stack of wood had disappeared. I had become a wood artisan and the hunt for more barnboard was on. Later my nephew, Richard, helped me build a 28 x 36 foot woodworking shop in our backyard, which I dubbed my Barnboard Woodart Studio. I understood that if you let folks know that you crafted your work of art in your 'Studio' rather than a garage or workshop, they will gladly pay you five times as much.

Since then I've "processed" dozens of other granaries and ancient shops and sheds. I had been doing well with sales at the Three Hills Christmas Markets, and now Betty and I began attending the regular Market from May through September. Her multi-grain bread and buns, sticky buns and freshly baked muffins were an immediate hit. She was soon selling to folks all the way from Calgary to Rocky Mountain House.

A lady from Rocky one day stopped by our table to admire Betty's wonderful lightly browned multi-grain loaves. I gave her a tongue-in-cheek caution, as I often did, "I need to warn you, Ma'am, that you must be prepared to deal with an addiction with your first bite of that bread!" She smiled and picked up a couple of loaves. Two weeks later she phoned Betty, and said, "Your husband was right, I need more of your multi-grain loaves." She often passed through town to pick up several freshly baked loaves of multi-grain.

Tuesday was Market day so Betty would bake all day Monday, prepare four large pans of sticky buns to rise over night, and get up at 5:00 am on Market day to bake them. At the same time she would bake six dozen muffins so customers could purchase fresh products. I would pack up these culinary delights and get them to the Market where we also served coffee and tea. Then on Wednesday she would bake for local customers who would drop by the house to pick up their special orders. This was our schedule for the Market season from May through the end of September. During her last two years I also managed the Market.

Christmas Market 2006. As regulars we got the best spot just inside the door. Three tables, two covered with woodart, and the first one by the door with bread and buns and Christmas tea rings. I sat waiting for customers when Betty walked in, just back from a visit to the doctor which just happened to coincide with Market day. We looked at each other for a moment and I knew immediately that the news was bad. "The doctor says it is cancer." I was dumfounded. The perpetual optimist, I "knew" the pain she had been experiencing in her breast was not from Cancer, the Big C. But now I just stood there, with dozens of folks all around, both vendors and Christmas shoppers – speechless. It really was Cancer.

More medical appointments as the doctors did tests and decided on a course of action to fight the cancer. I went with her to all of them. Finally, the cancer surgeon at the Calgary Foothills Hospital removed the cyst as I sat in the room and chatted with them and with Betty. In the middle of the surgery I offered to get them a hot chocolate or coffee, attempting to bring a bit of levity to the situation. All three declined.

Betty soon started a six-week regime of radiation at the hospital and then stayed during the week at our daughter's in Bragg Creek, a half hour away. For the next six years she regularly went for tests and they never did find any more Cancer in this area of her body.

I think that Betty expected to get cancer. Several relatives had died of cancer and her father had cancer when he passed away. The Big C was part of her ancestry. Medical folks assume that if it is prevalent in your family your chances of having it are very high.

Betty knew about pain, diagnosed years before with fibromyalgia, an arthritic-like condition only in the soft tissue rather than in the joints. Well acquainted with all the available pain killers, she often took them in the evening in order to sleep through the night. And every time she would discover a new pain, for the six years following her bout with breast cancer, we would fearfully wonder, "Is the Big C back? Is this the cancer returning?"

But it was not; her first cancer did not return. When in October 2011 she was diagnosed with pancreatic/liver cancer, the nurse in the oncologist's office (the chemical poison doc) told her that she was one of the few people on the planet who experienced a second cancer that was in no way related to the first. Not a very satisfying statistic!

We met with the oncologist (the chemotherapy guy) a couple of weeks later. Here four different medical personnel interviewed her with the usual questions and a few more. Long before this she had learned to bring a list of her half dozen meds along with a bag of them in bottles to show these interrogators. Everywhere she went for various tests they asked her the same list of questions about her medical history and current situation. Even I had it all memorized, although she could also spiel off the technical names of all her meds.

I questioned the doc when he arrived, "What is the life expectation for this type of cancer?" He said, "We don't know." Not an answer. "Well. . .what do the statistics tell you?" He realized that we wanted the facts, so said, "Five or six months." I was shocked. We were assuming several years. In the Foothills I had said to Betty when we received the diagnosis, "We are going to do this right. Our first goal is to reach our 50th Wedding Anniversary." We had just celebrated our 48th a couple of weeks previously, so that seemed a reasonable goal. Not to be. Two months later she was gone. Forever.

Betty had assumed she would be taking chemotherapy, just as she had done the radiation for her breast cancer six years earlier. But I had done my own research so had a couple more questions. I asked the oncologist what he could promise us the chemo would do. He said that symptoms may improve so she would not have to take as much pain medication, or they might not. She may live another month, but may not. "So the only thing that you can promise us is that her immune system would be compromised," something he had not mentioned. He agreed and informed us that she would probably get sores in her mouth and other conditions could develop. "But," he said, "I would like to confer with four of my colleagues before recommending chemo treatment. I will telephone you with our recommendation." He then went on a week's vacation. Ten days after our visit he informed Betty that they wanted her to start the chemo.

I was angry. What kind of logic was this? We cannot promise you anything good, only the misery provided by the chemotherapy. And prolonged misery at that – but do it anyway. These docs, I concluded, were knowledgeable about how to poison you with their chemicals but did not know a whole lot about cancer. I had questioned the oncologist about the cause of cancer. He had hesitated, sort of shrugged his shoulders, and said, "Probably all the chemicals we are exposed to." What did they want, her to be part of some kind of experiement?

The diagnosis of pancreatic cancer was a death sentence. Her pancreas would gradually shut down and she would starve. Already in the Foothills Betty was finding it difficult to eat. Her desire for food was entirely gone and she ate very little. The thought of eating turned her off, and from that point on her intake continued to decrease until finally she only took a bit of applesauce only to help her pain pills go down. She starved to death.

This book is our story, my story. How do I describe it? The devastating news of a second cancer. No real treatment for it. Sent home from the hospital with no hope but a visit with an oncologist who wanted to make both our lives more miserable, with more suffering and then starvation death. Watching my wife of 48 years gradually deteriorate at home for a month then a second four weeks while living with her in the palliative care suite at the local hospital. A lovely, wonderful, caring lady gradually ravaged by this evil disease. Gradually starving to death while her lower body ballooned from water retention. A very efficient hard-working caring woman – my Country Girl I called her – now helplessly lying in bed for most of the 24 hours each day. Fading, drugged, and me, her primary problem solver for 48 years, helplessly standing by, watching her and wondering where God was.

This is our story, my story, and how we dealt with this heart rending devastation of a gruesome dying by cancer. And my grief and loneliness.

The next chapter includes excerpts from Betty's journal of her first experience with breast cancer. It is her personal record of the pain and fears during this difficult period, and how she dealt with these. Perhaps her struggle will encourage you to carry on when you are living in not the best of times. I have significantly condensed it, and include some of her comments.

But my story is not over. As the book title says, my journey into grief and super loneliness morphed into hope, new love and renewed life. I tell about my exciting deliverance from this loneliness.

But first, read Betty's part of this story.

3

Fear and Faith

This first section was written by me, Arnold, based on Betty's comments and actions. I wrote it as though she were writing it. In doing this I intended to give Betty the encouragement to start recording her experience as I knew it would be good therapy for her. I have condensed her journal in order to tell her story, and have included some of her key comments as quotes.

November 30, 2004.

I telephoned three brothers (Betty said), "I have some news for you that I have always hoped I would never have to give you! On November 26, three days before, I was called to the doctor's office to be informed of the devastating fact that the biopsy taken a week earlier in Calgary was cancerous."

My brothers tried their best to give me encouragement and hope. . .in spite of the fact that cancer was rampant in our family. An uncle with this cell destroying disease in his pancreas, an aunt with cancer of the ovaries, three cousins – two with breast cancer – one died. My Dad had prostate cancer when he died. This was all on my Father's side of the family. My Mom's brother died this year with cancer.

The dreaded question at the doctor's office was, "What is your family history?" I have a lousy family history. Oh yes, my Grandfather also had cancer.

Questions and terrorizing fears fix my mind and emotions all day and keep me awake at night. Like a horror movie with me as the star that keeps playing over and over because I cannot find the off button.

My breasts. They are a vital part of what I am, of my femininity. When people find out are they going to look?

My husband enjoys them – what will he think? Will this affect our relationship if surgery leaves me malformed? How will he deal with this? Will he think less of me?

I cry. Sometimes in the darkness of night when Arnold is doing his usual snoring. Sometimes in the middle of the day with him holding my hand.

Betty started her journal on December 8, 2004. It was hard for her to go back over all the pain, the unknowns, waiting, wondering, and sleepless nights. She had first heard the bad news in early October, at work. Someone at the Grace Hospital mammogram department phoned: "I'm Sorry Betty, but you will have to come back for a second mammogram. There is a lumpy area they need to look at."

Next the Doctor in Three Hills sent her to a specialist. On November 18 the lump was removed by local freezing. Arnold was present for the procedure, sitting in a chair a few feet from her.

November 26 the local Doctor informed her of a malignancy. "This sent shock waves through my whole body," she wrote. "I tried to prepare myself for that possibility but didn't want to believe it was true. The receptionist said I could have an appointment to see the Surgeon on Monday. There would have to be further surgery – possibly a mastectomy, radiation, chemotherapy. This can't be happening – *but it is.*"

The local doctor asked if she was a Christian, then prayed with her, asking for healing and God's peace. He had not believed the original mammogram. They had said to come back in six months for another look. With her family history of cancer he moved quickly by sending her to a specialist. She remembers him saying, "Thank Goodness, I did not listen to the advice of the mammogram report and wait six months!" The cancer surprised the Surgeon. He called it invasive duct carcinoma. They will have to remove more tissue and check the lymph nodes.

Saturday was a long day. Panic permeated and came in waves. Betty spent time at the Farmers' Market with Arnold because she didn't want to be alone. Both Lisa (daughter-in-law) and Tara (daughter) called during the day and were shocked by the news. Sunday the Elders prayed for us after the service. "Arnold," Betty wrote, "is being strong and positive and is a great source of strength, but it is so hard."

"One thing I am learning", she wrote, "is to not pull away from the people that love me when I am in a situation like this. I need their strength and encouragement so much. As we drove home that night, we talked about how this will affect me and us. I was overcome with sorrow and sobbed. It can't be real – but it is." She called her family with the devastating news and had our daughter phone Arnold's family.

Betty wrote: "Days were filled with grief. Nights – I have come to refer to 'the demons that come in the night.' I sing praise songs and quote scripture to put the tormenting thoughts out of my mind, but it doesn't always work. Some nights I take a sleeping pill, and that helps, but they do not work if I take them too many days in a row." Betty had some good days and some bad ones, some nights spent awake and often crying. Sometimes we cried together. I held her while she cried. She wanted to live!

Surgery in two to three weeks, more extensive than before. Healing for eight weeks, and then four to five weeks of radiation, five days a week. In the meantime she baked – did orange braids for her work mates for Christmas and delivered them. People were kind; many assure us they are praying. Betty reads her Bible every morning, crying to God for strength.

December 9 she read Psalm 63:6-8: "On my bed I remember you; I think of you through the watches of the night, because you are my help. I sing in the shadow of your wings. I stay close to you; your right hand upholds me."

"Last night I dreamed we were standing in a collection of something like Arnold's display of trunks. There was a box that was discolored and rusty looking and I kept staying away from it for a long time until I realized that it stood for a cancer survivor and it was okay to stand close to it. I slept more peacefully after that. Arnold says this is our answer to prayer."

On December 31 she had her second surgery. When we got home a message on the answering machine said, "When fear knocked on the door I answered it with faith and no one was there." She wrote: "Surgery is over and I'm home. What a relief! The past two weeks have been more relaxed then the weeks before. So many people have been encouraging and saying they are praying. There have still been some nights when sleep evaded me but I feel as though I'm being upheld. Lil has sent encouraging emails often."

The next day her devotional reading was Habakkuk 2:4b: "The righteous will live by his faith." Schwyn Hughes says, "Those who tear through life, never pausing for prayerful thought and consideration, must stop and get a hold of this: the just shall live by faith. God knows what He is doing, so trust him."

Another day she read Habakkuk 2:4, and then wrote this quote in her diary: "God is showing us that there are only two possible attitudes to life – faith or unbe-lief. . .philosophy of the just – those who have a sense of certainty in spite of adverse circumstances. Life, when stripped to its irreducible minimum consists of one of two attitudes: we take what God says and live by it, or else we do not." (*Everyday with Jesus*)

Daily she received strength and courage from her devotions. She read Luke 8:48, "Jesus said, 'Daughter, you took a risk trusting me, and now you are healed and whole. Live well, live blessed." She commented, "Trusting Jesus is not a risk for me as it was for the woman who touched the hem of his garment, but I want to hear him say to me, "Your faith has healed you – go in peace. Live well, live blessed."

January 12 we received the good news that no cancer was found in the sentinel lymph node or in the tissue that was removed during surgery. "Praise the Lord!! It was the news we hoped for," she wrote.

Hebrews 11:34 talks about Bible heroes whose weakness was turned to strength. They experienced triumphs through faith even though they were weak in themselves. The devotional author wrote: "If you knew – really knew – what spiritual forces are available to you through faith, you would never be afraid." Betty wrote, "As I contemplate what is ahead – especially the radiation, it is easy to be afraid and wonder if I am strong enough to go through it. My prayer is that in my weakness I will be strong. One day at a time, and not be afraid."

She quickly became busy at home, then in early February we met with the oncologist to discuss radiation. Her cancer was estrogen induced and could be treated with hormone therapy – which blocks the estrogen to the breast. This was instead of chemotherapy. February 9 she started a tamoxifen pills regime – one a day for five years. Her first radiologist appointment was Friday, February 11. She wrote,

"I've been praying that the right treatment would be chosen; now I pray that it will be effective."

She will have 25 treatments and will likely be sore and tired by the time she is finished. The radiation kills cells so your body has to work hard to grow the good ones back again.

On February 22 she read, *Whatever you ask for in prayer believe that you have received it and it will be yours* (Mark 11:24). "I asked that the cancer be healed and cleansed from my body" she wrote. "As this radiation takes place I pray it will be a part of that healing process as will be the tamoxifen. This morning I called the church to ask to be put on the prayer chain as I begin this journey."

February 24 Arnold brought the car home ready to go with a full tank of gas. We sat on the chesterfield and got choked up together and I prayed for Betty before she left. It was hard for both us, but has to be. She would stay each week two hours away at our daughter's place. This allowed her to be only a half hour from the hospital. When she arrived at Tara's, Jonah's first words to her were, "Grampa at home?" Tara told him ahead of time that Grandpa wouldn't be coming. He definitely is Grandpa's boy, she told her diary.

Betty was sewing together the parts of the sweater she had knit for Nathaniel. He had been watching her progress with much interest. One morning he came down to her bedroom at Tara's to encourage Gramma to get up and work on the sleeve. He kept trying on the parts that were finished and wanted to know if he could wear it when he was four – which was then. She had told him it was for next year when he is five. When she finished sewing the sweater, Nathaniel was quite pleased and tried it on several times. He was quite concerned that there wasn't a tag on it so he could tell which side is the back.

She dearly loved this time with her grandkids. Britni was a little sweetie – two dimples in her cheeks and looking a lot like Tara at that age. She regularly charms you with her beautiful smile. She was starting to move around on the floor quite well and did not stay still for long. Being there was a real treat, she noted in her diary.

On March 17 she found a reason to be encouraged. "I have been so looking forward to being finished with treatment but realized again today that when it's over it is not over. There will always be that repeated test every six months down the road and the possibility of it coming back. I was feeling pretty down about this when I came off the elevator I met a young fellow, eighteen or twenty, coming out of the treatment area. I thought how fortunate I am to have lived for 63 years already. If we look around there is always someone else whose shoes we wouldn't want to walk in."

February 5, 2013

After radiation, what? It is not over. Not with cancer. Betty's ongoing fear, and mine: Will this evil return? Or will Betty remain cancer free? Every usual and some-times a not-so-usual pain or discomfort brought this ongoing fear to the surface. Then we would have to wrestle it down again, sometimes by sharing those fears, and returning to God's promises and praying again. We desperately wanted to have faith that she was completely free, but often it was elusive. But life goes on. Every six months we went together for her mammogram, and a week or two later we got the all-clear again. Relief and thanksgiving.

In April, 2005, Betty was so relieved to be finished with radiation and home again. We went together for her final treatments and to see Dr. Corbett. It was so good to be done. We went to Phil's Restaurant to celebrate.

Betty retired from the Prairie Book Store the end of May, 2006. Her journal after April, 2005, was mostly filled with family events: her step mother's 80th birthday event, my oldest brother's 70 birthday celebration, and Betty's 64th birthday celebration when our kids and grandkids all came. Todd and Dave came to help replace the roof on our sun porch, and I fell off the roof on to the deck. Betty was in the wash room and happened to be looking out the window and saw me go by at a pretty good speed. I later told her it was my Peter Pan imitation but I forgot to think a happy thought as I left the roof. Nothing broken, just severe pain for several days and an elbow the size of a tennis ball where it had hit the shelf of the barbecue on the way by. Demolished it, of course. After viewing about 20 x-rays, the Doc says I have large strong bones – none broken. However, I did finally learn what "tennis elbow" really does mean! Betty wrote several days later, "I keep seeing Arnold tumbling off the roof. What a horrible feeling! Thank you Lord that he wasn't hurt any worse!"

In August, 2005, we celebrated Britni's dedication and her first birthday. Betty noted that, "Britni started walking that week. She was so excited at what she had accomplished that she stood there clapping her hands and jumping up and down till she fell on her behind. A little cutie with curly hair and big smile. She still walks like a drunken sailor but is very pleased with herself."

On May 26 she officially became a Senior and celebrated with a party organized by Tara and Merle, her sister. May 31 Praire hosted her retirement party. The President presented her with a gold Bulova watch. Workmates plied her with gifts.

Betty had a life filled with pain – very few days without any. Since high school she experienced the almost daily discomfort of fibromyalgia. She had two hip replacements, with severe pain during the many months waiting for her surgery dates. Often she had to take a pain killer in order to sleep at night, and became an expert on the variety of medications for pain.

Cancer is an insidious, destructive evil – aggressive enemy cells attacking a person's healthy cells and destroying them. Betty received a minor surgery as the Doc removed only a fairly small wedge from her breast, so she did not have to deal with a serious deformity. But the fear remained, just around the corner to pop out at a moment's notice. Her breast cancer was not the most serious kind. After weeks of radiation and during the five years of tamoxifen she was repeatedly cleared and free of cancer. God answered her prayers! She conquered her first cancer and remained totally free of it. We often thanked the Lord for this gift.

Betty knew the danger she faced, so she aggressively took action. She lost 55 pounds in a year and a half to achieve the slimness she sought. Together we walked a half hour four or five times a week. But for her, it was too little too late. Who knows? Perhaps diet and exercise could not have staved off her second cancer. Was the second onslaught of this horrible malaise related to the first? Not according to the oncologist's office. I wonder today if all the pain killers she took over the years and her five years of ingesting tamoxifen may have contributed to her second cancer. The jury is still out on the negative effects of the chemical tamoxifen.

Family members from three generations died of cancer. She made statements a couple of times that indicated she expected to die early, probably also of cancer. Did this expectation hurry on her double dose of cancer? I do not know. When she was diagnosed with the second cancer, this time in her pancreas and liver, I realized at the end that she knew from then on that this was a death sentence. I being the perpetual optimist believed till almost the end that she would be healed and would come home again.

Not so. The next chapters tell this story.

Part Two

The Second Cancer

4

The Support Group and Home Care

A t first I established the Facebook group mostly for convenience. Relatives and friends would want to know about Betty's health issues so I chose this means to daily communicate her medical progress. In Facebook I said it was a group to support Betty, but in a couple of months it became, "A group to support Betty and Arnold. We started it when with the receipt of the heart rending news in early October that Betty had untreatable liver/pancreatic cancer. She went to Glory December 14. That now makes this Arnold's Support Group."

Almost every day I reported to The Group, at first just the medical information. Soon, however, it became a daily journaling of our struggle with dying, and in two months my battle with the enemy, Death. And the aftermath of deep sorrow, anger, unanswerable question, digging deep into my life-long faith, painful loneliness that morphed into "aloneness". Throughout, I shared my emotional roller-coaster thoughts with the Facebook support group. These folks became my listening board, crying shoulders, encouragers, and faithful counselors and prayer warriors throughout.

Can there be more heart rending news than this surgeon's quiet comment? "You have inoperable liver cancer that started in your pancreas. We cannot operate." Later he sent us to the oncologist to discuss the possibility of poisoning by chemotherapy. That's another page in this painful odyssey.

When Betty left, "our" story became my story. Terrifying – the Big C always is, then morphing into grief and painful loneliness. But eventually hope arrived. Here is The Story, presented in the journaling format almost exactly as it developed on Facebook. I shared with the FB group my daily observations, comments, and sometimes deepest inner raw feelings about the horrendous events of Cancer, dying, death, grieving, the pain of loneliness after 48 years of companionship, then the "aloneness", and how I coped with all this, And finally, how I discovered hope and new love. I found at the bottom of despair that God dwells there too. His handprints are seen throughout this tale, from beginning to the end, as are the encouraging responses from Group Members. As you read this story, you will sometimes cry, and occasionally chuckle, but your heart will also be warmed as you sense the movement of God's Spirit throughout.

On my Facebook special page for The Group it says that, Arnold created the group October 27, 2011 at 11:17pm

The initial group members included relatives: Suzan, Cheryl (BC), Candice, Tracy, Tony, Bethany, Jan S (Denver), Irene, Tara and David, Lyle, Daphne, Lisa, Joli (New Zealand), Mahdieh and Anthony (Australia), Sheila, Raymond, Jane, Colleen (Denver), and Jan C (Saskatchewan), Wes (Nova Scotia), Farrel (Illinois), Curtis (USA), Rachel, Rebecca, Lacey, Ehud (USA). These friends joined, along with many others: Joanne, Gert, Tom, Sylvia, Jorlean (Florida), Michelle, Heather, Paul (USA), and Richard. I have identified in the brackets where people live if they are from outside Alberta. All these folks were already my friends on Facebook.

And my next door neighbour, Tammy, who I made co-manager of the group. Her first response to The Group was, "Awesome Arnold!!!. . .you guys know you're right up there at the top of our prayer list. . .LOVE YOU BOTH ♥

Eventually The Group expanded to 153. People would hear the devastating news, and that I was sharing our story on a daily basis. They asked to be part of it. At its peak, there were several folks whom I had never met in person. The Group members became my cyber sounding board, my therapists and counselors and prayer warriors, but mostly warm shoulders on which to unload my struggles and buckets of tears. Many of their responses are included here as they shared them with me and each other within the Facebook Support Group. Because of much repetition in these responses I have considerably condensed them. So often, the only thing there was to say was, "I am praying for you." For me, some days, this was sufficient.

You can now follow this story, as it happened. Here is my first day's entry.

October 27, 2011 at 11:27pm.
Betty's Physical Situation:
Description

Betty has been home from the Foothills Hospital since Saturday, October 24. We came home with the heart rending understanding that we are dealing with inoperable liver/pancreatic cancer. She was experiencing increasing pain around her tummy and back. After three months of tests: a CT scan in Drumheller which discovered a cyst on her pancreas, ultrasound, endoscopy to get a sample from her pancreas, then a visit with a surgeon at the Foothills Hospital in Calgary, who wanted more tests. Since she has had three more CT scans, the first of which showed a spot on her liver, and a biopsy of the liver which revealed the cancer. She spent 12 days in the hospital where they attempted to bring several issues under control: pain, major fluid retention, total lack of appetite, and no bowel movements. Now we are home continuing to deal with these same issues, about which the docs don't seem to know what to do. We picked up a bag of pharmaceuticals in Three Hills on our way home from the Foothills and a few more since.

Tomorrow we go again to the doc to check her phlebitis (inflammation of veins), which is getting worse.

We received a call yesterday October 25 for an appointment with the oncologist in the Tom Baker Cancer Centre in Calgary. We are well acquainted with this place from when Betty experienced breast cancer six years ago. They are the best. However, the promise offered by chemotherapy is not that great. The doc says you may have a longer life but not a better one. Five percent find their cancer reduced so they can live a normal life. (NOTE: He did not tell us that the five percent is of *all* cancer patients. No pancreatic cancer is cured by chemotherapy.) Betty told him we would pray to be in that percentage. Well, he says, some people call it a miracle; I call it genetics. We are looking at our Lord's intervention – that's our hope! We are making this information available to you as we covet your prayers for her healing. We will continue to update our cancer journey for your information. It would be nice to hear from you as well.

Friends and family immediately responded. So many assured us their prayers. Tammy wrote, "This is awesome, Arnold. Now everyone can know and be reminded to keep you both in our prayers." Nephew Tony: "Hang in there Auntie. I love you and so does God. He knows what he is doing whether we like it or not:) I love you always."

Jorlean reminded us that this did not catch the Lord by surprise. Nephew Farrel assured us that God will do what is best for us and brings him glory! Lyle: "Prayer can move the hand of God."

Mahdieh was grateful that I was keeping them in the loop and assured us, "I love you Auntie Betty." Suzan was asking God for a miracle. "You hold a special place in my heart. I am praying for all of you daily. Love you." Cheryl: "Love you Auntie Betty. Big hugs from Abbotsford. We are praying for you every day. Thank you for this Unc. We really appreciate it!"

October 28 through November 1

Over the next few days we began a difficult search for two immediate items: (1) getting a life, and (2) getting Betty's symptoms under sufficient control so that she can physically tolerate chemotherapy. Every day this week we visited the doc's office or the emergency for advice and care. The doc prescribed some heavier duty pain meds to add to her collection, and gave some advice regarding handling the fluid retention. He also suggested a couple more off-the-shelf meds for constipation (a by-product of the meds). Also, a home nurse spent a couple of hours at our house today and we had a very good discussion regarding Betty's long list of seven or eight symptoms/issues. She will contact a palliative care nurse to visit us. Palliative care sounds scary but I assured Betty that this is Home Care and this kind of nurse has experience with pain control, fluid retentions, appetite issues and constipation. We learned that "A Happy Bowel is a Happy Gal!" We will get there. As I look back I realize that I really did not accept the meaning of palliative care. The medical system assumed Betty was already in the dying mode. Not me. It had not occurred to me that this would be so. She would get better. Her total health would be restored. Some would call this denial. But I expected that God would heal her.

We asked folks to pray that we would make the right decisions regarding treatment. We intended to pursue natural medicine. And were in the initial stages of putting together a special praise and prayer event for Betty's healing.

People were amazing. Old friends visited with information about an elderly lady who has been completely cured from the same cancer as Betty. We both visited our neighbours to create some jack-o-lanterns. Three Hills folks were so caring. I did not gone downtown without one or three folks assuring us of their prayers – no matter what store we are in. We loved it! Family brought food, although it was mostly for me. Even then, Betty could not eat much as her digestive system was shutting down. She tried to get down a can of Ensure each day – the high protein editions. She needed protein to help diminish the fluid retention and tried to adjust to new and more serious pain controllers. Through all this Betty has never lost the spark in her eye and folk regularly comment on how fine she looks. We are blessed! I told Face book friends.

On October 30 I posted a picture of Betty and asked Facebook, "Don't you think my Honey looks like Princess Di in this pic?" I was so proud of her dignity and courage in the face of this difficulty. Jorlean responded, "There's a peace in those eyes that the princess didn't have, a peace that passes understanding! Louise remarked: "Yes she does! She is truly beautiful. We're so thankful that as a Daughter/ Princess of the King she is totally cared for in Him. Our prayers are with you as you travel this journey – through many toils and snares, but yet because of our King we need fear no evil. Blessing to you today!" Suzan: "She truly does and even more beautiful. Love u both. Praying always for all of you."

November 2 through 12

Medical appointments and discussions for the next several days were the norm. One day we had a two and a half hour visit with the palliative care nurse who helped us sort out our pain killer medley. Then we visited the oncologist in Calgary regarding possible chemotherapy. He said Betty had a bundle of an unusual combination of issues and of the nature of the cancer as he saw it on the CT scan. So he is sending her for more blood tests tomorrow and an x-ray to see how much water has collected in the lungs area. He will also consult with a team of five oncologists to see if they have anything to offer and get back to us in two weeks. At that time we have to decide if we want the chemo.

He offered very little hope with the chemo, from "it may do nothing," or it may reduce the cancer so that she gets some relief with her pain and lack of appetite. I asked him about life expectancy. He said stats say about six months for someone with her type of cancer.

The oncologist eventually phoned from Calgary and advised chemo. Betty is leaning toward this. The only thing they can promise for sure is that the immune system will be compromised, but it MIGHT help diminish the symptoms and MAY add to the fluid problem. Or might not. He said improvements would not kick in for two or three months.

There are too many IFS and NO positive promises. So why take the poison? I am getting increasingly angry with the medical industry. They beg us for money to find a cure for cancer, then spend the billions on finding better ways to cut, poison and burn instead of attacking the causes. People have discovered the causes and found cures, but the Drug Cartels in North America are ponying up to the Government Druggies who turn the other way and they all continue killing folks. Less than a 5% cure rate for chemo! You would think these educated folks would get tired after a while of being such losers! Who are the real Quacks?

I continued to investigate alternative/natural treatment. I had been studying one that totally cured a woman in Alberta of cancer. At the time I understood that she had Betty's cancer but when we visited her found out it was in her bowel so was curable. Her basic internal organs were not affected. She was on her last legs (in fact could not move her legs as they were swollen so badly), when her husband took her home from the hospital. She was given 90 days to live. The medical system had given up on her. He started her on a simple food product regime. Two months later she was up and walking and now apparently is cancer free. Eight months later she was up and about and still is cancer free.

Throughout this ordeal we heard several wonderful stories of healing through natural means. Jorlean, a retired nurse and friend now living in Florida, sent note this on FB: Arnold, you mentioned laetrile and I remember about 30 years ago giving it by IV to various people with cancer. It was illegal at that time so people would get it from Mexico and bring it to my house for injection. I know of at least one of those people being cured. She also went on a strict diet of mostly carrot juice. We continued to pray; prayed for Betty in our little group during the service at church. The Lord is our Healer! I remind him often of those grandchildren that need a grandma.

More recently one of our customers at the Three Hills Health Food Store, which I currently manage, came in to purchase several pounds of bitter apricot seeds. He stated that his cancer doc wanted to rip out his voice box along with a large tumor in his throat. But he adamantly refused and started taking 30 of the seeds a day, definitely a therapeutic dose. In a few weeks the tumor was gone. The medicinal component of bitter apricot seeds is laetrile.

Betty's total lack of appetite and difficulty in drinking continued to worry me. Food just did not want to go down the gullet! She will soon be in starvation mode, I thought, if she cannot eat more. For two days she did not gain weight from fluid retention but today she gained almost two pounds. Over the next few weeks I slowly realized that she was starving to death, as the oncologist predicted. With her pancreas failing to produce digestive enzymes and her liver losing its function, her system was shutting down.

She had gained 20 pounds in a month from fluid retention and getting a nice spare tire around her abdomen as a result. It put pressure on her lungs to the point where it was affecting her breathing. One day we spent the past five hours in the emergency getting blooded (testing for protein level), oxygenized, chest x-rayed, and latticed (IVing "water pills" into her blood stream). So that released a significant amount of the fluid (into the potty chair) and they put her on pills for a week. This was supposed to help her appetite also by taking pressure off her digestive system. We eventually started her on oxygen

Kim cried out on Facebook, Oh for freedom from pain and sorrow. My soul cries out to you Lord. Why do the faithful suffer and the wicked celebrate? Father God, my life is in your hands. Let me not forget your goodness. Suzan echoed her thoughts: Hi Uncle Arnold and Aunt Betty. I can't imagine what you have been going through every day except from what you have been telling us. My heart cries for you both and we also are praying diligently for you, that the Lord would guide and direct you. I can't understand God's reasoning for allowing Aunt Betty to go through this. She certainly doesn't deserve it. We love you both so much. You are ever and daily in our thoughts and prayers. Love from your little flower girl and her Hubby. A big hug to both of you from Suzan and Bob.

We are increasingly amazed at the support we receive from our Christian community and families. Both Betty and I come from large believing families. Yesterday we received a call from my cousin on Vancouver Island and today from a friend in Ontario. People from Canada, the US, New Zealand, Australia and several provinces have assured us of their prayers. We know God is at work in our lives as a result!

I was Betty's primary care giver, a full time job. Negotiating with the doctors, nurses and home care workers who came almost every day. I was desperately wanting to help her get better, at least feel better. It seemed every day was a failure. Of course it was. She was dying, but there was no way I was going to put up with that nonsense. She was going to get better! It was my job!

Lois, Betty's cousin, commented on my attempts to work with the healthcare system: Thank goodness for nurses! When my brother-in-law was training for MD in Calgary and first went on the wards, I asked how he knew what to do? He replied: I ask the nurses – they have all the answers. After Dad's (Betty's Uncle Armand) nightmare encounter with the medical system, I understand your frustration with doctors! Betty is lucky to have you, Arnold, at the helm and advocating for her. Navigating through the system is NOT for the faint-hearted. In my prayers, Lois. Joli, my niece in New Zealand commented: You two are doing such an amazing job of dealing with all this! I love the way you say "*We* had treatment, *we*. . . ." Love and prayers!

5

Praise and Healing Service

Facebook Announcement
Betty's Praise & Healing Meeting
November 13, 2011 at 4:00pm
Mt Olive E Free Church, Three Hills

L ooking forward to seeing you at our Praise and Healing Meeting. Praise, share testimonies and the Word, pray for Betty's healing. God is able. Nothing is too big.

Arnold: Introduction at the Praise & Healing Service

Thank you so much for coming. Betty and I very much appreciate your prayers and encouraging words.

During the past several weeks we've discovered how wonderful it is to be a part of the larger Christian community. Folks from several countries are praying for us, from as far away as Australia and New Zealand, as are friends and relatives from Vancouver Island to Prince Edward Island. Several churches from different denominations put us on their prayer chain. Over 100 friends on Facebook have joined Betty's support group, including several people from Mt Olive. Some have come to the house to pray for us and be an encouragement. Every day we get phone calls and Facebook messages and emails and visits to our home.

We asked for this Praise and Healing get-together for three reasons:

1. This event is our testimony to our strong and unwavering faith in our Lord and Saviour Jesus Christ. He is our peace and our rest. He created us and is our ultimate healer. In terms of curing Betty's cancer, the Health Industry has abandoned us. Even our oncologist, the chemotherapy doctor, has only "for sure" promise to us, that his poison will compromise her immune system. Otherwise it might help, but it might not.

Yesterday Betty told the Home Care Nurse that we were going to have this Praise and Prayer Meeting. I added that we are going right to The Top. We are going over the heads of the best Cancer doctors to our true Saviour. (By the way, the Home Care Nurses have been extraordinarily helpful and very compassionate and caring!) We are also getting first class care from Dr. Dada and his staff as well as those at the local hospital.

2. Secondly, we came here to praise our Living Saviour. I have learned over the years that in the time of deep diversity and heart ache, it becomes especially important to lift my heart in praise to our Lord. This gets my attention off me and my troubles to make sure the Lord is genuinely the centre of my being and my focus, and the source of my peace and strength. Then I always turn to the last chapter of Habakkuk. The Prophet says:

Though the fig tree does not bud
    And there are no grapes on the vines
Though the olive crop fails
    And the fields produce no food,
Though there are no sheep in the pen
    And no cattle in the stalls,
Yet I will rejoice in the Lord,
    I will be joyful in God my Saviour
The Sovereign Lord is my strength;
        He makes my feet like the feet of a deer,
        He enables me to go on the heights.

3. The third reason for being here is an act of obedience. James says: If you are sick you should call the elders of the church to pray over you and anoint you with oil in the name of the Lord. I think that one reason for James telling us to do this is that he knew that in a time of heaviness it is not easy to manufacture the faith God asks for. So the sick person comes to the church and its leadership.

Then he says that "the prayer offered in faith will make the sick person well." So we are counting on the fact that amongst this group of Believers, who come from various churches, there are those who can pray the Prayer of Faith.

Thank you so much for being here today.

Over 100 friends showed up, family friends and neighbors from several churches and communities. We sang, I presented the introduction, Sister-in-Law Pastor Irene led the Service, Son-in-Law Pastor David shared some thoughts from scripture and theology and experience, and then the Elders prayed. Then we all went home. No discernible physical results for Betty at the Service or later. For Betty and I this was an act of obedience based on James who tells us to go to the Elders for prayer if you are sick and the Prayer of Faith will make you well.

The day of this healing service had started at 7:30 am with Betty sitting up on her bed saying, "I think I am dying!" The Evil One obviously had heard about our

Praise and Healing Meeting in the afternoon and tried to head her off at the pass. Later we spent time together praying that she would be able to attend and sang some praise songs. Well, tried to! She made it to the meeting and came home exhausted. The meeting was a blessing! Our kids and seven Gkids then came for roast beef supper. I did the roast, the girls the veggies, Todd the gravy, and Pastor Dave brushed and cut up the spuds. Betty sat up a couple of times, including for the meal, although she didn't eat. Tara's family stayed overnight till noon. It was good for Betty and me to have our whole family home.

6

Henderson's Six-Part Cancer Cure Protocol

November 14 through 19

We continued to visit our family doc for scheduled appointments. He found some fungus in Betty's throat and thought it might be hindering her eating. Another prescription! He also prescribed a feel good immune moderator. We then went to the hospital for another chest x-ray. The x-ray technician brought her out later and hurried her over to emergency cuz she was fading fast. Her newly delivered portable oxygen had run out in the doc's office where she was on oxygen for an hour and then we went home. This brought her count down to about 78; it was supposed to be around 90.

Some days were promising. The evening following the service she was more upbeat than for a long time. Very encouraging to me, especially after two super busy days.

I ordered all the natural products for her Bill Henderson protocol treatments, including a water ionizer. This I believed was the means that our Lord would use to bring complete healing. The 80 year old lady we had visited recovered from bowel cancer by using this protocol. Now we just have to find a way to get it down to her tummy and into her bloodstream. For the first time this evening she downed a whole bottle of Ensure meal replacement in one sitting. Another good sign. These days I was thankful for small blessings.

Then we went to Calgary for an echo-cardiogram, a check of the heart. Another heavy day for Betty. That day she just drank one full can of Ensure – on her own accord! I reached for it so she could take half of it in 30 minutes with her pain meds. She pulled it away and drank it all! I thought my Country Girl was already on her way back! The evening before she drank another full one, but only with my urgings and gentle haranguing.

Late that evening I was praying about the Bill Henderson Protocol, a natural food product regime that builds up the immune system and attacks cancer cells.

The Lord gave me the most beautiful sense of peace and joy. He reminded me of Genesis 1:29 where God says, "I give you every seed-bearing plant on the face of the whole earth and every tree that has fruit with seed in it. They will be your food." Some say that for every disease and ailment there is something growing somewhere on the earth to heal it.

In 1535 Jack Cartier landed on Newfoundland with 25 severely sailors sick with scurvy. Another 25 had already died of it. Three native ladies brewed up some white pine needle and tree bark soup. "Drink a cup of this and they will be better tomorrow." They did and they were! It took another 400 years in the early 1900's for the medical establishment to discover that scurvy results from a lack vitamin C. Jack had returned to England and reported his discovery to the medical practitioners but they laughed at him, "What do those witchdoctors know about medicine?" It is estimated that 1,000,000 British sailors died over the years from scurvy. Someday current cancer cures will become so widely known that they will be accessible and affordable to everyone. And this will put the North American Drug Cartels and Government Drug Control Police out of business with their poison, cut and burn approach to cancer symptoms.

Thank you Lord or your provisions for our health and well-being.

The next morning I woke up at 5:00 am with a sense of joy. I suddenly realized that the heavy, heavy burden I had carried for weeks was gone. It is devastating to see your lovely mate of 48 years deteriorating under the evil onslaught of the destructive pestilence of cancer. I cried a lot, sometime uncontrollably. I am a "fixer" but could not fix this! But since our Prayer and Healing Meeting IT IS GONE! Instead of weeping I turned to singing (the alone in the shower kind). Well. . .I've had some tears of joy! So many people have come to our house and almost everyone prayed for peace for us. It has come! I no longer saw Betty devastated by disease but on the road to complete health by God's hand. Glory to his name! Last evening God gave Betty and me this: "For Jehovah hears the cries of his needy ones, and does not look the other way" (Psalm 69:33 TLB).

A friend sent this scripture for us. Psalm 91. *Whoever dwells in the shelter of the Most High will rest in the shadow of the Almighty. I will say of the LORD, "He is my refuge and my fortress, my God, in whom I trust." Surely he will save you from the fowler's snare and from the deadly pestilence. He will cover you with his feathers, and under his wings you will find refuge; his faithfulness will be your shield and rampart. You will not fear the terror of night, nor the arrow that flies by day, nor the pestilence that stalks in the darkness, nor the plague that destroys at midday. A thousand may fall at your side, ten thousand at your right hand, but it will not come near you. You will only observe with your eyes and see the punishment of the wicked. If you say, "The LORD is my refuge," and you make the Most High your dwelling, no harm will overtake you, no disaster will come near your tent. For he will command his angels concerning you to guard you in all your ways; they will lift you up in their hands, so that you will not strike your foot against a stone. You will tread on the lion and the cobra; you will trample the great lion and the serpent.*

"Because he loves me," says the LORD, "I will rescue him; I will protect him, for he acknowledges my name. He will call on me, and I will answer him; I will be with him in trouble, I will deliver him and honor him. With long life I will satisfy him and show him my salvation."

Notice the key words that were for Betty and me. Here is our response: My God. . . .will save us from the. . .deadly pestilence. . . .We will not fear the. . .terror of the night. . .nor the pestilence that stalks in the darkness, nor the plague that destroys at midday. . . .it will not come near us. . . .No harm will overtake us, no disaster will come near our house. His angels will guard us in all our ways. Our Lord says he will rescue us and protect us. When we call upon him he will answer and be with us in our trouble and deliver and honor us. He will give us long life.

Psalm 91 is a covenant between God and me. He promises protection from all kinds of harm: sickness, accidents, war, and natural disaster – if I dwell in the shelter of the most high. And this is done through faith, which comes by hearing the Word.

Facebook friends asked about the Bill Henderson Cancer Cure Protocol that Betty has started.

Betty started on the cottage cheese smoothie but immediately lost it. We tried more that evening a half hour after taking the nausea pill and it stayed this time. And for the second day she was able to take three cans of Ensure. We praise God for this as she was not getting enough nutrition to keep a sparrow on the go. I ordered all the Henderson products along with a machine to produce alkaline drinking water. We seemed to be seeing a bit-by-bit progress. We were still working on her oxygen level, trying to get it up to 90 consistently. The respirator guy brought a heavy duty Cadillac eight cylinder floor model which produced 10 litres per minute, double our current machine. This was the amount she seemed to require to boost her oxygen to 90. Terrible thing to wear, but she can exchange it occasionally for the nose gadget. But she threw up her alternative today. Probably because I encouraged her to eat it all at one time. I decided to not be so pushy. Couldn't heal her in one day!

Hallelujah! The next day Betty and I sang this to the tune of Amazing Grace (well, sort of). I started it after she completed eating her third portion of the cancer kick butt (CKB) smoothie! I could hardly wait for the next hour to pass this good new to our FB friends. It's an answer to their prayers! I waited, wanting to make sure she didn't barf it up, again. This is a major component of her alternative CKB Bill Henderson Protocol. The other components come in capsule/pill form which methinks she will down a bit easier. I experimented with several approaches to getting her to take in and keep down this stuff and looks like we found a winner. The other components will come by post so I was praying that the Custom Cops would be having a real nice day when they processed the items from three different States.

After four days of being down, Betty was slightly upbeat. Perhaps partly to the fact that all night and all day we have had her oxygen at around 90.

A friend told me at the Bank today that God is good – all the time.

Hallelujah!

We request prayer from our Facebook friends that she would be able to consume the Protocol products and keep them down, and that we would find a way to keep her oxygen level up.

You can read about Bill Henderson's Six-Part Cancer Cure Protocol in the Appendix. According to him, "If you follow this regimen diligently every day for about six to eight weeks you will not just improve your condition, you will probably be cancer free."

7

From Home to the Hospital

November 20 through 24

The next morning I returned from the hospital where the ambulance had taken Betty. She wanted to go. She threw up the alternative treatment again and was experiencing more pain than usual. I strongly objected to her going to the hospital, thought she was giving up. But after having a family conference with our kids and Betty's sister, a nurse (as is our daughter-in-law) I yielded to Betty's wishes. She will get better and more consistent care there. At this point I do not know if/when she will be back. The past few days she is talking as though her days on earth are drawing to a close and doesn't want to die at home. She is in the hands of our sovereign Lord who dearly loves her and me.

Suzan saw it more clearly than I did: Hi Uncle Arnold. Sorry to hear that aunt Betty is in the hospital maybe that was her way of giving you some much needed rest. I'm sure she is thinking of her wonderful, adoring husband even in her time of need. We pray for both of you daily that God would be your constant companion which we know he is. He will give you the grace and strength for each daily task. Of which I know you know. But doesn't hurt to just get a reminder. His grace is sufficient for your every need. We love you both. Give our love to Aunt Betty. God bless you both.

I soon came to realize how much better it was for Betty to be in the hospital. She was on IV to keep her hydrated and they utilized it for a continuous drip of anti-nausea. Otherwise she had to have a nausea pill every half hour before taking the hydromorphone. She also could take her short term pain med by injection directly into the IV site on her hand, which means when she required additional pain med it took only about eight minutes or so to take affect instead of waiting at least three quarters of an hour. The bed was marvelous with all kinds of adjustments. The doc comes every day and the palliative care specialist came from Stettler to advise us and to review Betty's situation. Then she advises the doc and nurses on possible changes in her care. I spent most of my day there but can now feel free to leave when I need to and not be concerned, nor have her concerned about me being away. As they got her meds adjusted she had more times of being alert enough to visit a bit. My beautiful niece asked me a couple of days ago what she could bring. I said I got lots of food, but she insisted. So I thought a bit and said brownies with walnuts and lots of icing. So today for supper she brought brownies with walnuts and lots of icing, strawberry ice cream to accompany them, a 10 inch heavy duty saskatoon pie with flaky crust. Oh yes, and a pot roast with veggies. Mama Mia! Life has its good moments!

At the hospital at meal time, the nurse said I could have Betty's meal. So she gets the first bites – maybe two or three tiny spoonfuls and I got the rest. Once we had turkey dinner with dressing and cranberry sauce, then breaded fish and the next day pork and mashed tatoes. No problem for both of us getting all we wanted to eat. Hospital food was not too bad by Niece gets first prize though!

On November 23 I spent a lovely time with my Honey. She was alert when I arrived and we had a couple of hours of chatting. She thought that after she is gone I would probably sit around for a couple of weeks and then see all the jobs around the house and shop needing attention and then would get up and at it. I told her I would probably be extremely lonely so would camp around awhile at my brothers' and sister's places. She thought that would be a great idea and mentioned a good friend of ours that did this when his wife died. When the Doc and Nurse came she sang her song for them and we had some fun talking about what it would be like in heaven, "Walking and Leaping and Praising God". My sister Lil stayed with Betty while I was home getting last minute chores done for the Christmas Market this Friday and Saturday. God is Good – all the time.

The next day they called me to the hospital at 10:30 pm. I had just left Betty after tucking her in at about 9:00. She was panicking, afraid that when she died it would be because she was suffocating. This thought terrorized her. So we talked and read some scripture and prayed. I asked FB for prayer that she would have a real sense of Jesus' presence. I think her meds are confusing her and affecting her emotions and spirit.

Betty's cousin, Sheila: About a year before my Dad died, he took a pretty bad turn health wise, and I believe at the time he was very fearful of the same thing, that he would suffocate. A year later the day he died (and knew he was dying) he said to one of my brothers "If this is as hard as dying is, I can handle it." I think when it was actually his time, he was given the strength to deal with what was about to come. Maybe it would help Betty to know that Uncle Dave felt the same way?

Here is Betty's Current Favorite Song

1 Peter and John went to pray;
they met a lame man on the way.
He asked for alms and held out his palms,
and this is what Peter did say:
2 "Silver and gold have I none,
but what I have I give to you.
In the name of Jesus Christ

of Nazareth, rise up and walk!"
3 He went walking and leaping and praising God,
walking and leaping and praising God.
"In the name of Jesus Christ
of Nazareth, rise up and walk."

Betty sang this for her doctor and nurse one day and we all had a time of rejoicing about dancing together in heaven.

November 21. I took a break from the hospital to come home and get the signs ready for this Fri/Sat Christmas Farmers' Market. It was too late to pass the job to someone else so I, the Market Manager, had to get things ready. I came home at 6:00 pm totally exhausted and went to bed at 9:00. Couldn't sleep so I sat up in my chair in the living room. At 11:30 I had a strong urge to get to the hospital so I packed a few things. A nurse quickly got a chair that made into a cot and brought bedding. I was able to sleep next to Betty and hold her hand. Well, I didn't sleep much. At 4:30 she woke. I had been asking the Lord for time to talk to her about final things and how we should say goodbye to her. She was quite alert and we had a beautiful exchange about how she wanted to leave and what she wanted at her celebration service. I later told FB, "If you come you might get a few surprises." I also needed to communicate to her that I am now willing to let her go. My Country Girl is so strong. I told her I weep a lot. She said she did her weeping "before", that is, for the several months, June through October, when the medical experts were attempting to find out what was wrong. During this period I think she knew that she knew what was happening to her. I the perpetual optimist didn't accept that her pain might be cancer. Now we had finally come together in how we viewed her final time this side of heaven and she helped me to know how to say good-bye and also to look to my future. She is such a lovely, strong person – my Country Girl. I love her so!

NOTE: Someone asked me why I call Betty "My Country Girl". Cuz she is. Growing up on a ranch with a Dad who raised Herfords and Percherons, the classy heavy duty work horses. As the oldest she got to get out and help with the chores and harvesting until her younger brothers were old enough. She knows how to put in a good days work from the start. Rarely complained, even though she experienced pain all her adult life. She is one of those folks who I call "the salt of the earth".

FB responses were again so encouraging. As you read these, perhaps they will help you to understand how to meaningfully communicate with someone whose loved one is dying.

Ehud: Arnold, you brought tears to my eyes now. At the same time, great comfort in knowing that "It is well with (your) soul." I continue to pray for both of you. I love you guys a lot and I just feel bad for not being there with you right now. Receive my love, dear Brother and Friend.

Gert: My heart is blessed by her faith and courage – and by yours. You are both continually in my prayers. Candice: Thank you for sharing Uncle Arnold. You have a beautiful love story. And I admire you both so much. We will be praying for comfort and the peace that passes all understanding! Paul: Arnold, my good friend, it is too hard to imagine being in your shoes. Please know that you and Betty are so special to so many who continue to pray for your two. . .that you would experience his amazing grace and peace in very tangible ways. James: Thank you for allowing us to share a bit of your journey and knowing how to pray. We love you both. Tammy ♥

Tara D: Arnold, you and Betty hold a special place in my and Andrew's hearts. We hurt for you and you are in our prayers. I just thought of all the reminders we have around the house of 'Grampie' Arnold's Christmas gifts: piggy-banks and snowman stuffies. Your nativity scene will be going up soon too. I was just listening to those Anne Murray records within the last month, not sure why, just thought. . .why not? I think I'll dig out Betty's cinnamon roll recipe soon. Send our love to Betty.

Marg: Our hearts are aching for you two after reading this tonight, Mom and I. Please tell Betty that we love her so much, and you too Arnold. I cherish the memories shared with her. Such wonderful memories of family get-togethers, waiting for the Stauffers to drive up the farm lane and add to the chaos, and of course the enhanced menu for the visit time. Betty's delicious baking! Picking saskatoons, and fighting off the mosquitos. Betty, you've taught us so much about patience, diligence and especially commitment. Big big cyber hug to you both!

Cherie: All of these friends have such a great way with words. All I got are tears and hugs and I will pray for peace. . . .sigh.

Suzan: Uncle Arnold. Thank you for allowing yourself to be vulnerable and open to us all. I can so understand what you are going through, not because I have gone through it but because your openness has caused us to walk thru every pain and joy with you both. I would fight for my husband the way you are fighting for your love. You are giving us all strength daily to be able to say goodbye to Aunt Betty even though we don't want to. It is bringing tears to my eyes as I even think of it now. I thank you for the joy long ago to be your flower girl. That has been on my mind for the last three weeks. Please give her a huge hug for us and let her know we love her very much and that she is an amazing example for all of us to follow and leaves us big shoes to fill. Love you both.

Ann: Dear Arnold and Betty, How precious your message and truly the Lord gave you those moments that so many would have wished for but were unable to either face or just didn't have the opportunity. Your updates have touched the hearts and have brought tears to many. Thank you dear friends for sharing your pain and sorrow. Surely the Lord has great rewards both here and there for you both. Our love and prayers, Len & Ann

Connie: Bill and I so appreciate your friendship, we keep you both in our prayers. May the God of comfort and uphold you in these difficult times.

Lyle: You are adding beauty and grace to a fearsome journey.

Makiko: Our hearts go out to you and Betty. Thank you for letting me be a part of this group to receive updates, so I might know how to pray for you better. Thank you for a glimpse into your personal life. What a beautiful love you have for each other – truly, "in sickness and in health". You guys are a great example to us all. Love from Scott and Makiko.

November 21. I met at 8 pm with a crew to haul tables for the Christmas Market taking place the next day (1:00 to 7:00) and Saturday (10:00 to 4:00). Our lovely daughter stayed with Mom overnight and for the whole weekend. Other family members spelled her off Friday and Saturday afternoon. Betty was a bit sleepier so the nurse said she would talk to the doc about backing off on her pain meds. This balance was not so easy to find and things change from one day to the next.

Betty had said before that she wants to go to Jesus. I told her that it was hard for me to agree with her, but I did. I asked our Lord a couple of days before to not let her be in this state much longer. We were sitting side by side on her bed. She had asked me, "How will I know when I die?" I told her that when she passes through the pearly gates angels will be lining both sides of the street. A great shout will go up, "Betty's here!" And family members will crowd around and join in her current favorite song, "Walking and leaping and praising God." She added, "And I will be able to dance with my four children?" (from miscarriages). Only one of the four has a name (Robert Lloyd, the child's two Gramps' names), so I suggested it would only be fair that we choose names for them now otherwise she would get to name them herself.;-) There is one other boy but we don't know about the other two, so we'll have to choose either a generic name of one that can be either gender. I asked FB, Any suggestions?

Gert: Bethany, Jamie or Jesse or Ashley or Courtney. Tammy: I say definitely Rachelle. Lacey: Alex. Mahdieh: Bobby after Grandpa. xoxo

Raymond: Arnold, I thank the Lord for giving you his strength right now. Writing this with tears. Betty was always our "big" cousin. She went before us to school, then on the bus to the school in Castor. When I moved to Calgary and knew no one you guys were already there. She was always so talented and the "pretty" cousin. We of course had almost grown up as brothers and sisters. Lived with four families in two and a half miles. We went to the same little country church and the same one room school, grades one to six and then the other school across the street in Fleet with grades 7-9. As to the names for babies there are a lot that can be for either gender: Dale, Leslie/Lesley, Dakota, Dana, and of course many others. God be with you both.

Suzan: Hi Uncle Arnold. Sitting here painting our basement and thinking of you both and names for your little ones already in heaven. I thought since you didn't know which two of them were that it should only be fitting for one to be named after Aunt Betty: Sarah Elizabeth or Julia Elizabeth. Not sure what you will think of those but you wanted suggestions. Not sure why those came to me but there must be a reason. Sarah was such a women of faith as is Aunt Betty so it just seemed to fit together. Think of you every day and anxiously wait for your updates. You're daily in our prayers. Please give Aunt Betty a huge hug for us and one for you too. Love you.

Arnold: Y'all are so encouraging! Thanks so much.

8

The Royal Queen Suite

November 25

Tomorrow the Hospital is moving us into the Penthouse Suite, my name for the palliative care unit. It's a regular living room with floor lamp, mag stand, microwave oven, coffee maker, etc., and a chesterfield that makes into a bed for me, as well as reclining chair. Huge picture windows with a view. So Sunday I am moving in with her and will be there for the duration. She has been getting panicky the past couple of days when I've had to be away for a few hours getting ready and doing the Farmers' Christmas Market. Wednesday should be good. With the Market history I'm at the beck and call of my lovely wife. She asked for pain med five times today, after not wanting any the past two days. The doc will likely increase her long term 12 hour dose. Tara stayed with her overnight and the same tonight. We will be having a family conference tomorrow evening to ensure we are all on the same page about Mom's situation. Me with Todd and Tara and then with Mom if she is able.

I said to FB: As we travel this path I have a growing understanding of why we call death the last "Enemy".

James: How true – enemy indeed! Yet an enemy that we can conquer with the power of Christ and we pray with you that this enemy will be conquered and that you both, regardless of which side of this life you stand, will be victorious. And how wonderful to know that for the Christian, death is the LAST enemy. Thank you for sharing.

When Betty moved into the Royal Queen Suite I changed the name from Penthouse. When I move in with her the next day I now get to be King!

It was nice to get the two-day Market done today. It distracted me from the real job of being with Betty but I found it a change I needed. I enjoy the Market. It was one of our retirement highlights as something we could do together. So many people pitched in to help with everything so that I didn't have to be there most of the time. A lot of fine folks live in this area.

We prayed together a bit ago. Betty prayed earnestly that our Lord would not wait long to come for her. She's had enough pain and wants to go home. That's a hard prayer for me to pray. But I joined her and asked FB to pray likewise. Mom, Todd and Tara and I shared a meaningful time discussing Mom's situation, how we wanted it to end and how we would say good-bye to her. Nothing mournful; she wants us to celebrate with her. We will. Certainly we will all sing her current favorite song, "Walking and leaping and praising God!" So, I told FB friends, if you expect to come, start practicing your leaping.

Gert: It's hard to know what to say, except I'm amazed at how faith in Jesus can turn something so horrible into something beautiful. You are an encouragement to us all. Tell Betty I think of and pray for her continually. Cheryl: Thank you for all the updates Uncle Arnold!! It makes it a little easier to be far away!! We love you both and pray for God's perfect peace at this time. You are an amazing support for Auntie Betty!! God bless!

Betty's condition continued to deteriorate. Growing pain but mostly under control, swelling of her legs and tummy from fluid retention, occasional anxiety, and total lack of appetite. She gradually required more pain meds. They attempted to control it with the long-term slow release hydromorphone she gets every 12 hours. When, in addition, she asks for short term pain med more than three times in 24 hours they raise the level of long-term. It's a catch-up business.

I am honoring her desire to go home in the midst of her suffering. I'd want to. However, I still prayed for her total physical healing. I told FB: Just wanted y'alls to know. I am asking this of my Heavenly Father. As I do, I say with the father who brought his son to Jesus: I believe – help my unbelief. And Jesus healed his son. God always works for good, in all things, so I am watching for his hand at work. We already have experienced his care in many ways.

November 29. Came to the house to do some chores. Driving home today gave me an opportunity to pray real loud, cuz sometimes methinks when I am praying quietly or silently he may not hear. I was complaining that he already has billions of folks dancing and praising around his throne so why does he need my Betty. I only have one! I am pleading with him to allow her to dance home with me. I want her whole and healthy at home. But if he thinks he needs her more than I do, I am reluctantly releasing her to his sovereign desire. (If I had created the world, I would have done things differently!;-) This morning Betty and I prayed together to Jehovah Rapha, God the Healer (doctor).

Kim: Thank you for sharing. I too wonder why God the father does what he does but I have learned to trust even though I don't understand. Hug Auntie Betty from me. My heart is with you. Another song. Faithful one, so unchanging, ageless one you're my rock of peace. Lord of all I depend on you. I call out to you, again and again. I call out to you again and again. You are my rock in times of trouble. YOU LIFT ME UP when I fall down. ALL THROUGH THE STORM, your love is the anchor. My hope us in you alone.

Karen: I am praying for her complete healing and many long years of life on earth with you Arnold. Let's keep on believing that our God is healer, he is awesome in power.

Cherie: So encouraging that God is big enough to let us rage sometimes, when we are done we can still feel him with us and giving us his assurance and peace. Tammy: Praying with you both. I need you guys to come home, I miss seeing the van and keeping track of you ♥.

November 30. I said to FB: Seventy years is not old. Probably 90 is and 95 and 100 for sure. What do you think? (I was implying that Betty was too young to die.)

Fay: Well, my Great Aunt in Germany used to say, "To live to 75, that's an accomplishment. To live to 100, that's a problem."

Arnold: I heard the other day about a 99 year old who said, "I am going to live to be 100 or die trying!" He did the latter.

Fay: At least you can't call him a quitter. Cheryl M: 70 is not old. My mom is 73 and I consider her still young! Marilyn: NO.NO.NO. 70 is not old!! And the closer I get to it the less I think it is old!! Suzan: Definitely not old and much too young to leave this world. But God does know best even if we don't always agree with his plan. He has her best interest at heart. He will look after you too, Uncle Arnold. There are tears coming for you as I write this. I love you. Kim: My father has renal cell carcinoma and is on an experimental pill. His goal is to be married to my Mom for 50 years – two more to go. Always set goals.

Arnold: We did set a goal – 50th Anniversary for our first goal. Just had our 48th October 5. That was before we knew how deadly pancreatic cancer always is.

Raymond: I agree! Many years ago when we were in our 20's, 70 was old. Funny how our attitudes change. I still pray for Betty's healing but who knows the Father's plan. God Bless and thanks for being there for Betty.

Jorlean: I agree totally! And 80 isn't as old as it used to be!!

Cherie: Gus Honecker was at church one fine Sunday when the guest speaker announced that it was his 89th birthday. Two kids that were sitting behind Gus were asking each other, "Who in the world would want to live to be as old as 89!?" Gus, in his late 80s turned to them and said, "Someone who is 88!" Hahahaha!

December 1. I posted some thoughts on visiting Betty. DON'T greet her with, "How are you doing, Betty?" (Our most common greeting to each other.) That makes her deal with the negatives of her situation. Rather, refer to something positive: the large picture windows with the great view, the snow, the neat room with all the conveniences, etc. Don't tell her you miss her multi-grain, which reminds her she is not baking this week. Tell her you are praying for her and me. We can't hear that phrase enough! When she prays she asks God to help her. You may have an encouraging scripture about God's grace, nearness, or his being our shelter. She won't say much and will soon fade away and close her eyes. Conversation completed. Now it's time to visit with me. I might even brew a cup of tea and offer you a munchie. Come and visit anytime. I enjoy lots of company.

Tammy; Reese (our ten year old neighbor) asked me a couple of days ago how Mrs. Betty is doing. I told him she's very sick and that we're still praying for God to heal her. His response was, "Well I bet God just wants her up in Heaven with him because she's such a nice lady. I would want her with me if I were God." Had to share that with you. Love you guys tons and tons.

Arnold: Yes but what about the fact that I want her too? Lovely thought, Reese!

Tammy: We are praying with you for complete healing. The other song that came to my mind was, "My God is so big so strong and so mighty there's nothing my God cannot do." But I loved Reese's simple pure thoughts on the situation, that she is such a sweet and special lady that God just wants his turn to Love on her ♥

9

Scripture Prayers for Healing

December 1

Not giving up, I posted a list of scriptures and a prayer for Betty's healing. Would you join me in earnestly praying this prayer? It is my job as Betty's advocate to appeal to hers and my Heavenly Father. It is his job to be true to his word.

Words of Scripture and Prayers for Healing to Jehovah-Rapha

Praise the Lord, O my soul;
and forget not his benefits—
who forgives all our sins
and heals all our diseases. Psalm 103:2-3
They cried unto the Lord in their trouble,
and he saved them from their distress.
He sent forth his word and healed them;
he rescued them from the grave. Psalm 107:19-20

My words. . . .are life to those who find them and health to a man's whole body. Proverbs 4:20-22. I am the Lord, who heals you. Exodus 15:26. Worship the Lord your God, and his blessing will be upon your food and water. I will take away sickness from among you. Exodus 23:25. By his wounds we are healed. Isaiah 53:5. Jesus healed many. "This was to fulfill what was spoken though the prophet Isaiah: 'He took up our infirmities and bore our diseases.'" Matthew 8:17. By his wounds you have been healed. 1 Peter 2:24.

Whoever dwells in the secret place of the Most High will rest in the shadow of the Almighty. . . . Surely he will save you. . .from the deadly pestilence. . . .You will not fear. . .the pestilence that stalks in the darkness, nor the plague that destroys at midday. . . .With long life I will satisfy him and show him my salvation. Psalm 91:1-6, 16. The tongue has the power of life and death. Proverbs 18:21.

Have mercy on me, Lord, for I am faint; heal me, Lord, for my bones are in agony. My soul is in deep anguish. How long, Lord, how long? Turn, Lord, and deliver me; save me because of your unfailing love. Psalm 6:2-4. For you who revere my name, the sun of righteousness will rise with healing in its rays. And you will go out and frolic like well-fed calves. Malachi 4:2. You are my refuge and my shield; I have put my hope in your word. . . .Sustain me, my God, according to your promise, and I will live; do not let my hopes be dashed. Psalm 119:114, 116.

Shouts of joy and victory resound in the tents of the righteous: "The Lord's right hand has done mighty things! The Lord's right hand is lifted high; the Lord's right hand has done mighty things!" I will not die but live, and will proclaim what the Lord has done. Psalm 118:15-1. Do you know that your bodies are the temple of the Holy Spirit, who is in you, whom you have received from God? 1 Corinthians 6:19. For his has rescued us from the dominion of darkness and brought us into the kingdom of the Son he loves. Colossians 1:13. Through Christ Jesus the law of the Spirit who gives life has set you free from the law of sin and death. Romans 8:2. The one who is in you is greater than the one who is in the world. 1 John 4. When I am afraid, I put my trust in you. In God whose word I praise--in God I trust and am not afraid. Psalm 56:3-4. Casting all your anxiety on him because he cares for you. 1 Peter 5:7.

My Prayer to Jehovah Rapha, the Lord who Heals:

Jehovah Rapha, Oh Lord, I am crying out to you in our trouble and ask you to save us in our distress. A deadly pestilence is attacking Betty. My once strong Country Girl, always so competent and able, is fading away. Lord Jesus, you took up our infirmities and bore our diseases. You rescued us from the dominion of darkness and brought us into your kingdom, the kingdom of your Son. I now reach out to you asking you to take up Betty's infirmity and to bear her disease.

The Gospels report many stories of all the folks you healed, as Matthew tells us, to fulfill what Isaiah said, "He took up our infirmities and bore our diseases." Lord, in the past you sent forth your word and healed many. You rescued them from the grave. Now I am asking you to do the same for Betty. You are the Lord who heals all our diseases, so now I claim that promise for Betty. Your words are life to those who find them and health to a person's whole body. We have "found" your word and claim it for us. You said you would take away sickness from among your people. We are yours, Lord, the recipients of this promise to Abraham and claim that promise for ourselves. You are the Lord who heals us! We claim healing by your wounds, as you promised. We dwell in the secret place of the Most High and rest in the shadow of the Almighty so we claim the long life you promised to satisfy us with. (70 years is not long; maybe 90 years is!) I ask you to send forth your word and heal my Betty.

The doctors and nurses all say that the best they can do now is take away her pain and make her comfortable. You promise so much more – healing and long life. You created her body and it would be such a simple thing for you to reach out and destroy the evil in her body that is destroying her and driving her into the grave. Nothing godly or spiritual about this activity and process. That is why we are casting all our anxiety upon you and calling out to you for salvation and complete healing as your word so abundantly promises. Betty's body is a temple of the Holy Spirit; it has been invaded by this evil pestilence, so we implore you to purify it, making it fit for your holy presence. We put our trust in you and claim the truth of your word. We are asking you to send forth your word and heal Betty, and to rescue her from the grave. We are simply asking you to apply your promised word on Betty's behalf.

I command this cancer to go in Jesus' name. You have no right or place in Betty's body for she is a Child of the King of Heaven and of Earth. Her body is the temple of the Holy Spirit; leave it now.

Thank you, Jesus, for taking her infirmity and for bearing this evil disease that has struck her down, and for forever delivering her from it. We rest in your protection and in your almighty shadow. You are our refuge and fortress, our shield and butler against this disease; in you we place our trust. Your word never returns void. She is healed in Jesus' name and will live, not die, in order to declare the works of the Lord. We receive his healing now.

Curtis: Uncle Arnold, I just caught up with many of your recent posts. My heart aches for you. I am praying for Aunt Betty's full healing but at the same time recognizing God's sovereignty and praying for his will. Not an easy thing to do. I wish I could be there to hold Aunt Betty's hand and give you a big hug. I love you guys! Arnold: Thank you. Great to hear from you Curtis.

Wes: thanks for sharing your journey. Unc, I don't have the words but be assured my heart is consumed with empathy and engaged in intersession for you (body mind and soul) and for Aunt Betty. All my love. Arnold: Thanks a lot, Wes!

(Curtis and Wes are sons of my two brothers who died several years ago.)

December 5

This morning this verse came up on the TV screen at the close of a program: "Have faith in God," Jesus answered (Peter's question). "I tell you the truth, if anyone says to this mountain, 'Go throw yourself into the sea,' and does not doubt in his heart but believes that what he says will happen, it will be done for him. Therefore I tell you, whatever you ask for in prayer, believe that you have received it and it will be yours." Matthew 11:22-24

Was Jesus just jerking Peter's chain, or joking around? Was he speaking hypothetically? Giving a theological theoretical treatise on prayer? No way! Jesus was speaking divine truth. He, while on this earth in bodily form, functioned in complete obedience to his and our Heavenly Father. He operated in the Father approved power of the Spirit of the Father. Can a statement hold any greater authority and power? No. This statement is from The Top, from the highest of the high.

Could this be any simpler? "Whatever you ask for in prayer, believe and you have received it." Would you join me and many others in claiming and believing for complete healing and wholeness for my (our) Betty?

One of our nurses spent some time in Africa where she and her team were privileged to pray for the healing of many. They saw several instant miracles, including one lady who received her sight after being blind from birth. A crippled man got up and walked. It's now Betty's turn to fulfill her favourite song: "Walking and leaping and praising God."

Suzan: Absolutely! We will believe God's word with you for complete healing. If we all ask and believe, then why aren't we seeing results? We are doing exactly as God is instructing us to do. Maybe some of us need to learn a few more lessons first. I can't think of any other reason. But Aunt Betty shouldn't have to suffer for others to learn. Don't understand. But I guess that's where faith comes in. Love you both. Can you explain this Uncle Arnold?

Arnold: My only answer is that it is my job to ask my Heavenly Father and it is his job to be faithful to his word. I am doing what Jesus complimented the widow for doing. She kept banging on the Judge's door until he answered. I'm banging on the portals of heaven! Jesus was illustrating persistence. Let's keep banging away!

Suzan: Ok I'll keep banging on his door with you. I'm very good at being persistent. My Hubby can verify that for sure. Believing with you for her complete healing. Thanks for answering my question. Have a good sleep.

10

Recipes, the Internet, Fasting and Deer Feet

D ecember 2. A GOOD DAY, Betty had a major bowel movement (we talk about those things at the hospital). The first in a month! She ate as much this evening as she has in a week. And she wanted to sit up more and was more lucid than she has been for some time.

On another note my neighbor clobbered me at chess. She skipped out when I was getting the best of her and then came back to finish me off when I was half asleep. Was that fair? God was with me through this trial though!

Had a great nurse, today. Gave Betty a complete bed bath with my help and completely changed the bedding.

I have been busy word processing Betty's stack of favourite recipes. I suggested over the years that I do this, but for some reason she liked to flip through the seven inch high stack with a rubber band holding them together. Many were hand written and some came from friends in the distant past. Many are yellowed with age and tattered from using hundreds of times. Like Todd's favourite spinach lasagna. Now I am sitting right under her nose and entering them in a file called, "Gramma Betty's Favourite Recipes". Got lots of time now, between doing small things for my Honey. You can find a few of our family's favourite recipes in the Appendix.

Senior Doc Reedyk connected me with the hospital's emergency Internet wireless. All I have to do is go to the other end of the hospital now for my email and Facebook. Instead of going home.

Betty's seven inch stack of recipes, collected over a period of 45 years. This is just the loose ones. She also has a 100 recipe books! The small pile is what I've word processed, about 20 pages worth. The large pile could take five years!

Well-worn "No Boil Lasagna" recipe. (See Appendix for a copy) This was Todd's favourite meal, spinach lasagna. Methinks we had this every week he was a teenager and again when he came back home for two different stays. Joli: Don't ever throw this copy away however faded – it's part of the story.

With Three Grandkids

Betty & Arnold with Todd and Lisa's three children on our chesterfield. They came to visit November 2, not long before Betty entered the hospital.

December 6

They came to clean our room. So I took 43 steps down the hall in 25 seconds to the tables and chairs at the Y in the hallway. Here I am close enough to the wireless to talk to you folks. Today, after discussions with Betty's sister, who was a palliative nurse at the Foothills for years, and Deb our official pc nurse, we convinced the Doc to remove the IV and discontinue the saline solution. She is taking water and a bit of juice all day long so I didn't think she needed any more than this. She is retaining massive amounts of fluid, making her exceedingly uncomfortable. Besides the IV is a big hassle. We are also changing from hydromorphone to morphine which apparently has less potential for being toxic. With no saline solution this seems to be a good move cuz she cannot be dehydrated or the pain med will become toxic. I am trying to figure all this out! Life is complicated right now.

A few minutes ago Betty felt a touch on her shoulder. She said, "Whoa!" and woke me up from dozing on the couch. Maybe it was the touch of her angel!

Just went for a walk with Betty. We slipped on her housecoat and slippers, took off her oxygen and hiked out the door and down the hall a few yards and back. She was quite alert for a while. Nice. We did take off the IV today but decided against changing pain meds after talking again with the head nurse. Betty has not asked for extra pain med for two days now. This was unusual, so we decided not to fix something that was not broken. Tara (our lovely daughter) is staying with her Mom tonight so I get to sleep in my own bed.

December 8

Went for a walk again – 15 feet to the hallway and 15 back to the bed. Found some air hose and attached it to give us a total of 45 feet which we walked and back again. And then another five to her chair. Short of the 25 minutes we recently walked.

One day is piling up on the last. The pain meds are working. Betty has asked for extra only once in three days. She is not eating, except for the tiny restaurant jam size packets of apple sauce she uses to help he pills go down four or five times a day. Sips water, apple juice and ginger ale throughout the day.

Betty wants me next to her. She even wanted me to come along when the nurse took her for a bath and shampoo, so I had to tell her that I didn't know anything about it but the nurse does! She trusts me, doesn't want me out of her sight.

I went to visit Habakkuk this morning, a place I go when I am in trouble. I got quite a surprise when Mr. Hab said the same things I've been saying the past few days:

How long, O Lord, must I call for help,
but you do not listen?
The Lord answered,
I am going to do something in your days
that you would not believe,
even if you were told.

Mr. Hab said,
O Lord, are you not from everlasting?
My God, my Holy One, we will not die. . . .
I will stand my watch

and station myself on the ramparts;
I will look to see what (God) will say to me,
and what answer I am to give to this complaint.
Then he prayed and concluded by saying. . . .
Though the fig tree does not bud
and there are no grapes on the vines,
though the olive crop fails
and the fields produce no food,
though there are no sheep in the pen
and no cattle in the stalls,
yet I will rejoice in the Lord,
I will be joyful in God my Savior.
The Sovereign Lord is my strength;
he makes my feet like the feet of the deer,
he enables me to go on the heights.

Some of the verses above are pulled out of their context. That's okay, I like them anyway! God is good, all the time. Even when he is silent.

December 9

I woke Betty up this morning and she almost immediately said, "I feel better this morning," and repeated this twice more in the next half hour. She asked for some apple or orange juice, something she has not done for many weeks. So she and I had breakfast together – two mandarin oranges. She chews the juice from a half section at a time then spits out the pulp. She also suggested that we get some counseling for what we should do about our situation. So I am going to phone Bill Henderson today, to discuss what he thinks we should do. I've got bottles of his recommended cancer fighting natural food products. See what he thinks of her current situation.

I've pretty much decided to fast for a while, perhaps a week, maybe longer. Betty has stopped eating again so maybe I will too. She only takes a little apple sauce to help her pills go down.

So what do y'alls think? Does fasting help bombard the gates of heaven to allow a more significant audience with the King of Kings? Is our Heavenly Father more likely to turn a listening ear to our pleadings when we demonstrate the seriousness of our entreaties by going without food so we can concentrate on our requests?

Although Jesus was led by the Spirit to go into the wilderness and fast for forty days and nights, he said very little about fasting in his teaching. He had fasted in preparation for his earthly ministry. Assuming his followers would fast, he later instructed them to do it in a humble spirit and not for show. His disciples did not fast while he was with them but Jesus assumed they would after he left them.

While prophets and teachers in Antioch were worshiping the Lord and fasting, the Holy Spirit instructed them to send Barnabas and Saul into ministry. Later these two men appointed elders in each new church, with prayer and fasting.

That's about all we learn regarding fasting in the New Testament. In the Old Testament most of the fasting is relating to humbling oneself before God in repentance, or to seek God's guidance and intervention. (See Joel 1 and 2 and Jeremiah 36; the Ninevites fasted in fear and repentance; Daniel fasted and prayed in sackcloth and ashes, confessing Israel's sin.) King David fasted and prayed for a week asking for the life of his child born to him by the wife of Uriah. When Jehoshaphat was about to be attacked by a huge Edomite army he called all of Judah to fast and seek God's help. Then he sent the choir out ahead of the army to sing and praise. Ezra fasted and petitioned God for safety on their trip to Jerusalem. Israel fasted to seek military victory over the Benjaminites.

Do I fast then to get God's attention to persuade him to act on our behalf, to intervene? Do I fast to seek the Lord's guidance in our present situation?

Betty and I walked again today. I keep thinking about when we will dance out the front door!

The FB response to my post on fasting was pretty much negative.

Makiko: Hi Arnold, Scott and I send our love and we think of you and pray for you and Betty. I appreciate your thoughts on fasting; however, I also would like you to know we care about your physical well-being as Betty's primary caregiver. With all that going on, I am sure you are tired and you are working so hard to care for her. I want you to stay healthy and not neglect yourself. So please be careful. I understand the spiritual aspect of fasting and wanting to see miracles and answered prayers. I am with you wholeheartedly and I would gladly fast with you to see miracles in your life! But please also consider your physical health. We don't want you to get sick! Take care, Arnold. Give our warm greetings to Betty.

Ehud. Arnold: I totally agree with Makiko. God's in control and knows what's best for Betty and you. He knows your heart and how much you want her healed. I don't think he needs your fasting; just continue to trust Him in everything. Much love to you and Betty.

Bonny: We too want you to look after yourself and keep your strength up. It is hard work to stay strong for your love ones, and I'm sure that God knows your hearts deepest desires and prayers. Please take care

Cheryl M: Does fasting make us weak so we can't do anything physically? I suppose it may. Maybe a Daniel fast would be good. Just vegetables. Or juices and broth. I often do liquid fasts and I feel better than when I am eating full meals. I think when we fast for spiritual reasons we are seeking God's direction. We are showing that God is more important to us than even food. We cannot do it to manipulate God. Fasting isn't something that we Christians do very much and I think we are losing out because of that.

Merle: You know how I feel about the way you fast! (Arnold's NOTE: Not much!)

Arnold: Ehud, what happened to your Old Testament theology? If Daniel fasted for the confession of the sin and the deliverance of his people from Babylon, and Jehoshaphat fasted for deliverance from the Edomites, and Israel fasted for victory over the Benjaminites, and Ezra fasted for safety in traveling to Jerusalem, why wouldn't I fast for Betty's deliverance from the evil cancer eating away at her innards? If he doesn't need my fasting, then he doesn't need my prayers or pleadings either, right? So it sounds like I just sit back and wait for whatever cuz God's got it all figured out. I thought seeking after God was supposed to mean something significant!

Cheryl M: I have read a couple books on fasting and I would read more if I had them. These books both say that we need to fast. People are healed when we fast. There is something that happens when we fast that is amazing. Arnold, I say that if the Lord is calling you to fast then you better do it. He will give you all the strength and the energy you need to take care of Betty. When we fast we do this in God's strength not our own. If we do it in our own strength then God is not glorified.

Mahdieh: I'd say you need to be on top of your game. Eating healthy and getting enough exercise. You need to be healthy to fight! And you are helping Auntie Betty fight! To fight this disease you need to be mentally, physically, emotionally healthy just as an athlete is when they step into the ring to fight. With healthy food and drinks you are mentally alert and can make quick and accurate decisions. Auntie Betty needs you so you are right near her side fighting.

Arnold: Mahd, you sound like your mother (Merle)! Why do you assume I need calories to be mentally alert? Besides, the doc told me awhile back that I am allergic to calories. He discovered that when I eat them they break out into globules of fat. Not good!

I thanked my FB friends for their caring comments on fasting. I pointed out that there are some specialized clinics that successfully utilize fasting as a treatment for a number of health problems. Why most people view fasting as un-healthy I don't know. Probably they have not ever fasted for more than a day or so.

Fasting gives your body a rest. For most people, this is much needed as most of us eat twice as many calories as we need for comfortable survival. I have completed several long fasts without any negative consequences, including a 30 day fast when I went to work my usual five days a week. My brother fasted for 40 days and then ran a mile the next day. Fasting does not give you a foggy mind. Rather, going without food allows your mind to clear and your body to concentrate on healing and health, instead of managing the overload of calories we press into it every day. The clue to remaining strong and able during a fast is to drink lots of pure water. Actually I did have one negative result during my most recent 30 day. About half way through, I lost a wee bit of hair off my scalp, but these hairs were probably already dead! I think they've grew back. Perhaps I will try a week, but if I experience negatives I can return to food. I will keep in touch.

Well. . .I fasted for a total of six hours. Couldn't do it. I lost heart, I guess. Maybe it wasn't God's calling. Ehud was probably right.

11

Is She Going to Get Better?

D ecember 9 was a good day for Betty. She asked for some fruit in the afternoon and chatted a bit more than usual. She has usually been confused from the meds, so our discussions are in her reality rather than mine. A couple of nurses made up my bed and another completely took Betty's apart, washed it and remade it. We had five star accommodation in the Royal Queen Suite! My sister-in-law stopped by for a few hours to give me a break to go home and do phone messages and shower. And our lovely daughter is doing some Christmas shopping for us today. I am getting used to living here. A couple day ago when I went home for the night while our daughter stayed overnight with Mom, I just about came back instead. The house now seems so big, empty and silent. But tonight I'm with my honey – albeit across the room.

One nurse who looked after my Mother in Continuing Care several years ago and now works in Acute Care said that Betty is an icon in this town, implying they are taking special care of her. She is known far and wide for her multi-grain bread, cinnamon/sticky/white/brown dinner buns. She spent all day Mondays baking for the Market and was up at 4:45 to bake the sticky buns that had risen all night. Then put together the Market muffins: rhubarb, orange/date, and raison bran. Almost always sold out of everything. The last several markets in September were tough for her, but my Country Girl always came through!

Tammy: I Love watching you care for your Country Girl. Your Love for each other is such a Blessing and inspiration to witness first hand.

Arnold: Just can't help myself – got such a lovely lady!

December 9. Gotta tell you this. I was walking back to the room and heard, "ARNOLD. ARNOLD!" My Betty was calling at the top of her voice – using her good old country "Come bossy" bellow. She wasn't upset, just calling me to the task. All she needed was something to drink. She asked for ginger ale so I got some. I turned around after a bit and discovered she had guzzled ¼ of a can, then some more. She does not guzzle; for two months she has taken liquids a sip at a time. So this was a good, not a great day. We also went for our usual 45 foot walk for the 4th day. So will you pray with me that tomorrow will be even better? Hungry and thirsty seems to me to be good signs, along with the return of her good ol' country cow call!

I requested a new diet for Betty of soft foods, mostly fruit. They brought a tub of pureed apricots, which Betty ate 2/3 of – the most she has eaten in one "sitting" for six weeks. Gave her a "sit-on-the-bed" wash and put on her brand new hunter green night gown. She came to the hospital with two ten year old ones. Those shiny silky ones never wear out. So I had Tara pick out a couple of new ones. She found a couple same style and material Betty likes. Our daughter knows how to get things done.

December 10. Went for our walk for the 5th day. Betty ate a couple ounces of apple sauce and drank two ounces of fruit juice. She was a bit more alert today. Do you suppose our Lord is reducing the tumor?

December 11. I wanted to read some praise Psalms this morning and this is what I opened to. These are excerpts from Psalm 116, 117, and 118; the verses are all about praising God for delivering me from trouble, sorrow and death. We shout victory for he has given us life.

I love the Lord, for he heard my voice;
he heard my cry for mercy.
Because he turned his ear to me,
I will call upon him as long as I live.
The cords of death entangled me,
the anguish of the grave came upon me;
I was overcome with trouble and sorrow.
Then I called on the name of the Lord:
"O Lord, save me!"
The Lord is gracious and righteous;
our God is full of compassion.
The Lord protects the simple-hearted;
when I was in great need, he saved me.
Be at rest once more, O my soul,
for the Lord has been good to you.
For you, O Lord, have delivered my soul from death,
my eyes from tears
my feet from stumbling
that I may walk before the Lord
in the land of the living.

Great is his love toward us.
and the faithfulness of the Lord endures forever.
Praise the Lord.

Shouts of joy and victory
resound in the tents of the righteous:
"The Lord's right hand has done mighty things!
The Lord's right hand is lifted high,
the Lord's right hand has done mighty things!"
I will not die but live,
and will proclaim what the Lord has done,
The Lord has chastened me severely,
but he has not given me over to death. . . .
I will give you thanks, for you answered me;
you have become my salvation.

Is this a Word from our Lord, or what? Give thanks to the Lord, for he is good; his love endures forever.

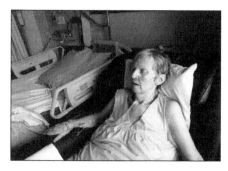

Betty caught snoozing – her main occupation now. In a first rate fancy recliner with just about every movement control possible.

Marg: Thanks Arnold for this photo. She's still such a beautiful woman. Arnold: I hesitated to include this pic, but she is whom I relate to every day and who greets visitors. You can see the hardship she is enduring. My capable Country Girl is fading. I cry. Suzan: Aunt Betty looks like a sleeping angel. She is a beautiful woman. She is truly an example of faith to us all. Joli: Thanks for sharing the picture Uncle. It shows us so much.

Arnold: Betty continues to amaze me. She has not missed once. If you touch her hand and say her name, she will open her eyes and in a moment say Hi and name you by name. Instant recognition in spite of the heavy pain meds. Her mind is still sharp. That's my Honey!

12

Royal Treatment

P alliative care doesn't have an encouraging title so I dubbed our new abode, The Royal Queen Suite. Best in the house, that's why I chose this name. Fully equipped with fridge, microwave, coffee maker with coffee, tea kettle, sink, bath with shelves and shower, double closet, chesterfield with a Murphy bed in the wall behind (just remove four cushions and tip down bed), TV with VCR and CD, sitting area outside of room (also for public) with a patio and another great view. The local Palliative Care group has done a terrific job putting this together. Also have access to the main kitchenette to make toast. This is now our primary abode.

The lounge viewed from the Royal Queen Suite.

These frosty scenes outside our window. I enjoy these views every day. Nice patio but not very accommodating in November and December.

Looking out our "Living Room" window. The two toys in the window are the twins' first birthday gift – November 30.

13

Some dude took a bite out of an apple

It was December 12, as I sat looking across our Royal Queen Suite at Betty. She was completely disoriented, confusing the bed table for a bath tub and wanting to have her feet in a "sweet place". The day before as she ate an orange she repeatedly insisted it was cheese. Serious conversations are now history. Her bed sore was looking horrible as it turned black as the surrounding tissue dies. She leaves blood on the toilet seat. Thrush, a fungus, keeps reoccurring in her mouth. She moans and groans continuously as she sleeps, day and night. I wondered where God was. Maybe in Kansas. Or Timbuktu. Perhaps he was visiting Mahd and Ant in Australia? Or Jolie in New Zealand.

It seemed totally unfair that because some dude took a bite out of an apple 10,000 years ago that my Lovely Betty should suffer such a lingering dreadful death. From the waist up she is skin and bones and below she is grossly ballooning from fluid retention. My Beautiful Betty! Dying such a death is cruel – unjust, and unfair. If it was blizzarding today I would be sorely tempted to take her and go out for a long walk in it. Maybe the Indians and Eskimos had something going for them with this practice. But out the window all I see is fog.

I opened a file I had put together years ago regarding fasting. Here is a summary.

The Ezra Fast: finding solutions to a complex problem. What do you do when you bump up against a serious problem? Somehow we expect a perfect world and are surprised when we have problems. When they come we develop poor attitudes like: I am unusual. I am unspiritual. God has forsaken me. Three problem solving attitudes: You cannot run from problems. You cannot keep problems from happening. You can solve your problems.

The sin of Adam brought pain into this planet. Job said, Man who is born of woman is of few days and full of trouble (14:1). Man is born to trouble as surely as sparks fly upward (5:7). Jesus promised us trouble and hardship. Everything any human being makes breaks. Everything God made he cursed. Problems are a part of life and learning to solve them is a part of becoming spiritually mature. Look at the problem facing Ezra and how he solved it.

Prescription from the Ezra Fast. Share the problem. Fast seriously. Withhold food and agonize in prayer and intercession, "that we might humble ourselves before our God." A decision to fast recognizes the seriousness of the problem. Fasting produces: introspection, examination, confession and intercession. What did Ezra do? He gathered at the river and waited, then sought solutions to the problem. He called a fast "to seek of (God) a right way" (KJV). This problem-solving Ezra fast is not an attempt to escape a complex problem but to enlist the Holy Spirit's aid in tackling it.

By setting aside to seek God I declare that he is more important than anything else. I am paying more attention to my own inadequacies and to God's adequacies. When we fast the Lord pays increased attention to our heart motives. The essence of our faith is oneness with our God. Focus is the issue; a changed heart is the result. "The Kingdom of God is not a matter of eating and drinking, but of righteousness, peace and joy in the Holy Spirit" (Romans 14:7). Prayer needs fasting for its full growth.

Guess I will attempt to pay attention to my own words. God says, You will seek me and find me when you seek me with all your heart (Jeremiah 29:13).

True fasting results: Your light will break forth like the dawn, and our healing will quickly appear; then your righteousness will go before you, and the glory of the Lord will answer; you will cry for help, and he will say: Here am I. Isaiah 58:8-9

I posted these thoughts and received quick responses:

Kim: This morning you both came across my mind as I prayed. I know where God is. He found you both faithful and chose you to carry a burden that myself and many could not. And even though it's hard and you grow weary, he is near. I too join in the fast for better days.

Miriam: I am praying for you and Betty more and more. Last night I even prayed in the moments when I woke up during the night. Keep hanging in there! Keep clinging to God, as his right hand upholds you!

Louise: This was in my devotional this morning. . . and my heart went immediately to you. Lamentations 3. "He has driven me away and made me walk in darkness rather than light; indeed he has turned his hand against me again and again, all day long. He has made my skin and my flesh grow old. . . Even when I call out or cry for help he shuts out my prayer. . . I have been deprived of peace; I have forgotten what prosperity is. So I say, "My splendor is gone and all that I had hoped from the Lord." I remember my affliction and my wandering. . . I well remember them and my soul is downcast within me. Yet this I call to mind and therefore I have hope. Because of the Lord's great love we are not consumed, for his compassions NEVER fail. They are new every morning; GREAT IS YOUR FAITHFULNESS. I say to myself, 'The Lord is my portion; therefore I will wait for him.'"

Sylvia: Our family experienced what death was like this past Fall when my Mom went Home. Death is not a pretty thing; it's downright ugly. It's painful; for the one suffering as well as those faithfully watching by the bed side. I'm reminded that Jesus' death was not pretty. Why did God make death this way? I don't really know, but it made it easier for me to say good-bye to my Mom knowing she would be without pain and suffering. If God has laid it upon your heart to "fight for her life" then he will give you the strength, but it may be that you need to put Betty into God's loving arms. If that is so, I pray he will give you the courage and strength to let her go. Just think, when Betty crosses over and "steps on shore and finds it HEAVEN, of touching a hand and finding it God's, of breathing new air and finding it celestial, of waking up in glory and finding it HOME." We are praying for you and your family.

Wes: Arnold, my prayer for you is that you will hear the words Jesus is speaking to you. That you will hear through the anguish, pain and confusion. I dare not write anything as I find my words inadequate. Jesus' words and comfort will be perfect as he gives them to you. I believe he will embrace you in strength.

Ann: Dear Arnold and Betty, We keep following your updates and marvel at the tenacious faith you have had as you trust our loving Father to do what he thinks is the best. In our Sunday School Class we read from the scripture about the question John the Baptist asked as he sat in prison. Was Jesus really the Messiah, when he did all those miracles? He was told that "Blessed are those who are not offended because of him." Then there was the Saturday between the cross and the resurrection when his disciples asked lots of questions. There are many Saturdays in our lives when life is perplexing. BUT we know that our Father is faithful. Sending our love and prayers, Len & Ann.

Joli: He is here with me and he is there with you. I pray that you will feel his breath on your cheek; He is that close to you in your darkness. Makiko: Arnold, what I appreciate about this site is that you are real and you don't sugarcoat what's happening. It helps me understand the reality of what's going on. Thank you for being willing to share with us. We continue to keep you close in our hearts and lift you two up in our prayers. I am sorry for your pain. Irene: Sometimes the Lord sustains us one step at a time! One foot ahead of the other! Arnold: I agree, but the walk is getting long.

On FB I thanked them all for their kind and encouraging comments. I very much appreciated them taking the time to post them. Their words helped me to think outside my own cocooned experience and to understand this major event in my life in a more improved context.

I had been so inspired by the scriptures that opened my day, then Betty woke up having a real downer. Wouldn't take her pills, sip water, or eat anything, and wanted to die. She was very unhappy. I endured this for several hours then needed a break. So I decided to walk home as I was not getting enough exercise. I also needed to complain out loud to God and cry in private. Needed someone with a physical body to talk to so phoned my neighbour whose wife was about to start watching a crazy movie with a houseful of ladies. He was heading out of town so we went to Drumheller and had broccoli soup and coffee at Tim's. I came back several hours later and Betty got up, drank some apple juice, and ate apricot puree. And my Honey and I went or our sixth 45 foot evening stroll. So the day has ended much better than it started! Finished all the veggies and fruit in my fridge and tomorrow I am on juice only for a couple of days. Well, maybe some coffee. Perhaps I can hear God better with an intake of fewer calories.

Tammy: It was ten ladies, my friend. Thank you for the candies. Big hugs. Sorry I didn't read this before I dropped off the care package of more fruit and veggies today xoxoxo. And by the way it wasn't a crazy movie it was just a sappy girl movie: P. Arnold: Is there a difference? Tammy: lol Be nice. Arnold: Will I get extra points? Tammy: Nope ya already got them when ya dropped off the candy for us. Can't get double points in one day ya know.

14

"Is it time to go?"

O n December 13 the nurses gave Betty a subcutaneous injection site. It func-
tions similarly to an IV but puts the goodies just under the skin into the fatty
tissue. She refused the anti-nausea pills twice and as a result threw up after the
second. As a result she had severe pain for a while but now that problem is cared
for. Now they can inject the meds instead of attempting to have her swallow them.
Apparently this works almost as quickly as injection into the artery via IV.

I finally turned an important page yesterday. In the current chapter of Betty's
and my story, the pages are heavy, not easily flipped over. I had struggled for days
with how to understand healing as related to Betty. Finally I decided that I needed to
give her over to God as some of my FB counselors suggested. Others continued to
encourage me to claim complete divine healing so that she could come home with
me. The evening before I had a lengthy discussion with a Christian nurse who helped
me finally lay this page down. I can no longer pray for her healing. Others can and I
hope they do. While watching her gradually fade away I could only turn her over to
God. And I have told Betty the same. I think she is still lucid enough to understand
this. I thanked FB folks for helping me turn this page.

Today she took a turn for the worse. Fluid was collecting on her lungs to make
her breathing noisy. She groaned and moaned while she slept most of the time. She
absolutely refused to take her meds first thing this morning but did take her pain
pills later.

I said, "Betty, I give you to our Sovereign and Loving God. Still, my heart
pounds, my lips quiver and my eyes drop tears; my legs tremble as I wait. Yet I
rejoice in the Lord and take joy in my Savior. He is my strength and will yet make
my feet like the deer. I hope in the Lord who will make me soar on wings like an
eagle." (Adapted from Habakkuk 3 and Isaiah 40) After all, "Arnold" does mean
"Strong as an eagle." God is Good, all the time!

I shared these thoughts on FB, and as always, received so many encouraging replies.

Ehud: Arnold, I was praying for you to release her. I understand how difficult it was for you but I know that God is being glorified and that he is very close to you and Betty right now. Romans 11:36. With much love, your brother and friend.

Kevin: My heart aches for you, Arnold. You're not alone in this struggle, yet I know it doesn't feel that way. In many ways it seems like the world churns on, oblivious to our private pain. The fact that there are "a great crowd of witnesses" who have suffered the same and triumphed, is supposed to comfort us (Hebrews 12:1). But in the moment it does little. Yet, cling to the hope that one day you will see Jesus face to face, he will wipe the tears from your eyes and say, "You did it! You stayed the course. You kept faith in me, even in the darkness." A song I say so many times while watching over Alyssa, was "Christ the Solid Rock." One of my favourite stanzas is, "When darkness hides his lovely face, I rest in his unchanging grace. Through every high and stormy vale, my anchor holds within the veil." Like Job of old, your faith is a living testimony that there are people who will love and trust God, even when he isn't giving us what we want. "Therefore we do not lose heart. Though outwardly we are wasting away, yet inwardly we are being renewed day by day. For our light and momentary troubles are achieving for us an eternal glory that far outweighs them all. So we fix our eyes not on what is seen, but on what is unseen. For what is seen is temporary, but what is unseen is eternal." 2 Corinthians 4:16-18. Grace and peace.

NOTE: A few years earlier Alyssa was born to Kevin and his wife with severe brain damage. As an Elder, I and Betty, with others, prayed for her complete healing. She died a year later. It was from folks like Kevin, who I knew understood my dilemma that I received the most courage and encouragement.

Tammy: Teary eyed hugs xoxoxoxox Love you both. Marilyn: Oh, Arnold. My heart aches for you. I too sometimes question why God allows us to go through such pain and yet God loves Betty and you. There will be healing for Betty, although it may be when she is with her Savior. You are in my prayers.

Gabriela: Dear Arnold, thank you for sharing this part of your life, my heart even far in distance is with you and Betty. The love you have for Betty will last forever. Separation hurts, but love heals. Please receive a big hug from me.

Jan: I so remember when I came to this point when Walt was close to entering Heaven's Gates. It is fresh in my memory. I will pray much for the Holy Spirit to be all he has promised to be, strength, peace, joy in the middle of tears and anguish and all you need. It is amazing and beyond understanding. I will continually pray for Betty's healing that his name will be glorified. NOTE: Jan was married to my brother who died a few years ago. Her first husband, Walt, died of cancer. She knows!

Suzan: Hi Uncle Arnold. I have felt for the last week that you should do exactly what you did yesterday but didn't know if it was my place to tell you to turn your dearly beloved completely over to the Lord. He knows the cry of your heart. I have felt that her pain may have been decreasing because then the Lord would just see to it that she would go peacefully. I know I would have as much trouble as you have had in giving my dear love over to the Lord in that way even though I know it should be done if I was ever in that place. I know God will honor your heart but in the way that is best. He will honor you for taking that incredibly hard step. You are in my thoughts each day. I pray that God will give you an exceptional peace in knowing that you have done the right thing and that he is completely in control. Wish I could give you a big hug. Give our love to Aunt Betty too. God is with you.

James: Praise the Lord for the Christian nurse and the freedom to minister in such a powerful way. My heart also aches for you Arnold. I am sure that you have heard this before but I want to encourage you. Remember that trusting God to be God and trusting that God is loving and good and compassionate and wise, even if he takes Betty home, is as big a step of faith. It's as big a step as believing that he can heal her and keep her here on earth. God will decide whether her healing should be on earth and temporary or in heaven and eternal. It is my prayer that you will be overwhelmed with the love of God, so that there will no room for fear or doubt or discouragement. Love you brother.

On December 14, at 10:08 pm I posted this on Facebook:

My Betty is now pain free and dancing in heaven with her children. She quietly stopped breathing at about 1:45 this afternoon. I am so happy for her. She experienced pain all her life, suffering from fibromyalgia since high school and often over the years having to take pain meds to go to sleep at night. These past four months have been very difficult for her. Not anymore!

At 4:30 this morning she called for me and we had this little discussion.

I asked what she wanted. She said, "Is it time to go?" I replied, yes it is time. She said, I'm going but you're staying? Yes, Betty, you are going and I am staying. Then she repeated four times, I am going but you are staying. (I think she wanted me to come along, as I usually did when she asked.) She spoke quite clearly in spite of a rugged voice due to all the fluid in her lungs, whereas a few hours earlier she had tried to tell the gathered family something but couldn't. This was the last time she spoke. I am grateful for this last bit of sharing. A treasure to remember.

Betty's Celebration Service will be at 1:00 pm next Wednesday at Mt Olive Church in Three Hills. Burial will take place in the Didsbury cemetery following the Service. Viewing for the family and invited friends will take place at 10:30 am on Wednesday. A feature of the Service will be a local group of performers leading us in singing Betty's recent favourite song.

My heavy burden is starting to lift.

Responses, December 14 through 18:

I include all these responses because these wonderful folks knew how to talk to someone whose loved one has just left in death. A lot of people can only come up with the usual clichés, like, "Now she is in a Better place", or "She is now pain free". Most of them will be true, but I needed more than that. Most of us really do not know what to say. These comments may help you next time you feel inadequate.

Tammy: xoxox. Ehud: May the Lord bring all the comfort that you need right now, Arnold. I am praying for you and for your family. "The LORD cares deeply when his loved ones die" (Psalm 116:15, NLT). Gert: Praise the Lord; praise God our savior! For each day he carries us in his arms. (Psalm 68:19 NLT)

Cheryl: I bet she's walking and leaping and praising God!! We will be praying for you and the kids. May God give you peace like a river and the strength to carry on. We love you all. And you Uncle Arnold were an inspiration to us all. What dedication and support you showed to our dear Auntie B!! Hugs to you across the miles! Louise: Strength to you as you begin a new leg of your journey with the Lord. We're sad and happy at the same time. Psalm 116:15.

David H: We love you Uncle Arnold. You can count on a lot of people to continue to keep you and the kids and grandkids in our prayers. Joli: God bless you Uncle Arnold with peace. We rejoice that she is pain free and with the Lord and her children. We sorrow for you. Lots of love. Malcolm: Arnold, I'm glad you had those precious moments with Betty today. I pray God fills you with peace now.

Ruth: Dear Arnold, Tim and I continue to pray for you. Betty was always such an encouragement to me with her smile and kind words! It was good to see you this morning at 7:00 am. My thought as you and Tim laughed together was how obvious the light was in your eyes – in spite of your pain. May you know God's Presence and Peace more than ever before. Much love. David & Wendy: We are so sorry for your loss, Arnold, yet we rejoice that Betty is in the presence of her Lord and dancing, free of pain. May you know the deep peace and comfort of that same Lord as you enter this new phase of your journey with him.

Amanda: Oh Uncle Arnold my heart aches for you. I am so thankful you will have the Lord's peace and comforting voice with you through this difficult time. Love from our family to yours, Ryan and Amanda. Mahdieh: Love love love to you. We are all still here for you Uncle Arnold. Auntie Betty is with her babies, her Mom and Dad and her brother. We will see her again. How wonderful is that?! We will all be together one day in Heaven.

Ann: Dear Arnold and family, our heartfelt condolences and prayers are with you. Your faithfulness and sharing of your burden and journey have been a great blessing and challenge to your family and friends. We hope to attend the Celebration service. Love and prayers, Len & Ann. Cherie: Arnold, thank you for letting us come on this journey. I feel that I can mourn and rejoice with you and your family and I have no doubt that she is dancing and singing pain free now. God blesses you always.

Kevin: May Jesus bring you much comfort and peace, Arnold. Fay: Sad, yet rejoicing with you and Betty. (((big bear squeeze))) Bethany: Thank you for letting her go. God is good and he knew what was needed. Kyle and I send our love to you! xoxox Heather: Praying for you, that the God of peace surrounds you. Thank God Betty is free of pain; God is good, all the time. Thank you for sharing your journey, what a testimony of God's love and grace. God Bless

Kim: My heart is united with yours. May God give you peace. Blessed are they who mourn for they shall be comforted. Alana & Richard: Our hearts and prayers continue to be with you during this time. Sylvia: I am so sorry for your painful loss. Thank you for sharing your journey with us. We will continue to pray for you and your family.

Suzan: Hi Uncle Arnold. Just checking to see how you are doing. I pray as you build Aunt Betty's resting place you will enjoy lots of special memories. May your days be peaceful and your burden lifted. I know she is watching down on you with great admiration and pride. See you on Wednesday. Marg: This morning I took the time to make a delicious pot of Betty's corn chowder soup. My gang loves it. Bless you brother and see you next week.

Lyle: Thank you Arnold for keeping us all involved in your journey. You have shared your heart with us and you have taught us something about what community means. And I have learned some new things about how to grieve. Please continue.

Jan: Thank you so much for sharing Betty's Homegoing. It touched me deeply! I'm sure she did want you to go with her. When Ray went so suddenly, I said, No, No, you can't go without me! I wanted to go too. I know the Lord will lift you and surround you with his presence as you could never imagine. Praise be to God! The Holy Spirit and Betty's presence will be so near.

Martin: Dear Arnold: I thank God for Betty's release and pray for your comfort. It has been a blessing to see you support her through this difficult illness. May you experience the peace of God through these days.

Cheryl: Happy memories of Auntie B. I was always impressed and amazed by the snow white divinity fudge she brought to Gramma E's at Christmas time. She was the auntie who always had a camera in here hand – documenting life:) She was my mentor! Her amazing bread and buns. Christmas letters in January:). Her love and pride of the grandbabies! These memories will live on and on. OXOX

Cheryl M: Oh, Arnold, I am sorry to hear of Betty's passing. I am so glad we don't mourn as others mourn but we will all be reunited in eternity where we will not have to say goodbye again. May you and your family be carried with the shalom of our Father. Watching you through all of this has really been a testimony to me.

James E: Dear Arnold, I have been following the posts over the last few weeks, and I wish you God's peace and grace at this time, as you both celebrate and grieve the passing of Betty. Your posts have shown me a model of love and faithfulness that is truly Christ-like, and that I can only hope to emulate in my marriage. May you know God's nearness and comfort as you are called to walk through the 'staying'. Your brother in Christ.

Rennie & John: Arnold, our deepest condolences to you and your family. Our prayer is for strength, peace and the comfort of the Holy Spirit. Thank you for allowing us to share in your journey as Betty fought this noble fight. Glad that she is free and home, but so sad for your loss and grief. She will be missed by many many people. She is healed. Now we pray for the healing of your broken heart and that peace that passes understanding. Blessings and much love to you. Tammy: ♥ xoxox

15

Betty's Final Resting Place

Two of my brothers, Curly and Lyle, and I are building Betty's final resting place in my Barnboard Woodart Studio. This is our act of love in together contributing to our Goodbye to her.

Most Facebook friends were not able to attend our Goodbye Service for Betty, so I posted the obituary that I placed in the local paper. I also included the order of service.

Obituary, Betty Stauffer

Betty (Margaret Elizabeth) Stauffer was born in Castor, Alberta, May 28, 1941. Her Dad, Robert Murray Holloway, a cattleman and grain farmer, also raised Percherons. Mother, Rita Irene (Weaver), had been a school teacher before Betty was born, walking two miles each day to school often through three feet of snow.

Oldest of a family of seven, Betty was also the firstborn in her generation. But she was soon surrounded by a host of cousins who grew up on nearby farms. She completed early grades a small rural school in Fleet and later finished High School in Castor. She studied for three years at Mountain View Bible College in Didsbury, Alberta, where she had an on and off relationship with Arnold. At the end of the third year he finally fell permanently under her charms and they married October 5, 1963. They recently celebrated 48 years of a wonderful life together. During the past four years of retirement they were seldom apart.

Arnold and Betty raised two children: Todd (married to Lisa Hegedys) who have three children (Makayla, Chelsea, Janessa), and live at Sunnyslope; and Tara (married to David Zimmerman), who have four children (Nathaniel, Jonah, Britni, Aliyah), who live at Bragg Creek.

She is survived by brothers David (Mary), Keith, Jerry (Rebecca), and sister Merle (was married to Javad). Brother John died at six weeks and brother Ronald at age 17 in a vehicle accident along with Betty's mother.

Robert married Enid (Hahn) Mitchell in 1971, who brought with her to the Holloway home three lively daughters, doubling the previously rather quiet household. The first time Betty was home for a meal, she said, "Wow, this is like a birthday party every meal!" In addition, Betty also gained three step brothers and another step sister.

Betty is survived by numerous cousins and nephews and nieces, one aunt and one uncle.

Arnold recently commented several times to Betty's about her beautiful hands, which were slightly knurled by rheumatism. They sewed baby clothes for her children and blue jeans for them into their teens until they discovered they were not the designer type worn by their friends. For many years she created cross stitch pictures which grace the homes of many friends and relatives. Friends and family members have long encouraged Betty to sell her unusually delicious bread and buns. Her baking was always enjoyed at family gatherings and by guests. In recent years she brought them to the Three Hills Farmers' Market and usually sold out. In addition she baked her famous multi-grain bread and buns for many folks. Wherever we lived she became well-known for her amazing sticky buns. For the past two seasons she and Arnold Managed the Market when it grew to over 50 vendors and up to 80 tables.

For many years Betty and Arnold have been members of the Three Hills Good Health Club which holds meetings to encourage good health and operates the local Good Health Store. For the past three she served as secretary to the Club. She also served as Deaconess at Mt Olive Church.

Betty was a singer, starting as a preschooler soloing at the rural Markham church in Fleet, Alberta, and at school concerts. She sang in trios and the choir at College and in many church choirs as well as with the Seminary choir while Arnold attended Asbury Theological Seminar for four years in Kentucky.

She dearly loved her seven Grandchildren. Her greatest sorrow when she was recently sidelined by pancreatic/live cancer was that she would no longer be able to look after them on occasion. The family always came home at Easter, Thanksgiving and Christmas where we all enjoyed Betty's delicious turkey dinners.

His "Country Girl" will be deeply missed by Arnold, and by his children and grandchildren and a host of relatives and friends.

Her Celebration Service will be Wednesday at 1:00 pm at Mt Olive Church, with Son-in-Law Rev. David Zimmerman officiating. Burial will take place at the Didsbury Cemetery following the Service.

In lieu of flowers, donations may be made to the Three Hills Good Health Club, at the Good Health Store. A memorial to Betty is being established to pursue research and to promote the prevention of disease.

Cheryl: Thank you for this Uncle Arnold! What a beautiful tribute to a lovely lady. We think about you often and pray for you daily. All the best to you and your family. Hugs from afar. Mahdieh: Thank you Uncle Arnold for sending this. Today Anthony and I walked to the ocean with a little bouquet of handpicked flowers and read aloud the obituary that you wrote. We said a prayer then put the flowers for

Auntie Betty in the sea. I hope that the service is very lovely for you all tomorrow. We are all there with you. I love you xo. Arnold: Mahd and Ant: Beautiful. You have been so caring. Thank you.

16

Why Dying can be so Unpleasant

O n December 18, at 7:28am, I posted this document on Facebook. I wrote it in the wee hours of the morning in an attempt to understand why Betty had to suffer. I said that this may be a note that that they would not find pleasant and maybe should not read. Parts of this article are a repeat of The Story. They are referred to because I had to re-think what had happened and mull it over trying to make sense of it. Life does not always come as a puzzle that can be put together by the best of the puzzlers. Maybe it is not really supposed to make sense – in the here and now. Some questions are not to be answered this side of heaven. But we still desperately, at times, want to understand difficult events that invade our lives, unwanted.

It is 2:30 AM Saturday, and I cannot sleep, sitting in my chair in the living room. Thinking of the terrible things that happened to Betty during the past six months. My Beautiful Betty.

Since June when the cancer pain started it gradually got worse. It took our brave folks in the Health Industry four months to figure out that she had liver cancer that probably originated in her pancreas. By October we finally checked her into the Foothills Hospital through the Emergency, because we just could not wait any longer to see the Foothills specialist. That took five hours and the necessity to be interviewed by staff in four different offices. They all asked her the same basic set of questions.

It was in the Foothills where the surgeon who was to operate on a cyst in Betty's pancreas decided to do another CT scan. Through this procedure along with a biopsy he discovered the cancer in her liver, which he said originated in the pancreas. This was a death sentence as they cannot treat this kind of cancer. (I found out later that in Canada 12,000 people are diagnosed very year with pancreatic cancer. And that many die from it. No research is done for this type of cancer because the North American Drug Cartels cannot make enough profit from selling drugs for such a low number of patients.)

Later a nurse in the oncologist's office told us the Betty was one of the few people on this planet that has experienced a second cancer. She had breast cancer six years ago but this new disease is not related (as most second cancers are) to the first. So a resident doc dropped by on a Saturday, after 12 days in the place, and told her to go home, without any doctor giving us further advice or providing pain medication. She had experienced increasingly severe pain over the preceding several weeks. So I brought her home and with the wonderful compassionate assistance of the Three Hills Home Care nurses looked after her for four weeks. Finally we called the ambulance which took her to the Three Hills Hospital. Within a week she was moved to the palliative care room in the Acute Care section of the hospital where she died three weeks later. A wonderful room where I lived with her and observed the tender and loving care of the nursing staff and Doctor Dada.

I watched her die – slowly, mostly without pain which was controlled by hydromorphone. But with discomfort from lying down for most of the 24 hours each day. And every waking hour trying to break through her drugged fog to relate to people. I would help her sit up on the edge of the bed and give her a back rub and take her to the bathroom. Once I had to clean her up when we did not make it in time. I would take her around the bed to a comfortable recliner chair which gave her some relief from a change in position for a few hours each day. Near the end I took her for a short walk six days in a row. She slept well at night, only occasionally calling me for help. During the day she slept most of the time. We had quite a few visitors; someone came every day. I told each one to touch her hand and say her name. Until her last few days she immediately opened her eyes and said "Hi" and called them by name. Within the fog of the medications she still had a sharp mind. I was word processing her hand-written recipes. Not too many days before the end I took one to her which had no title and asked her what it was. With just a glance at it she said, "That's Rhubarb Cake. From Merle." During her hospital stay we did have a few wonderful exchanges that were so meaningful for me.

But her body gradually became grotesque. During her final two weeks from the waist down she ballooned from fluid retention as her liver gradually shut down and failed to do its job. Her arms and shoulder lost their firmness and her bones showed through as she lost fat and her body began to feed on its tissue. One day as I sat across the room looking at her, I said to myself, "That's not my Betty." The last few days she would groan and moan, sometimes loudly, during the night and also the day. I could hardly tolerate these sounds coming from her. My gut ached in sympathy. Her eyes became glazed and focused off somewhere else. The suffering look in her eyes and on her face made me cringe.

Why am I telling you this? Because dying is evil and ugly. Especially with cancer. I've mentioned this to several folks each one whom commented about a relative who had a similar experience to Betty's. I have always thought of cancer as an evil thing – like sin. It eats away at the body and finally destroys it. Sin does that to the soul, if we allow it to take its course. Now I've seen cancer do this to the lovely lady whom I dearly love.

But after her spirit left her body, I stayed with her, along with our son and daughter, for a couple of hours. We immediately packed up my belongings in the room as I didn't want to come back to this place of suffering, dying and death. Then I sat a bit longer, alone talking to my Betty and just enjoying her one last time. I kissed her lips and brow and the beautiful knurled hands that had helped and cared for so many. As I studied her face, I was surprised to notice that her beauty had returned. It was beautiful again, and I wondered. No longer did it reflect any pain or suffering. Later I shared this observation with a nurse who had experience with many deaths in palliative care. She said that when Believers die often their faces portray a look of peace and quietness. Other folks sometimes fight death and this violence shows on their faces after they die. Betty went quietly in her sleep; she just slowly stopped breathing. She wanted to be in heaven, away from her pain and suffering.

As I pondered why such a beautiful, innocent and wonderful person should suffer so, I suddenly realized I had been wrong. Several weeks ago I told folks that I was not angry at God because he did not give Betty this cancer. But he did! He did. I opened my Bible to Genesis 3. Eve sinned, blaming her disobedience on the serpent that had deceived her. Adam sinned and blamed it on "The woman you put here with me – she gave me some fruit from the tree, and I ate it." God did not accept their lame excuses. Because they disobeyed God's instructions to them, he cursed them. "By the sweat of your brow you will eat your food until you return to the ground, since from it you were taken; for dust you are and to dust you will return." This is the curse of death, which often comes to us through disease.

I was wrong. Totally wrong. It was God who cursed mankind – we whom he created to love and serve him. We did not do a very good job if it; he had no choice but to send us back to the dust from which we came. God caused death that day and still does for every living human being. But in death Betty's face became beautiful again as she reflected the fact that God gave us all a way of escape from this body that returns to dust. It was his necessary curse because of the disobedience of mankind that caused the cancer. But, wonderfully, he allowed her to escape this curse the moment he rescued her soul and spirit from her cursed body, which at 1:45 on Tuesday began the process of returning to dust. I am almost laughing now. Mama mia! She got out of there in a hurry and did not stick around to see it happen. God instantly freed her and took her to her new eternal home.

So I wondered, "Is death so terrible, perhaps deliberately so as God the Father intended? As a result of original sin, so that we can better understand how excruciatingly evil sin really is?" If we can understand this fact, it should drive us away from sin into the arms of our Saviour who also suffered a terrible death long ago, so our very moment of death can be one of victory over the dying, and of extreme happiness. So after all, God really is Good, all the time! Now I really can laugh at death because in it I found sweet victory. My Betty is her lovely self again, and more so. Beautiful, beautiful, and wonderfully happy.

Now I am going to go back to sleep. It's 4:17 AM.

Bethany: Thank you thank you thank you for posting this!!! Lisa C: Made me cry! Thank you for sharing.

Gert: Thank you, Arnold. Your transparency through this journey has blessed me. I pray that writing and sharing all these things over the past few months has brought you healing in the midst of grieving. My prayers for you continue. Joli: God bless you Uncle Arnold! To find such loveliness requires the whole journey, doesn't it? Irene: I'm so glad you can process your thoughts the way you do. You are blessed and helped and so are we! I too will be with you all in spirit as you celebrate Betty's life.

Mahdieh: Ok, it took me a few days but I have now read your words. I didn't want to read it, thinking maybe I could deny that Auntie Betty has left this Earth. I am very thankful that you wrote this Uncle Arnold. Thank you for sharing your journey. Even though I am on the other side of the world I feel very connected to you. I hope that you feel that we are with you. I can feel the love in your words. I am trying to find what your and Auntie Betty's faith has given me – strength, hope. Thank you for this. Thank you for sharing. I love you.

David & Wendy: This was a hard read, Arnold, but powerful. Wendy has many fond memories of working with Betty in the Book Room. I know you better from our days on different sides of Distance Education. Your journey in these past weeks has been something to observe – a testimony to yours and Betty's relationship with your Abba Father. Betty is now in his presence, restored and whole, something we can all look forward to one day, but in the meantime, we deal with all the fallenness of this world. Thank you for showing us how to do it in his grace and with honesty. We trust Wednesday will be a special celebration of Betty's life. Grace and peace to you, Arnold, as you grieve and celebrate.

Tammy: Arnold, sorry it took me this long to read this. . .like Mahdieh I didn't want to read it, but my reason was because I was sure it would make me cry (which it did) but I must say you've also made me smile. We are so blessed to be part of your family. Thanks for sharing your heart.

17

Good-bye to Betty

December 20
Tomorrow we say Goodbye to my Betty.
Precious in the sight of the Lord is the death of his saints. Psalm 116:15
Betty now resides in her permanent home in heaven
And her beauty will remain forever in my heart.

Saying Goodbye to Betty (Sections copied from the Service Bulletin)
Betty (Margaret Elizabeth) Stauffer
Celebration Service ~ 1:00 pm, Mt Olive Church, Three Hills
Burial at Didsbury Cemetery ~ 3:30 pm
Betty was born on May 28, 1942, in Castor, Alberta, and went to be with our Saviour
December 14, 2011, in Three Hills, at 70 years of age.

Celebration Service
Welcome and Prayer: Pastor Dave Zimmerman (Betty's Son-in-law)
Congregational Song: Everlasting God
Betty's Story: David Holloway (Betty's Brother)
A Picture Story (Prepared by Tara [Daughter] and Friends)
Solo: Larry Hooper: The Lord is my Light
Scripture and Prayer: Pastor Rod
Congregational Song: Because He Lives
A Tribute from the Community ~ Len Perry, President of the Three Hills Good
Health Club
A Tribute from the Family ~ Lillian Nobert (Betty's Sister-in-law)
Duet: Larry & Debby Hooper: Find us Faithful
Message: Pastor Dave
Stix N Stuff Team (Tammy Roberge, Fay Issac and Kids) Song:
Walking and Leaping and Praising God: By kids, then the congregation joins.
Pianist: Charlene Cole

Following the Service you have opportunity to greet the family in the foyer before Betty's final trip to Didsbury.

Burial Service at Didsbury Cemetery, 3:30 PM
Led by Pastor Rod
Communion with a loaf of Betty's bread led by Pastor Dave
Closing by Pastor Rod

Pallbearers
Todd Stauffer (Son) Arnold (Husband)
Keith Holloway (Brother) Jerry Holloway (Brother)
Curly Stauffer (Brother-in-law) Lyle Stauffer (Brother-in-law)

Memorial to Betty
Donations. In lieu of flowers, donations may be made to the Three Hills Good Health Club, at the Good Health Store ~ for the research and promotion of the prevention of disease ~ As a Memorial to Betty.

I n Appreciation. Thank you for your many prayers and generous kindnesses in word and deed during this time of Betty's illness and passing. Your prayers and many encouragements have been very gratefully received. Thank you for helping to say Goodbye to Betty today. Lunch for the family is provided by Duane and Carol Dobson.

Betty's casket was lovingly crafted by Curly and Lyle Stauffer, with some assistance by Arnold. Lining and pillow cover was provided from Betty's stock of sewing material and Lisa (Daughter-in-Law) sewed the pillow. The brown stained wood was from Prairie Tabernacle balcony pews built by Prairie carpenters in the early 1930s. (Both Betty and Arnold were working for Prairie when they retired.)

Suzan: Uncle Arnold, that was such an amazing day. It was hard but also a joy to know that "our beautiful aunt Betty" is dancing. I will never forget having communion with her precious last loaf of bread. She would have been so pleased with all that you did for her today. She was truly deserving of it all. I had tears when I saw you dancing at the end and kicking up your heels. That would have made her smile. You have two wonderful kids and a family to love and support you these next days and months. So please take advantage of all that love and care. We are looking forward to you gracing our home with your joy and laughter. We love you dearly and you are always in our prayers. May God's love enfold you daily. All our love. Bob & Suzan. Arnold: Suzan, you are such a sweetheart!

Fay: That was a real inspiring and encouraging service, and it made my heart smile to see you kick up your heels with Tammy – I'm sure Betty would be pleased;P Sylvia: Fay, the dancing kids were great! It was a fitting way to end the service. I can just see Betty encouraging them on.

Betty's Final Earthly Resting Place

Lovingly crafted by my Brothers Curly and Lyle, with me providing plans, some advice and help along the way. The final touch was The Old Rugged Cross crafted from weathered barn board.

Tammy: Arnold I have yet to see a more beautiful resting place. Sylvia: What wonderful memories you share with your brothers as each of you contributed your gifts to make such a precious resting place for your Betty.

December 22

Several folks said it would be a hard day. Not. My hard days were past. Betty asked for a celebrative send off so that is what we gave her. She had picked the songs and in every one she was singing to me. She knew what I needed to hear. Sure I cried. But she was already in Jesus arms, pain free. So many wonderful things were said about my gentle, caring, beautiful Betty. The high point was when the Stick Kids pantomimed Betty's song, "Walking and leaping and praising Jesus." I wanted to dance that song with her, so the second time several of us did. The Stick Lady came whistling up and together we did a couple of rounds with Betty. Others joined us. That made my day! Then I drove her, by myself in our Grand Caravan, to the burial site in Didsbury where 40 family and friends said a final goodbye. Together we shared communion using Betty's last loaf of multigrain bread. Then we placed the remaining bread on her coffin, lowered it and shoveled enough dirt in to cover the casket. I was so tired that when I arrived home I parked the vehicle down the street, moved the phones to the other end of the house, closed the door and had a fairly good sleep taking most of today to relax, talk a bit to Betty, and visit with some neighbors, and go down to the church to pick up some extra Celebration Service bulletins. So many prayed for peace for me; God answered their prayers.

Betty now resides in her permanent home in heaven.
And her beauty will remain forever in my heart.

I posted this to the Facebook Group
So ends a chapter. I probably will add some notes in the days to come, starting a new chapter. Please feel free to leave the group if you want. It's easy to do. And eventually I will close the Support Group.

This Group has meant so much to me. What started out as a convenient way to get updates about Betty's health to a few relatives and friends snowballed into something totally unexpected. I was planning all along for Betty's healing and that she would come home whole and healthy. Now she is, but in her heavenly home. As this chapter unfolded I found some difficult pages that were almost too heavy to turn. But you assisted – you helped me turn them. To know that in the midst of my hurt and pain, and Betty's suffering, you all were praying for us meant so much to me. I cannot thank you enough. Your kind words were more encouraging than you could imagine. What started as a newsogram became a journal of pain and sorrow. But I decided early if this was to be meaningful sharing for both me and you, I needed to be frank and open. I was. And this helped me from going "over the edge" and to find healing. Thanks for being part of this journey and helping me along the way. Some of you have said how much this journal has meant to you and has been a blessing. That makes even greater meaning for me. Not many of us have the opportunity to walk with someone travelling along the path of a dying loved one. With your help I have learned and grown, as I trust you have. Thank you! May your blessings continue. God is Good, always!

Kim Stauffer: God is good and his love endures forever. Grief is like a rock in your shoe. You learn to live with it, knowing that one day you will meet again. "Walking and leaping and praising God," you will be comforted. I love you Uncle Arnold, and Aunty Betty is at peace. Thank you for reminding me how happy we can be in Jesus.

Building the Coffin

This brown wood was taken from pews built in the early
1930s. I salvaged from the Prairie Bible College Tabernacle
just before it was demolished.

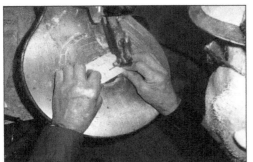

Curly, the master craftsman, made the detailed hinges and clasps entirely from wood. Crafting the hinges. Curly is especially talented at making intricate pieces.

Lining with the backside of blue jean material was taken from Betty's material stash. Brought from Kentucky where she purchased it from a blue jean factory.

Staining all the markings in the former Prairie Tabernacle balcony seats, made there by hundreds of folks visiting the Tab from 1933 till over 60 years later when it was demolished.

Betty and I had one last ride together in the Grand Caravan – to the church and then to Betty's final location – the Didsbury Cemetery.

The eight decade old well-used wood makes it look like an antique piece of furniture, perhaps something like Great Grampa would have made.

Forty family members shared communion at the graveside using Betty's last multi-grain loaf of bread, and placed the remaining bread on the coffin. Then we stood by as a crane picked up the cement cover and placed it over the coffin. After lowering it we covered it by shoveling dirt, one last way of saying good-bye.

Part Three

Loneliness and Aloneness

18

Betty's Gone. No, She is Everywhere

O n December 29 I posted some ramblings about what I have been thinking and
doing for the previous five days. It got longer than I intended.

The past five days

My Betty's gone. No. She is everywhere.

I spent Saturday and Christmas Day at Tara's, my Daughter. And they and our
Son's family came to our place to celebrate our Christmas on Monday. So I was
with Gkids from Saturday and some through Tuesday. This was good. Having ram-
bunctious kids around is fun and distracting. For the first time I cooked the turkey
and also made double cooked mashed potatoes. The girls did the rest. Yesterday I
was alone, except for two friends that came sequentially: a lady who had lost her
husband a few years ago and a neighbour who lost his wife to cancer this past year.
They came to comfort me. It is meaningful to share experiences with someone who
has been there and understands something of what I am experiencing. Along with
several phone calls, this filled my morning.

One call was from a credit card company cuz I'd missed two payments. For the
past two months I was preoccupied with caring for Betty. The bills and statements
were stacked in a box in the living room. I tried to do some online banking, which
Betty always did. Had to call the help desk for assistance so now that account is up
to date. It's garbage day. Bags had piled up; I'd missed several weeks of getting it
out on the street for pickup. Today I caught up. Eight bags (grocery size) instead of
our usual two or three.

Betty is everywhere, but she is not here anymore. I move around the house
doing stuff. Suddenly something reminds me of her and I get another shock; she's
gone. Sometimes I have to stop and cry again. I miss her so much.

This morning I looked around the bedroom. On the wall above our bed are
several things. Our wedding picture. A note on a little plaque above my side: "If I
could choose again, I'd choose you." Betty gave it to me several years ago. On her

side one I'd given her: "Love conquers all things – even snoring." In the middle was a big "Sunny Girl" craft she had made years ago. On another wall was a large garden hat she'd decorated with flowers and ribbons. On her dresser was a picture, my gift to her long ago, of a lovely lady knitting, with the caption: "Thy love satisfies my heart." Above the dresser sits a little stuffed honey bee holding a card I made: "To my Honey, You've made my life sweet! Let's keep on buzzing together."

In the kitchen she is all around. Four timers magnetized to the metal fan cover above the stove. Her blender and bread mixer sit on the counter. Against the wall are two cupboards made from barnboard, the siding of an old home on her Castor farm that I salvaged years ago just before they tore it down. A barn window on the wall, with four mirrors and two shelves holding mementos, including her parents wedding picture. I just toured the house and counted eight of her cross stitches. For years she did these fine works of art for gifts and then did some for us, her family. She, being very meticulous perfectionist, would painstakingly take several rows out and re-do them if she found even one stitch in error. I'd say, Nobody will notice that error. She would reply, No, but I would!

That's our house, forty-eight years of memories.

Tuesday morning Tara helped me go through Betty's clothes. A few I will give to individuals but most will be taken to the local thrift store. Two years ago over a period of a year Betty had lost 55 pounds, for health reasons. Didn't help, but she had purchased some real nice clothes, classy looking tops and slacks. I felt I was betraying her as I took them off the hangers to give them away. Somebody asked me if this was too soon. But the Pastor said to not wait too long and a book on grieving given to me by a friend said the same. It is not good to wait; her things can become a memorial and even a shrine. Pass them on so that others can benefit. And I needed Tara's help so decided to sort them out while she was here.

Betty's jewelry is spread out on the LR table. She wanted our oldest grand-daughter to have her rings. I gave a special set of jewelry to Tara, which I had specially made for Betty from silver last Christmas. I saved a selection for Betty's sister and some for her niece in Australia. I invited our neighbors over for turkey soup and to pick out a couple of pieces. I'll save the rest for others and for the granddaughters when they get a bit older, so the jewelry will go into their dresser instead of the current toy box. I cry. Giving away Betty's nice things tears (double meaning intended) me up but I think it is best to do it now and see the smiles of appreciation on the faces of those receiving something from their Mom/Gramma/ neighbour/friend.

Betty's sewing room was packed with dozens of knitting needles and all kinds of sewing paraphernalia. And a lot of treasures from her mother and grandmothers. They are now mostly in Tara's hands to decide who should take responsibility for these precious antiques, such as crocheted doilies, dresser scarves, knitted baby clothes, hers and her mother's wedding dresses, and more. Gramma taught grand-daughter Britni how to knit, so perhaps she will one day take up sewing and benefit from some of the sewing items. Some will go to a Grand Niece who Betty knew would appreciate and value them. These treasures are now passed on to the next generation. That is what Betty wanted.

100 cookbooks. I counted them: in a kitchen drawer, on the barnboard shelves, in the hall closet. A community or church ladies cookbook from every place we lived (quite a few!). A worn out falling apart 1950s edition. A number from the 60s and 70s. A Better Homes and Gardens Dessert Cook Book dated 1960, three years before we married. Inside the front and back covers are ten hand written recipes. Several with interesting added notes. Jelly Roll from Enid (Betty's step-mother-in-law); Christmas Cake (Aunt Ruth made for the folks 40th anniversary; Made for Tara's wedding cake August 16/96); Carrot Cake (tried the first time for Arnold's 39th birthday – Good cake!); Maple Walnut Butter Cake (Lou's Mom's recipe); Cheryl's Blackberry pie; Pie Crust (Ruth Norris – Eaton's); Jell-O Fingers (Kids love 'em).

Someone described Betty as a "Foody". A good name for someone who collected recipe books for 60 years and added to them others she gleaned from magazines and the Calgary Herald which she recently read on her iPad every day, my gift to her for her 70th birthday. Cooking and baking was her occupation, her hobby and her joy. People loved her for it.

Two of my favourite books I've pictured here. "Cook Book" by the Farm Women's Union of Alberta, published in 1956. (I wonder if Betty got it for a Bridal Shower gift). It's the bluish one with the back cover missing and falling apart from extreme use. You could order it from an Edmonton address for the sum of $1.50. It contains recipes from women all across Alberta. You can tell where the most used recipes are by the food stains and comments. Cornflake Cookies – "tasteless"; Chocolate Frosted Squares – "good!". "Nanaimo Squares, p. 104"; Shortbread, checked on p. 108; Rhubarb Meat Relish, p. 166; Date Loaf underlined, p. 18. And Griddle Cakes or Pancakes, circled p. 25.

The other book titled, "Favorite Recipes", is a small ring binder chuck full of her hand written and collected items, many supported with a comment about who liked this one. Each section starts with a pocket stuffed with the collected ones. She says the Beef Broccoli Soup is "good". Two recipes for Corn & Black Bean Salad, one from Canadian Living Magazine, the other from Merle. Enchiladas from Lorrie Lott, our neighbour in Wilmore, Kentucky. Mary's Brown Bread (brother's wife) which Betty developed into her great multi-grain bread, Dan Atkin's Cinnamon Buns, Marilyn's Buns (Arnold's sister-in-law), Mrs. Neff's Red Cabbage from Thompson, Manitoba, Dumpling Pudding from home ("Todd used to like this"), Apple Pandowdy (also from home), Sticky Toffee Pudding from Simons Bistro in Calgary Herald ("Todd and Lisa both like"), Salad Dressing, old fashioned, from Rita Holloway (Betty's Mother) before the days of Mayo, Huli Huly Pork ("Arnold likes the flavour in the meat but not for dipping"), Tuna & Rice from Corky Bell (Vermilion), Boiled Raisin Cake ("Todd likes this combination"), Jumbo Raisin Cookies (Todd's favourite), Orange Blossom Cake, "from my Mom's cookbook", Forest Rangers, "used to make these cookies at home (Castor)", Best Ever Chocolate Cookies, "we like this one best", Apple Butter, Lisa. And so on.

Telus just phoned; I'm two months behind in paying the mobile phone bill. It comes online and I have to figure out how to pay it. The Telus lady told me how. I mentioned why I was two months behind and we discussed how I could return Betty's cell for credit. Someone else would call me.

Betty's gone. I am alone. What do I do now? That's the question I have been pondering the past week. I am going to visit Merle, Betty's sister in Calgary. She has been a lot of help during Betty's sickness. Having worked four years at the Foothills Hospital as a palliative care nurse, she was able to give me a lot of advice on Betty's ongoing condition and some key questions to ask the nurses and doctor. We talked a lot on the phone and sometimes cried together.

Another call from Telus. They are canceling Betty's phone number and letting me keep the phone, with no penalty. Now that's decent! I have found the credit card folks also very caring and helpful in sorting out the overdue finances.

I have talked to several siblings about me dropping by to stay with them for a day or two. Think I will take a week or so and tour the province: Merle in Calgary, sister in High River, brothers in Didsbury and Ponoka, and nieces in Edmonton and the North Country. That is, when I get all the bills paid and the house straightened out.

I talk to Betty every day. I lament that you had to leave, and that I miss you so. I feel bad about giving your things away, but think lots of folks will benefit and appreciate them. I got lost in the Mall last Saturday; your super developed sense of direction never got us lost. Every day little things pop up that I miss. Can't reach out to hold your hand for a bit while driving somewhere, or to touch your arm or briefly hold your hand to say good night. Sometimes I feel lost even in the house.

Since our Goodbye Service to Betty I have had an inner peace. The gut ache is gone; methinks because all of you and many others have promised to pray for me. I am gradually finding my way and intend to be happy. Betty would not want it otherwise. She told me she wants me to have a good life. And that "I love your forever and ever, amen!"

Betty's Recipe Books

Two of my favourite books from Betty's collection of over one hundred

Left: One of her earliest cook books, described above
Right: A binder of hand written recipes and collected ones.
Some from her mother, others from friends, relatives,
magazines and the Calgary Herald

Betty's sour cream lemon pie, worth crossing the ocean for! I word processed it to pass on to others. See the Appendix for some our family's favourite recipes.

19

Will the Tears ever Stop?

D ecember 31. It was 6:29 AM, that last day of 2011. I was lying in bed with tears in my eyes and sobbing. Didn't sleep well. Kept dreaming about Betty in the hospital. Some of the negative things. Went to Olds yesterday to take some of Betty's things to her oldest Niece who is visiting from BC. I cried when we hugged. Later at Walmart I met a family from Three Hills whom I hardly know; she said she was going to miss Betty's muffins that she bought at the Market every week. I talked about her and cried again. A guy from church stopped to give his condolences at Canadian Tire and I cried again. Can't even get any solace out of town, 45 minutes away. Then in the evening the Deacons brought flowers and we mostly talked about Betty for an hour and several times I cried like a baby. I AM TIRED OF CRYING! It's embarrassing. I should be done crying by now. But I can't help it. I talk about Betty and get choked up and the tears come unbidden. When will they stop?

I remembered that Jesus wept. He cried at the sadness of his friends when Lazarus died. I tried to understand why I keep crying but I didn't know why. Because I miss my Betty. Because my heart is broken? My grief from watching Betty suffer has turned to the hurt of loneliness. I know tears are supposed to be healing but they were hard work. The ache in my gut is back.

A new friend brought me a book on grieving, written by a man who had lost his wife to cancer. The writer reminded me a couple of days ago in a devotional called "Bottled-up Tears" that God "kept my tears in a bottle" (Psalm 56:9). God did this? God collects my tears I guess because they are precious to him. The author says, "If I try to bottle up my tears I do myself psychological damage – I know that. . . .Crying provides a welcome catharsis for me. I must release my tears!. . . .I attempt to control my tears, but they break through my defenses and spill over the dikes. Help me to accept and even to be thankful for my tears. They are an important part of my grieving. I must not quench them." I could have written that! Father invented tears. They are supposed to be therapeutic and cleansing, so I should be thankful for them. I tried to be. But I cannot cry forever.

Kim reminded me that the tears need to flow. It's part of the process, she said, and I cry with you. And 13 years later I still cry when I hear "You are my sunshine" because Dallas and Emma used to sing with me. I still weep when I ride my motor bike. . .and much more. If I keep them in I find I get angry and then they turn into the wrong kind of tears. Above my bed is a cross stitch Aunty Betty made for Trevor and I, and I cry with you again. Blessed are they who mourn for they shall be comforted. (NOTE: Kim's husband, my nephew, Trevor, and their two small children, were killed in a motorcycle accident. Kim was riding along on her bike behind them and saw this accident take place. So I highly valued her advice and consolation.)

Merle: Kim, you said this so well and you truly are an expert. I told Arnold that the doctor had me on Prozac at one time which may have helped some symptoms, but it also took away my tears. It was an awful time in my life. Without tears, I could not express my joys, my hurts, or sadness and I became morose and depressed. (NOTE: When she was 13 Merle saw her brother die. She sat in the middle of the front seat of the truck as he sat next to her, badly hurt from the crash of the vehicle. Her mother, riding in the back with two other brothers, also died. She helped me so much as Betty lay dying in the hospital.)

Irene: Yes, Arnold, I feel so deeply for all you have to go through now. Tears are hard work and very extracting but eventually you feel after a good cry that another layer of healing has happened. At least that's the way I found it. I still get "ambushed" at unexpected times. At a memorial service yesterday they sang "I shall know him" and I dissolved into tears. A person can get so lonely for heaven sometimes! From what you write I can see that you are doing well and you can be assured that the healing will continue, although gradually! I know he will be faithful to give you the courage you need one moment at a time! (NOTE: Irene was married to my brother. He was killed in a highway vehicle accident. She hung upside down in the overturned vehicle as she watched her husband die in the median. She has been a model to me for how to grieve Christianly.)

It was January 1, 2012, as I sat in Lazyboy chair that Mom gave me for my graduation 27 years before. Just finished playing a couple of games of Solitaire on the iPad. Seems like an appropriate game for a Widower. From this vantage point as I looked around the living and dining room, nothing much has changed. Betty must be around somewhere.

Even after six months of pain, numerous medical tests and appointments, two months of knowing about her terminal cancer, one month of caring for her at home and a second living with her in the hospital, suddenly it seems she must still be in the house somewhere. I had sat with her for two hours in the palliative care room after she died. I planned her Goodbye Service with the kids, songs and singers she had already chosen. And helped carry her from there to the burial site, where we shared communion using her last multi-grain loaf of bread. Placed the remainder of it on her coffin – which I helped two of my brothers build. Then I covered her coffin with dirt, saying my last goodbye to her. But now I almost have to pinch myself to realize the reality of her absence from this house and physically at least from my life.

I've known her for 60 years. Met her at Camp Meeting as kids in Didsbury and we knew each other as teenagers at Gull Lake Bible Camp. Spent three years in Bible College with her, often working together on committees and for three years as the Annual staff photographers. We wrote to each other over both summers, and dated a bit. We had been married for 48 years and 69 days.

I guess such a firmed up reality over this long time, most of my life, refuses to accept that she actually left. Oh, I knew she did. But for a few moments today, as on other days, my mind doesn't want to accept this new reality. Maybe I should just try to enjoy those moments when they come, I thought. I could talk to her for a bit.

Irene agrees with me: Yes Arnold, she wrote, on the 28th, our wedding Anniversary, I took Poinsettia's to Virgil's grave site and spent two hours reminiscing about what a wonderful life we'd had together. I looked through our albums, then went to one of my treasured pictures of him and told him all about it. I still find such comfort from those times!

I am a Widower. Discovered this fact last evening. Neighbours had invited me to their church's New Year's Eve Shindig. First public event without my Betty. There were couples all over the place of all ages. And yesterday I noticed in various stores that most shoppers were couples. But January 1st I sat by myself. It dawned on me that I am now a widower. Not a husband.

Never thought much before about what a widower is – a guy who had a wife but no longer does. Most whom I was acquainted with were old guys I didn't know very well. But I'm not 70 yet. Well, not for 22 days.

A widower. My new identity. Canadian Oxford says a widower is "a man who has lost his wife by death and has not married again." There is only one instance of this word in the dictionary, but "widow" is mentioned eight times. A form of the word "widow" appears 109 times in the Bible, "widower" is not there even once.

Oxford is wrong. I had not "lost" my wife. I knew when she left, at 1:45 pm December 14, 2011. And where she went. She went to be in Jesus' presence. I know where she is. She is not dead either, Mr. Oxford, she is very much alive experiencing eternal life in its new and better phase. A very better place.

A widower is a guy whose wife went somewhere else. It's me that is lost. I wander around the house feeling that way, directionless. A widower is a guy who mostly sleeps, eats, buys groceries, and goes out alone. I'm alone. I get lost in the Mall because my Navigator who had a highly developed sense of direction is no longer with me. I drive places by myself. There is nobody else in my bed or across the table from me. Or beside me watching TV. And what's a vacation going somewhere all by yourself?

Now I can eat whatever I want for breakfast, lunch and dinner. I go wherever I want and can buy anything without consulting anybody if I don't want to. When driving in my Grand Caravan I can play whatever music as loud as it pleases me. I am now going to use glass food storage containers instead of the old scratched up plastics. I now have plans to put a TV upstairs in the LR. Everything, house, property and everything on it, money, investments, vehicles – whatever, it's totally mine to do with whatever I please. I am a widower.

I get to do all the cooking, cleaning, scrubbing, washing clothes and windows, driving, making the bed, paying the bills, planning, gardening, etc. I am a widower.

Is this some kind of freedom to be enjoyed? I loved being a husband. Had someone to love who loved me. We did everything together and went everywhere beside each other. We talked, laughed and walked and shopped with each other. All significant decisions we faced together. Neither of us bought clothes without the other there to discuss the purchase and give appreciated approval. Now I must do all this – and more, by myself. I just bought a food processor because I want to eat more veggies. The first time I purchased something significant on my own volition in 48 years. That's cuz I am a widower.

When we found out that Betty had incurable cancer I said to her: "We are going to do this right." Now I have to find out how to do widowering right.

Tammy: (hugs) xoxox tears (see I told you I cry). Our hearts break for your loss Arnold but please, please remember you are not alone. We can never fill that empty place but God and wonderful memories of Betty can help fill it so it doesn't hurt so badly. Love you tons and tons. And when you're feeling like ya need some noise in your life you know you can just head next door (we're family remember).

Lisa C: It is so precious to read these thoughts and to see how much you loved and cared for each other. A marriage like this is not to be taken for granted. What a model for marriage that I want to follow. I will pray that you find courage, and even joy, though it may be hard to imagine now, in this next stage in your life. And that you may know you are not alone. Betty is still with you and always will be. There are many caring people in the community, and of course the Lord, who is "the best company of all".

Joanne: Good Morning Arnold, Your reminiscing brings back a lot of memories that I totally relate to. That feeling 'lost' goes on for months but eventually as you find meaningful things to get involved in, it will lessen. All your memories of Betty are pretty acute right now but that will fade a bit too with time and be more bearable to live with. For now you are deeply grieving and that is good to give yourself to it and journal too so that in a year or so, you will be able to go back and read it and realize how far you have come. The Lord is with you to bring his comfort and his sweet presence. God Bless my friend. (NOTE: Joanne's husband died in a vehicle accident several years ago. She has been a wonderful counselor and friend and advisor for me. Helped in so many ways.)

Pictured are several of the family heirlooms Betty, as the oldest of her generation, held "in trust". These three ladies made decisions on where they should go. Merle (Betty's sister) on the left, Cheryl (Betty's oldest niece, and the next generation's holder of the "trust"), and Tara, our daughter, who I gave prime responsibility for the distribution of these treasures.

Three Ladies

Cheryl: Spending time with Auntie Merle and Tara, going through family heirlooms that had been faithfully cared for by Auntie Betty for many many years. Thank you Uncle Arnold for making it possible for us to share in these treasures.

Arnold: Wow! Thanks for sharing this. You three have helped to make this very special for me. Three very fine ladies! Hugs all around. It was time to pass them on to the next generation. Betty wanted this.

Cheryl: It was an honor. Merle: These little dresses look amazing for being just short of 100 years old!

Arnold: Did y'alls ever see three such sweet ladies?!

Cheryl: Uncle Arnold, we had such a good time at Auntie Merle's going through all the treasures Tara brought along. We all left with beautiful reminders of Auntie B and the past generations. I enjoyed seeing all the pretty things from my great Grandma and Grandma Reta too. Thank you for passing on these heirlooms. Also glad we got to have lunch together and share a hug that was long overdue. I LOVE these treasures. You are very gracious in making sure we got these things. Thank you from the bottom of my heart! xoxo

December 31. I was so glad that you three: sister, daughter, oldest niece, could do this together for Betty and me. Betty wanted you to have these heirlooms. She trusted you with them; not everybody values such things, but she knew you do. Your timing was good after all. You give good hugs!

20

New Plans and Goals

On January 2 I decided to make some goals. There was no way I was going to sit around and pout or pine away feeling sorry for myself. Here they are.

My New Plan and Goals: What am I going to do now?

I usually woke up at 5:00 am or so. Started thinking and couldn't go back to sleep. So I would get up and word process my thoughts. Another day of sharing my thoughts, wonderings and troubles with my FB group. I always appreciated the encouragements from this wonderful group of caring folks.

I pondered the question, What am I going to do now? What is my life going to look like without Betty? Without a loving wife, a 24/7 companion. It seems like a big blank. But I could not go on forever just asking that question, so I've decided to attempt to set some detailed goals and make some plans. I had been toying with a bunch of ideas so I started crystalizing them by putting them down in black and white.

ONE. I am going to be happy. Betty would want that for me. Not going to immerse myself in self-pity or prolonged sadness. Happiness is a decision, an idea I have to explore. I need be with people, to do stuff together, talk and laugh. And I have discovered that being busy, for one thing, helps. Ecclesiastes 2:24-26 says, "A man can do nothing better than to eat and drink and find satisfaction in his work. This too, I see, is from the hand of God, for without him, who can eat or find enjoyment? To the man who pleases him, God gives wisdom, knowledge and happiness." So I will eat well, study to please God, and do some work. How can I keep busy?

TWO. I am going to be busy. Betty said in the hospital that I would sit around for two weeks, then notice all the things around the house that needed to be done. Then I would get up and start doing these jobs. She was right. Yesterday I caught up in paying the bills that I neglected for the past two months. It was a good thing that all of our utilities were on automatic bank withdrawal. We worked this summer at downsizing. Seven garage sales. Seven loads to the dump. But that was only a start, cuz we have been collectors. Not throwaway people like the younger generation tends to be. Lots of work here to do. I planned to put a Grand Caravan load of stuff together to take to the auction mart in Blackfalls. It turned out to be three loads for which I received a tidy sum.

Cooking and baking is fun. My Dad couldn't boil water without burning it, a standing joke at our house. So Mom made sure all her seven boys could cook. At Boy Scouts we learned to bake buns and roast chicken over the campfire. So maybe I planned to find some recipes and throw a supper party. Perhaps I'll find some guy who will work with me on this. Maybe some mature lady. Maybe host a bachelor party. Or have some couples over along with several singles. There are 100 recipe books in the house along with Betty's seven inch high stack of hand written and collected recipes. And a ring binder of a hundred more! No excuses here.

I wondered, should I attempt to make some of Betty's multi-grain bread? I'm thinking about that. I've seen her do it often enough. The ingredients are fairly simple, as is the process. But working with yeast is something that can be a bit complicated and also to know when you have just the right amount of moisture and flour in the dough. You learn that, I've figured out, by a sense of touch. That comes only from experience. Maybe I will.

In a month or so I expected to make myself available to go back to Substitute Teaching. I can make $200 a day, so three or four days a month will buy my groceries and provide spending money. Without Betty's income I am going to have to be careful in my spending. Avoid dipping too much into our savings. Besides, it is good to get out and about. And I enjoy the kids. (Well, some of the time!)

THREE. In the hospital Betty said one day that I should get married again. My response, "Betty, I can't even think about that!" But she continued, "You need to find a real nice person. Don't make a mistake and get the wrong one. Take your time and find someone like (she mentioned the name of a nice outgoing lady we know)." For me this is a scary thought. Even thinking about such a thing seems to desecrate Betty's memory. But maybe she knows me better than I do. If I live for another 20 years I can't imagine doing so alone. A widower said to me the other day, "My wife died 19 months ago but I am still married to her." But I know several guys who have re-married within months or a year of their wife's passing. Others waited for years. My father-in-law took five years to find his second wife. However, today I am going to put this idea on hold. First I need to learn how to be a good Widower, and properly grieve. But when you think about it, this can be a special gift from a dying spouse, to give the remaining one permission to re-marry. She didn't want me to feel guilty thinking about it, I guess.

FOUR. But I think I do need some feminine friendship. Don't know how to do this. But my neighbours have been helpful. Both he and she have been our very good friends for two years and especially during this past couple of months. This has been very meaningful to me. I need to feel the freedom to chat occasionally with a woman without the expectation of getting tangled up. Don't know how to say that right, but I think you know what I mean.

FIVE. I am not going to be a Hermit. Although I will never be a socialite, I do not want to be a loner. For a start I am going to buy two tickets for the basketball game later this month. I'll find a guy to come along. Maybe my neighbour. Then I'll find some guys to do other things with.

SIX. I should join a small group from the church. I need some spiritual and social accountability. Need to make sure my spiritual life continues to be healthy. Gotta find others who will help and who I can help. Over the years this is how I have maintained and grown. Hebrews 10:24-25. I also need to watch out for others who I can help and minister to.

SEVEN. Woodwork. I love making things out of wood. Over the past three years the bottom has fallen out of my woodworking business. So I am re-tooling. There is a future, methinks, in birdhouses. I have numerous ideas and a ton of items and materials to make some funky creations. People also like my blue jean covered chests. So I will concentrate on these two products and keep my eyes peeled for other new ideas. I have a large, well equipped wood-working shop. So, put it to work, Arnold!

EIGHT. Maybe I will travel. In Bragg Creek the other day I picked up a brochure about the Cowboy Trail. Hiway 22 from Mayerthorpe north of Edmonton to the SE corner of Alberta. Maybe a good way to spend a couple of weeks this summer. Museums, rodeos, all kinds of summer shindigs. Also visit my siblings, kids and Gkids. Go up north. I've got a motor home, "Emma", named after my mother. Bought it with my inheritance money from her. Old and expensive to drive, so I'll stick to this province. Betty and I were planning on an Alaskan Cruise. She told me in the hospital to find a friend and still do it. Don't know about that.

NINE. Eat well. With a 100 recipe books (no kidding, I counted) and stacks of hand-written and collected recipes, no excuse. However, eating well has come to mean for me focusing on fruits and vegetables. I do not want to become a religious type vegan, but focusing on veggies rather than animal protein seems to be a good emphasis. That is what I discovered in my research on cancer. Animal protein is the primary cause for most "western" diseases like cancer, heart problems, diabetes, obesity, autoimmune problems and so on. I will continue to explore this. That was another thing Betty told me. In fact she wrote it out: "Have a good diet." Maybe I will make my own whole wheat blueberry or cinnamon/raisin bagels. And grow a nice variety of herbs and use them in my cooking. Etc.

TEN. Property Improvement. Betty would love this! Finish the sun porch. Complete the final coat of crack fill and paint. Put up the chimney so that we can use the antique stove that's been sitting there for several years. Finish tidying up my piles of barnwood. (Betty figured I have enough to last 50 years!) Improve the gardens. And more. Paint the house exterior. Maybe the interior.

In Summary. 1. Be happy. 2. Be busy (downsize, cook and bake, try Betty's multi-grain bread, substitute teach). 3. Don't think about getting married again, not yet. 4. Feminine friendship (untangled). 5. Be sociable. 6. Join a small group and help others. 7. Get into my shop. 8. Travel. 9. Eat well. 10. Improve the property. Looks like I've got lots to do. But first I will clean and tidy up the house to keep it from looking like a bachelor pad.

After posting these goals on FB I received all kinds of suggestion. Several FB ladies responded to number two.

Fay: Sounds like a good plan. I'll share a little piece of advice I got that might help you with #2. I couldn't make good bread when I first got married, so one friend, a pastor's wife no less, offered this gold nugget. "You beat the h@#*# out of it!" I hope you're not as shocked as I was. But it works!

Arnold: Betty mixes her dough in her Bosch for ten minutes that lets it rise for ten minutes three times. She then would punch it down the first and second time, then on the third cut it into loaf size and put it in the baking tins. Sounds pretty simple, huh? Carolin: You go do that Arnold I bet it will be good enough to eat. Arnold: You wanna be the 1st guinea pig? Carolin: Sure why not. It can't be worse than the stuff I make. Arnold: OK. I'll take your word for it.

Anthony endorsed #8, inviting me to Brisbane. Cheryl M said don't forget the Israel trip. Heather, Gert and Carolin wanted me to publish my journal, my ponderings. Makiko said, "Yes, please come back to substitute teach! I know my girl enjoys you!" Connie wanted to make sure that I planned to continue being a Course Instructor for Prairie Distance Education.

Marg reminded me of the first line of one of Mr. Lightfoot's songs, "Picking up the pieces of my sweet shattered dream." Go for it Arnold! There's so much life to live in you and we're all praying that the sweet strong renewing winds of God blow into your sails! That wind always comes as a result of surrendering it all and submitting to our Beautiful Heavenly Father. God wants to make all those shattered pieces whole again. The dream may never be the same, but healing and restoration will bring the picture into beautiful focus. Think of how good it feels to get your camera in focus manually. Does that analogy work? Keep your focus on God and the new picture will happen! We love you Arnold and are praying every day for you! (Marg had just gone through a divorce, something akin to your spouse dying, so her words had a depth of meaning for me.)

I responded to her encouraging advice: Sweet words, Marg. So appropriate. I know you are speaking out of your own experience – that makes it most meaningful. Refocusing. I like that. It almost seems wrong to be happy again. But I know Betty would want that for me. So I am working at a re-focused picture of the present and future, with sails furled to catch the sweet winds of the Spirit, and anticipating renewal and healing from the shattered pieces. There. I got all three of your analogies in one sentence. I am a visual guy so your word pictures help make things startlingly clear. Thank you! Now I am going to go put some of your Huckleberry Jam on an English Muffin and drink my second cup of coffee. LOL.

Suzan's invitation: In your travels to the north country you are welcome to come here. We could figure out when Bob and I would both be home from work that way we could spend more time with you. But you would also be welcome to just rest here too for as long as you want even if we did have to work. We have lots of good places to relax and ponder. Even a horse or two to take for a ride. You are often in our thoughts and prayers. I know. God is with you each moment of each day. Pray you have a good day today. Love you.

21

The Importance of a Hug

J anuary 4. I got a hug from a nurse at the hospital. Got hugs coming and going from each of my three neighbours last evening. Got a hug from my new lawyer the same day. I asked, "Do Lawyers give hugs?" She stood three feet away as we were on the way out of her office. She looked at me for a brief moment, and then smiled, and stepped up with a warm hug! And from my brother and sister-in-law.

Why did I seek hugs? Hugs produce endorphins. "People's endorphin levels rise when they hug," says a hug authority. The feel-good rush arrives if the hug is safe and wanted. "A simple hug is not simple. It's powerful." Brings comfort, can relieve stress and make you feel better. Endorphins, endogenous opioid peptides that function as neurotransmitters, are produced by the pituitary gland and the hypothalamus. (See http://www.redding.com/news/2007/apr/15/embracing-hugs/)

Why a hug? A hug will bring a smile to anyone's face. Hugs release endorphins and serotonin into the blood stream which cause pleasure and negate pain and sadness, lower blood pressure, decrease the chances of getting heart problems, help fight excess weight and prolong life. Hugs will also release oxytocin, which stimulates and sharpens the senses and increases the functionality of your body. A hug will also help you relax the muscles and stretch them out, especially the facial muscles, erasing age lines and slowing the aging process. Hugs will make you healthier, younger, thinner, more relaxed, live longer, fight depression and make you age slower. Doctors actually recommend getting 15 hugs a day for a healthy life! (http://whereisyourlightsource.org/freehugs.aspx)

Grieving and lonesome folks have a special need for your hugs! Next time you see sad people, ask them if you can give them a hug.

The next day, January 5, turned out to be another fantastic Hug Day! Started out at the church office with hugs from the Secretary and a friend, then went to the Bank to change some accounts and got hugs from all four office gals (even the Manager, and a new lady who said, "I love hugs!). Then I visited my accountant and got a hug from her (I guess it's okay my husband's here, she said.), and a one handed version from her husband. Fish, chicken, stir fry, strawberry/almond salad at my neighbors along with hugs. This is one huggin community; think I'll take advantage so long as it works! All in all a very successful day, including a couple hours of divine inspiration from the Pastor while coffeeing.

I think I got so many hugs because when I warmly grin at them when asking for a hug, they think I am probably just a big fuzzy Teddy bear. I got a zillion hugs in that month. When someone reached out to shake my hand I responded by extending both of mine and saying, "I am only accepting hugs today." It worked every time. I'm grinning!

That evening I started a 1000 piece puzzle and invited FB folks to drop over and place a few pieces. I promised a supply of coffee, tea and crumpets. Never did complete it. I eventually gave it to my sister-in-law who is a fanatical puzzler.

22

Christmas without Gramma

L isa and Tara laid out the preparations for each of us to make a tree decoration or two in memory of Betty, Mom, Gramma. Here are three.

Gramma often patched jeans and "blankies", and of course regularly brought bread and buns and sticky buns. We had said good-bye to her just four days earlier.

The Christmas celebration was difficult for everyone, especially me. Gramma was the centre of the major part of this tradition, the turkey and ham dinner, with all kinds of side dishes and a special dessert. Of course no meal would be completed with her white and brown dinner buns.

Last Christmas Tara gave Jonah $20 to go to the store to buy anyone a Christmas present. He chose to give this to Gramma. This Christmas we set it at Gramma's usual spot at the dinner table, and Jonah read it before we gave thanks for the food. So appropriate! We have such fine Gkids!

GRANDMAS have a FOREVER PLACE in our HEARTS, where every HAPPY MEMORY is tucked away WITH LOVE.

I found this neat Christmas train at Home Hardware in Didsbury for 60% off. Couldn't resist. Sound, lights, goes forward and back, notice Rudolf in the driver's seat. Got it going today before breakfast! Sometimes old men still need to satisfy a boyhood dream to have a train! The kid that forever exists in every grown man.

My Grandniece, Holly, offered that the "Christmas Town Express" was her favorite movie as a kid.

Betty loved everything about Christmas – lights, decorations, searching for just the right gifts for family, especially preparing an elaborate turkey/ham dinner for the whole family, and then gathering around the tree to open presents. We always waited to take down the tree till Ukrainian or Orthodox Christmas. I wrote this on FB, January 7, Orthodox Christmas Day that year and wished everyone, Merry Ukrainian Christmas.

23

Life is for the Living;
Joy Comes in the Morning

At 5:01 am, Wednesday, on January 4, 2012, I concluded, it feels good to be alive. Twenty-one days had passed since my Betty died. It seemed I was getting used to the idea that she really was gone. I finally began looking more ahead that backward.

I knew she's gone. I was there for all of it. I sat with her warm but lifeless body in the hospital. I kissed her lips when they were still warm and then called the funeral guy to come and get "it". I helped build her casket, her final resting place, as we say. Before the Celebration "Goodbye to Betty" Service I closed her coffin. But before I did, with Todd at my side, I took off her gold retirement watch, her engagement and wedding rings I gave to her over 48 years ago. And her necklace and earrings. The body was cold and stiff. Later I stood at the graveside as my brother held the button that allowed her to be lowered into the grave, six feet under, as we say. All the others had left because it was too cold for them to wait any longer. The Town guy finally brought the bucket of dirt I had requested to be there after I had accosted him at the far side of the cemetery. He was sitting in his monster front end loader in which he had just arrived. The gal in the office had promised the dirt. It was supposed to be there so everyone could help do this. But alone, I shoveled it on to the cement box that now enclosed her coffin.

She is dead. It sounds calloused to say it like that. We prefer, "passed away". Because nothing about death is pretty. That's why we use flowers. And usually hire some "professionals" to care for the body. We normally get them to remove the jewelry because we don't want to touch a dead person. We leave the graveyard before the coffin is lowered into the ground; it's too hard to watch it go down into that dark hole. But I wanted to do all this myself, with help from family. My family considers it an act of love, and the proper way to say good-bye to our loved one.

In most places around the world the family, with the help of friends in their community, care for the whole process of preparing the body and burying it. In the west we usually forego this proper and loving way to say good-bye. Many folks were so surprised when they found out we built the coffin ourselves, and no funeral professionals showed up at the church or burial site. Someone asked the Pastor, "Are they allowed to do that?" We did it. It has become a family tradition that started with her eight children doing all this for our Mother. We all dearly loved her and wanted to say good-bye properly, like 95% of people around the world would do.

They say I lost my wife. Not true. She is gone all right, but now lives in Jesus' presence. And visiting with her relatives and friends who got to heaven before her. Pain free and walking, leaping, probably dancing a bit. My (not "ours" anymore) house is no longer a cavern, as it seemed when I first came home alone. When I am gone now, I look forward to getting back home again. Reality is finally setting in; I really do know she is gone. I am often able to talk about her to someone else and to her when I am alone, without choking up or crying. My house is warm again. I am starting to enjoy occasionally being home alone.

I had done my deep grieving during the two months before she left. She had excellent care from a team of caring nurses and a doctor, as did I. But I cannot imagine a more terrible way to torture a person than to every day have to watch the one you love gradually become less and less a person, slowly losing the ability to eat, communicate, stay alert and alive. The medical folks kept most of her pain at bay, but they could not keep the devastation from showing on her once beautiful body.

But now I think of her pain free in Glory. The suffering, dying and death are history. I am slowly turning the page to this new reality. I am getting busy doing worthwhile things. The legal and financial things you must do when a loved one passes away. Getting "my" house in order. Visiting relatives and friends and joking and laughing again. I am determined to be happy. Yesterday I found a store in Didsbury that had 60% off on all toys so I bought things for my seven grandkids, a year's supply of gifts. And some half price Christmas wrap.

A week later I took my neighbours to watch the Harlem Clowns clobber the local high school lads. Lots of laughs! Life is going to be good; that's my plan. I want to do this right.

Life is for the living. I started living again. Lonesome, of course. And I still cried some, not so much anymore. But I now began see light at the end of the tunnel. That's where I was heading. With peace and joy deep in my heart. I deeply missed Betty, but I now expected to make it. It felt so good to be able to finally say that.

On January 8 I finally got back to church. The previous Sunday I stayed home, didn't want to face 17 folks in the foyer and cry with 100 watching. Stayed in my jammies all day and paid two months' worth of bills. This day I wanted to go. Had to get back into circulation, after not attending church since Betty got sick two and a half months ago. So I went late and intended to leave early.

The Host, an old friend, greeted me with a grin. "So, I suppose there is no point in asking you if you are staying out of trouble." I said, "Well, I am just starting to look for trouble again!" And we had a brief chuckle. Then a couple stopped and I got a hug and a word of appreciation for my journaling. I intended to "escape" into the "Sanctuary".

I stopped just inside the door and was slapped in the face with, I have to sit alone. Where am I going to sit? I found a spot, appropriately, next to an empty seat. For 48 years I always led the way in finding seats for My Betty and me. Now I was alone. Couldn't keep from crying. This was a surprising shock. I tried to sing, but all that did was bring more tears. And the ache in my gut returned. I used to enjoy snuggling against My Honey during the service. And sometime hold her hand for a while. When we stood to sing, I would often wrap my little finger around hers as we put our hands on the seat ahead of us. Now all I could do is reach over and touch an empty cold seat. The Pastor thanked the Lord for his special healing for those recovering from surgery this week. My thought, "You didn't do that for Betty!"

I thought I had been doing quite well. But no doubt there will be other times when memories will surprise and shock. I was expecting the foyer to be trouble but it was in the "Sanctuary". So I asked Jesus what he had for me today. I needed to take something home. He had a song, "Jesus. . .comforts those who mourn."

And a sermon: I will instruct you and teach you in the way you should go; I will counsel you and watch over you. Psalm 32:8 I needed to know that. John 15:16: I chose you to go and bear fruit. I do want my future to be fruitful, not self-centered.

A question: I wondered, What is God going to ask me to do?

Planned on leaving early but changed my mind as I thought about that. These are my friends, brothers and sisters. I needed to be a significant part of this fellowship again. One lady touched my arm on the way by, another smiled. And I did have two nice conversations. The first from a person who was a help on FB. The second with a lady who had been a wonderful encouragement to me when Betty was sick and again after she died. With hugs and words and books, including two on heaven for kids which my daughter and son read to my Grandkids. She had lost her husband, so her caring was of particular significance. She knew what I needed. Thank you. Thank you!

I went home and made some lunch.

I posted my first visit to church on FB. Again responses were positive and encouraging.

Mahdieh reminded me that even though I write and then press send into a virtual world, she always received my messages. "When you feel that no one is beside you Uncle Arnold please know we are all there with you. We are all there in your heart xo."

Kim noted that in her own journey through grief she related to my emotions. "Mine are always more raw when I'm in the church. I still struggle with communion and certain songs of worship, but I know I need them and fellowship and sanctuary for healing and worship. Draw near to him, Arnold. Love, hugs and prayers."

Pastor Rod blessed me for my courage in coming and allowing others to connect with me.

Joanne: Yes, Arnold: The Lord comforts us in our sorrow so that we can share that comfort others when they are sorrowing. There is nothing like a great loss to teach us how important that is. God bless and continue to encourage you and comfort you today as you take this journey. You may feel lonely, but you are not alone. Blessings!

For supper I had one of Betty's sub buns. Mmmm! Only three left:-{ and just four whole wheat cinnamon buns. They are now rare and increasingly valuable!

January 14 I noted that Betty had left one month before. Left a huge vacancy in my heart and our house. But, surprisingly, I recognized that I was adjusting to my new life. Keeping busy and getting out most every day with people, even though I'm not normally a people person. Didn't need to be; I had Betty! And my deliberate decision to be happy was working.

I still cried most every day. Usually when I noticed something that startled me with the reality that Betty was not here. Or a flashback to her suffering in the hospital. But the deep ache is gone. I am learning to marvel at her new reality: no pain, no sorrow, no worries. I wonder if she misses me. And I do have peace and often joy. Again I thanked FB for their prayers; God was answering them.

Had lots of stuff to do. Continue the downsizing Betty and I had started during the summer. Months of work left; sorting and packing stuff for an auction in Blackfalds.

I collected Betty's Recipe Books from drawers, shelves, and cupboards all over the house and put them together in her sewing and snapshot room. They took up more than eight feet of shelf space. Over 140 books, and magazines, some more than 50 years old, including several of her Mom's. That's besides her eight inch high stack of clipped and hand-written ones and two vertical files of booklets. Brought back many good memories. None of these were going to the auction or anywhere else! She was a "foody', as someone recently described her. A day seldom went by without her studying the recipes in her online Calgary Herald. Or searching one of her 140 books or magazines. She loved to cook and bake. From her bread profits she purchased mixers for our daughter and daughter-in-law, and had started teaching them to bake. She made the best stir fries, spinach lasagna, and spaghetti sauce. There were no written recipes for those favourites, all in her head. For years I enjoyed sitting at the kitchen table watching her punch and roll out the dough for her bread and buns, an amazing expert at work. Lots of good memories.

I listened to my Long Play record collection and added to it every time I went to the city. Yesterday in Olds they sold me ten LPs for $1, a Funky Friday Special. Found some of the records we had sold in our Gospel Books 'n Music store in Red Deer that Betty and I owned and managed from 1971 to 1977. It had since morphed into Parable Place. Praise series, Communion, Evie, B.J. Thomas, 2nd Chapter Acts, Oak Ridge Boys, Stattler Bros, Blackwood Bros, Phil Keaggy. You old guys will remember these songsters. And the records I collected during High School and later. Amazingly, these 30 and 40 year old records still provide music superior to any CDs! Chet Atkins, Neil Diamond, Wilf Carter, Sons of the Pioneers, Ann Murray, Burl Ives. Right now I'm listening to "Joy Comes in the Morning". I was pleased to find this LP. Twenty-five years ago we had a cassette of it and wore it out playing while we were recovering from one of the most difficult events in our life together. For me the joy of morning is arriving! See some of the words below. So many memories.

I so miss the touching. She would meet me coming up the stairs. Her on the top, me on the first step down. Just the right configuration for hugs and kisses. Most every day we walked, even in the winter – always holdings hands. Often folks commented on watching us walk by, connected. I would sometimes saunter up behind her while she worked at the kitchen counter, put my arms around her and she would put her hands on mine and we would nuzzle. I missed the touches and hugs. Guess that's why I so much appreciate when someone steps up and offers me a hug!

Twice this week I went to the city with my neighbour, Jerry. Calgary then Red Deer and Olds. He's a yacker and likes debating theology. Well. . .I like debating; he prefers dialoguing, so I'm going to have to tame my arguments. I grew up arguing with seven siblings, six guys, he was the only one. After completing our business we would go to thrift stores. He buys books and me records. One day I also purchased a large bag of blue jeans with neatly embroidered pockets for my Jean Chests. Then we go eat somewhere. He came over a couple of days ago and we totally re-organized the LR to get ready for my 59 inch flat screen that goes on the West wall. Going to throw some game or movie parties. (Don't tell Betty I am bringing the TV upstairs!)

I totally embarrassed myself. Bought two loaves of multi-grain bread at Super Store. However, it is more or less edible!

Yesterday I reduced our 92 x 42 inch table. Took off the four layers of Betty's special event table cloths: the bottom pad, a powder blue spread covered with Christmas bells, then a lacy top, all covered by a heavy plastic protective sheet. Had to fold these large pieces by myself for the first time. Then took out the two 15 inch leaves, until the family returns for Easter, or we have a supper party!

JOY COMES IN THE MORNING
(William J. and Gloria Gaither, 1974)

> If you've knelt beside the rubble of an aching, broken heart,
> When things (the person) you gave your life for fell apart (left),
> You're not the first to be acquainted with sorrow, grief or pain.
> But the Master promised sunshine after rain.
>
> Hold on my child, joy comes in the morning.
> Weeping only lasts for the night.
> Hold on my child, Joy comes in the Morning,
> The darkest hour means dawn is just in sight.

You can read the complete lyrics and hear this song by Barbara & John Tubbs on: http://www.angelfire.com/oh3/kenskorner/joy.html

Other songs on this LP: Jesus Draws Me, He Careth for You, Jesus Loves Me, Lay Your Burden Down, God Understands, It is Well With my Soul, It Won't Rain Always, and Angels shall Keep Thee. Ruth Bell Graham said about these songs: "People will often listen to music when they cannot listen to words. This is true particularly when one is devastated by loss, deep hurt or loneliness. These songs will have a unique ministry in relaying God's comfort to those who need it most."

When you do not know what to say to someone who's spouse or other loved one has died, just let them know that you care and are praying for that person. If you want to do something, give them a CD with songs of hope. Music soothes my soul, quiets my heart.

Facebook folks, the older ones, did identify with my songs. Dan: So good Doctor, talking and expressing like you are is so healthy and healing. Keep it up – you are certainly blessing my socks off (maybe my slippers). I love reading your epistles and yes those music artists named are some of my favorites too. Next time you have a Neil Diamond record on, tweet or text or call me. I am having trouble getting my 8-track machine going. Just like the Jackson five sang, I'll Be There.

Jan: "Joy Comes in the Morning" After Ray died, I sang this over and over with the tears streaming down my cheeks and wondering which morning the joy would come. Really, it ministered to me so much and I did have much joy at all times even the tears wouldn't stop rolling. I would explain the family and friends. Many can't know how there is joy in the middle of tears. We serve an amazing God! I pray for you much!

Tammy: I love Evie! You so have to put that on when we come over.

24

Things are Different Now

By January 15 I could say that things are different now. Almost every day I discovered some little, or not so little, thing that I was so used to Betty doing that I decided to make a list. All the things I was now doing which I had taken Betty for granted, or she just did them.

- Now I put only 4½ cups of water in the coffee maker and 3 scoops ground coffee for two cups of brewed coffee. Instead of 6½ and 4½ for 4 cups.
- I cracked open the 1.5 k of mixed nuts from Costco. Right on the top was a huge brazil nut. It was Betty's favourite nut so I always saved them for her. This morning I ate it. (Wish I didn't have too!)
- I now phone my neighbour for kitchen advice. A lovely caring lady who is always very helpful! Nothing like having a great neighbour.
- I play FB Wheel of Fortune by myself at 10:00 pm, if I play at all. Betty and I always played together and between us we almost always solved the puzzles.
- When I need a hug I have to go next door. But they hug real good!
- I have to search on my own for a chili recipe. Betty could have gone right to it. Tomorrow friends are coming for chili on Johnny Cake. Found one in *Joy of Cooking*. Simple to make.
- I get to clean the bathroom sink and toilet. Well, I should pretty soon!
- Make the bed, weeeeell, one of these days.
- Wash my clothes.
- Wash dishes.
- Vacuum. Dust. Soon.
- When the phone rings I know it is for me.
- Open all the mail. Including Betty's. She was intrigued with mail and wanted to pick it up every day. I usually said, "You know, it will still be there tomorrow." With a twinkle in my eye, of course, and went to get it.
- Water the plants. Two died in the past two months. Another is half gone.

- Watch the gas gauge. And oil change sticker. I never worried about the vehicle cuz Betty kept track of that stuff.
- I am the one who has to figure out how to get the grease splatters off my favourite green shirt before throwing it into the washer. The turkey I cooked must have splashed me.
- Betty's name will soon disappear off all our documents: bank account, insurances, will, financial documents, property, etc. etc. Visiting the lawyer today and accountant Thursday.
- I now get to be totally in charge of the finances. Keep track of expenditures. Pay the bills. Check out the bank statement. And the Visa. Just caught up on January 1 and mailed a handful of cheques, hopefully to bring everything up to date. That's after getting a phone call from a nice American Express lady who informed me I was two payments behind. And the next day the same message from Telus Mobility. I figured out how to settle those accounts online. Gotta order some more cheques.
- Take the Christmas tree and decorations down by myself. Maybe I'll invite the neighbours over for a de-tree decorating party! Fold up the four layers of 100 inch table cloths by myself this year.
- Re-new mag subscriptions. Won't do it through. With only one income and household expenses much the same except for groceries, I gotta cut back. Going to shut down our business account; they want $30 a month just for keeping it alive, even with no transactions.
- Make lists. Keep the calendar. Put on my memory cap every time I come or go. Or sit or rise. Betty always reminded me of stuff. Sometimes I received her reminders with a bit of irritation. But I knew, and now know more than ever, that this was just one of her ways of loving me. She wanted to keep me out of trouble, knowing I could take ten steps and forget two of the three things I was supposed to do. She was so organized. And practical. And foresaw things needing doing. Me, I just mosey on through life. Unless I'm in charge. Guess now I am. Mama Mia! That's scary. I now own a 3½ x 5¾ pocket calendar and actually have things written in it.
- Order my own prescription pills refill.
- Before I go out check in the mirror for rooster tails.
- Plan the meals, buy groceries.
- We have been downsizing all summer. Now I have to decide what to sell, dump, keep, or give away. If it's nice I'll give it to somebody I like, otherwise to someone I don't like.
- Garden. We always did it together.
- Drive. By myself. When I get tired she takes over. She is a better driver.
- And probably a lot more stuff in the next days and weeks to which I still have to look after.

Joanne picked up on my need for some female advice: I noticed you needed help getting grease spots out of clothes. Before laundering them, put some dish washing detergent, full strength, on the spot and rub it in a bit, then throw it in the laundry.

The dish detergent is good at cutting grease. Hope this helps. Once it has been in the dryer, the spot is pretty well set so I don't know if this will work for old spots, you could try it though. Best advice is "wear an apron in the kitchen". LOL

25

Betty is Back

On January 16 I enjoyed a Betty's Whole Wheat Cinnamon Bun for breakfast. Only three left. Tara brought them from her freezer at Christmas. Was going to feed them to the four Gkids who love Gramma's rolls and buns, but I forgot – tehehehe! They asked for waffles anyway, as they always do when staying overnight at Gramma's. So I made them in our antique electric waffle iron my mother found for Betty and me at a garage sale many years ago. Makes waffles much superior to the modern cheapoes, crisper! I had a half a leftover waffle, too. Had a little cry when I was done eating.

Tammy had to confess she "may have eaten a few sticky buns from the bag Betty gave Jerry for 'his' Birthday last year." Makiko reminded me of her 'ritual' on Farmer's Market mornings to take her kids to pick up a bag of Betty's buns home to go with homemade soup!

Betty is back. At least not so far away anymore. I'd selected some pics for the kitchen table. Now I could have meals with her. Cutting her 70th birthday cake May 28, holding her GGirl, and us together at her party and sitting out in the Stauffer Family farmyard on and ancient piece of machinery.

My favourite of her newest tops, along with the necklace and matching earrings. I was always with her when she looked for new clothes. She wanted to know if I thought they looked good on her. Usually her picks did. It took me a long time to give this one away, but I finally did, to my sister-in-law.

Betty is back! She watched me as I word processed. Smiling. I occasionally would look back and return her smile. I was learning to find ways of enjoying happy memories.

26

For this One I was Alone

By January 26 I began thinking I was doing okay and it may be time to shut down Betty's Update Group. I probably wouldn't have much more to say. And I seemed to be pretty much done crying. Done heavy grieving. Still lonely though. But I was planning on dealing with the loneliness by keeping busy, getting out, being with folks, and watching some good movies, etc.

Then I went to Red Deer today for an MRI. The Doc wanted a better look at some issues in my lower back. Betty and I have been to a 100 medical appointments in the city in the last decade, almost all them for her.

All the way to Red Deer I had tears. Betty and I always went together for medical appointments, but for this one, mine, I was alone. Checking in at Admittance the lady looked at her computer and asked me the usual questions then startled me with, "And the person to call in case of emergency is Margaret Elizabeth (Betty)?" "No", I said, and gave her my son's name and phone number. I headed toward the Diagnostic Imaging Department (DID). The sobs started. I could not stop them. Looking down I tried to hide from the hall full of people coming my way. But they didn't notice. It was the hospital and they had their own issues. A long walk, alone. No hand to hold. But I managed to control the sobbing before checking in at the DID.

A lady took me to a changing room, handing me two hospital gowns. "We do not have a house coat your size. Put one on, tying it at the front and wear the second as a house coat." (They don't make cars or clothes, sometimes, for real men!) I changed and came out to the small waiting room. Sitting there was a young raven haired lady in street clothes. I felt half dressed. Maybe her husband was getting an MRI. I sat four seats from her facing in the same direction. My two "skirts" came down to four inches above my knees. It felt like I was wearing a mini skirt. I practiced holding my knees together. That's hard work. Finally I figured that the most modest way to sit was with my legs stretched out and ankles crossed. I noticed my hairy legs. Took Betty awhile to get used to them. (I grin.)

After waiting a half hour I went across the hall to wash my eyes. Maybe no one would notice then that I had been crying. They'd asked on the form if I was claustrophobic. Scary thought. I figured I better pee while in the washroom. Wouldn't want an accident in the "tunnel". It was easy – just lifted my two skirts!

Waited another half hour, then decided to take a walk down the hall. Surprisingly a big door opened and a short swarthy older man said, "Mr. Stauffer, come in we're ready for you." He told me where to lie down head first in front of this too tiny too long tunnel. I suddenly realized why they asked if I am claustrophobic. He gave me ear muffs to deaden the loud sound of the machine and asked what kind of music I liked. "Country and western," I shrugged. After he handed me a bulb to squeeze if I panicked, the cot started to move and shoved me into this tunnel. My arms squished against my sides, and soon the machine started to roar. I tried to imagine running and jumping across a wheat field to get my mind off this tunnel I was just squeezed into. A cowboy started to croon into my ear phones, "The next 30 years are going to be the best of your life!" Then he sang something like, "I've got a girl now and everything is all right in the world!" Should have asked for some Gaither. My girl is gone and the next thirty years, at present, do not hold much promise. Well, the cowboy accomplished his purpose of turning my mind from getting squished or suffocating in this tight tunnel. Twenty minutes later the cot started to pull me out and there stood a lovely blond haired young lady. Thought for a minute I must have gone down this tunnel and ended up in heaven! Sent in by a short dark old man and brought out by pretty young blond gal!

I had left home this morning not expecting a hard day. But everything about the day was Betty. We always went to the food court. I have Chinese food and Betty a wrap. Then she has Yogen Fruze. I had to walk by it, however, being stuffed with pork, chicken and noodles. Then I bought groceries, which we always decided together what to get, besides what was on her list.

Crying is hard work, thought I was done. At Tara's for three days this week; I cried myself to sleep one night after sitting on the bed bringing up Betty's picture on Facebook. I gently touched her face. We had just sorted out her two boxes of music so Tara could choose some to keep. Betty sang ever since she was two feet high. I cried.

Don't understand all this crying. I have cried before but hardly ever, now I cannot stop. Sometimes it is embarrassing. It is one thing to have tears but this sobbing? I am a grown man with seven grandkids. You'd think by now the fountain would be dry. But the tears seem to be waiting just below the surface to gush at a moment's notice.

My grieving, the deep intense sorrow I think is mostly gone. Now loneliness replaces it, a big ache inside somewhere. How do you deal with loneliness when you have no choice but to spend most of your time alone? Betty and I did everything together, so now she is still in everything I do, and she goes everywhere I go. But she is not and does not! She is here but she is gone – everywhere but nowhere. Loneliness is a powerful hurting sense that no one else is here. You are all by yourself – forever. The one who is always here is not and never, never, never will be. Being with other folks may take your mind off it for a while, until you have to go home again. Or to your own room. Then it calls to you again from deep inside. Sometimes yells. At times, harshly.

I decided to watch some movies. So one is about serious suffering, in another a person slowly dies and I yelp with hard memories.

I visited my daughter and family for three days. Four GKids are distracting. That's good. But as soon as I am by myself in the same house and loneliness hits again. Betty's supposed to be there with me. My niece and her husband came Saturday to clean my house; here for seven hours, and I fed them lunch. Had a good time. As soon as they left a deep sense of aloneness again hit me. I wept.

When I get lonesome I sometimes think about what Betty said about getting married again. I look around in my mind's eye and see several ladies: too quiet, too giddy, too young, too old, too fat, too. . . . No one can match Betty's perfectness for me. She was just the right wife I needed. The last four years together were very special; we enjoyed 24/7 togetherness. Could another woman find a place in my heart? I don't know, and I do not need to know now. I don't want to know, yet.

People who have been there say, "Time heals. The hurt will gradually fade." That doesn't help me for today! Reminds me of when my mother used to say when I was crying because of some hurt, "It will get better."

Somebody else says, "Just think one more first behind you." But how many more firsts? Guess I should not worry about the tomorrows, just deal with today. Sometimes I get the feeling I'm the only guy in the world who has to deal with these things. Not true, though. Death is part of life and sooner or later every person loses a loved one. I need to complete this day and get ready for tomorrow. Hey! Tomorrow I get to substitute in the Grade Six class, the finest group of students in Three Hills. How better could I spend a day, with 25 wonderful, lively kids? See, there is hope! Lots of fine days ahead. Maybe tomorrow I won't have to cry even once.

I include the following responses to show you how important my journaling was. It helped me immeasurably to share my inner feelings. To put them in black and white. By passing my struggles on to this wonderful, caring group, I opened up to them. By doing so they were able to help me. In response hundreds of folks were praying for me and my family. Each time I posted on Facebook, replies would be immediate, loving and encouraging. Do not ever avoid "The Community" when in trouble. Christians are created for each other, to carry each other's burdens. I discovered a depth of community in a new and heartening way, and successfully passed through the deep waters of grief and loneliness as a result. Again and again, God spoke clearly through these individuals.

It was surprising to me to hear so many say how they were encouraged through my postings. They learned also, and sometimes passed my ramblings on to encourage others. I am so grateful. I earnestly hope that you, The Reader, will also be challenged and nudged along your life journey.

Grand Niece Amanda encouraged me: You are an amazingly talented writer Uncle Arnold. My heart aches with you every time I read your journals. But it's so refreshing to see such an honest expression of grief and hope. Think about you often! Much love.

Nurse Miriam wanted me to keep the group going a little longer. "I am honored," she posted, "that you trust us all with your precious personal ponderings! I really appreciate this group and pray for you after each entry you share with us! Please keep it going as long as you feel like it! It is good!

Sister-in-Law Tracy said, "Yes don't stop writing. I enjoy the stories of your life, and one day you will have happy things to say. I know what it's like to lose a spouse as I was with Al for14 years. It was hard; I cried for a month but then like they say, time heals and I did. Music Professor James: Please don't close it down. Your insights minister to me. Friend Terry Ann: Been there, and sometimes I still end up there, though not as often as before.

Friend Louise: It's so tough – the aloneness. Thanks for sharing. Yesterday I came across this comment by D. L. Moody: "It is comforting to know that the God who guides us sees tomorrow more clearly than we see yesterday." I like that; it helps me through.

Sister-in-Law Irene: Your ability to articulate your journey so authentically is indeed a gift to yourself and also others! I, for one will miss the privilege of knowing the graphic truth of your journey, being able to empathize and pray specifically for your need. Thanks for being so candid with the challenge of faith and human struggle that you have experienced because you have loved and lost – one who has been there.

Long-time Friend Ann: Dear Arnold, Your journaling of your grieving is amazing, putting into words what many feel but are unable to express so well. You must put your journey in a book sometime. I have passed on some of your posts to another friend who is going through the same. As you refresh and bless others, may you yourself be refreshed and blessed! Love and prayers.

Colleague Dan: So well said Ann. Who knows it could hit the New York Times best seller list. Arnold, your prose is such a great ministry to so many.

Old Bible College Mate Joyce: I pondered your post, Arnold, as I crawled in to my bed and spent time praying for God's peace to surround you and be yours. You are a gifted writer in that you are able to articulate your thoughts and emotions so well. I'm sure it is cathartic for you, as well as helpful to others who have gone, or are going through similar circumstances. You give us a lot to think about. Continuing to pray for you.

Betty's Workmate Andrea: I have hesitated in sharing, but last night I had a dream and Betty was in it. We were working at the Bookroom, again, and she was unpacking a new shipment of books. What caught me off guard in my dream was her humming. She always was humming! From the back of the store to the front, at her desk, behind the counter, or when shelving books. I cannot recall the song from my dream, but I do vividly remember what peace it gave me. Thank you, Dr. Stauffer, for sharing your heart and for sharing Betty.

Arnold: This is beautiful. Betty was a singer all her life. When the kids were young she would be always "attaching" one of her songs to an event, or something that happened around the house, or what the kids said. Whatever, she would sing a line or two from a ditty. And then I would hear the kids, "Oh Mom!" Like, "not again!" I was proud of her gift; she so often ministered to me.

131

27

I Needed Her More

January 28. Had been watching a few movies. Started one the morning of the 28th and the thought hit me, "Maybe I should read my Bible and devotional book first." Well. . . I didn't. God and I had not been on super good terms lately. He took My Betty from me. That was after giving her pain for four months plus another two months as cancer took its devastating, evil toll. He took her at 1:45 December 14. My ten year old neighbour thought that God needs her in heaven. Yeah, well what about me? I needed her more. He already has billions, I just had her. I wanted only one. For a while longer, at least.

I really did think all along that she would come home, healthy and happy. That's what I had prayed for, for months; many others prayed the same. I had believed till the last minute, as did others, for her healing. "Nope!" God said, and took her to himself.

He did me a courtesy, however. In the evening of December 13, it was obvious to me as well as the medical staff that Betty's time on earth was quickly drawing to a close. Her breathing sounded gurgling as her lungs filled with fluid. Her body was shutting down. As I pondered this development, I reached a decision. God is supernaturally omniscient, absolutely just and loving, and in charge. So I turned My Betty over to him, with almost complete trust that he would do the right thing. Heal her or take her home. Sixteen hours later he came and got her, leaving me with her cancer ravaged body to say good-bye to a week later. He got by far the best deal! But I really do believe that he gave me the courtesy of waiting for me to finally give her back to him. A hard decision, but I really had no choice.

There was another courtesy from him that I will always appreciate and treasure. Three of our kids were at the hospital a good part of the night. They were all gone by 2:30 when it appeared Mom was not going to go during this night. We had all said a verbal good-bye to her earlier, giving her our permission to go. She tried to say something in response, but could not get the words out. I was so, so disappointed for her sake and for all of ours.

I had been holding her hand for most of the night, but finally went to sleep. At 4:30 am she woke me calling, "Arnold" and asked, "Is it time to go now?" I said it was and she wanted me to come along with her. Her final words, "I am going but you are staying?" Sometimes I still wish I could have. God blessed me, allowing her to say this good-bye to me, all alone with her in the hospital room. Her last words. It was a tender, loving last moment just the two of us shared. She trusted me with one of the most important questions she ever asked. An eternal treasure.

God took her. But he did so with these two courtesies which continue to stick hard in my mind and heart.

People say, "Well, she's now in a better place." "She no longer has pain or sorrow." "God gave her the ultimate healing." And lots of other clichés we use when things don't go our way. They all sound really good, I suppose, to the "comforter". But they bring little comfort to the hurting person.

Sure, I attempted to cut into my grief by seeing Betty pain and sorrow free in Jesus' arms, the ultimate hug! He gets to hug her now; I do not. A "better place"? Sure, but we both, together, loved our current place. Why would either of us want to go anywhere else? Not now, maybe later, but not yet. The timing was not good, very bad! I know what you are thinking: "God's timing is always best."

"Ultimate healing." Now there's a major cop out. How can God give us dozens of promises of physical healing in his Word, and not follow through? That's not God's nature. Those verses do not imply "ultimate" healing, but immediate earthly getting better and going home *to 614 – 8 Street North, Three Hills, Alberta*, now! To the guy who battles grief, hurt, anger, sorrow, sudden severe loneliness, a scramble of mixed up emotions, this is really the "ultimate copout". Not logical. Not comforting. Not the healing we all wanted, we asked for, expected. God let us down.

So where do I go with this? Same place I've gone before with these unanswerable questions. Habakkuk. He listed the most severe tragedies and calamities imaginable. He was so terrorized; with a pounding heart and quivering lips, his bones were decaying and legs trembling. As he imagined the worst possible things were happening to him, he said:

Yet I will rejoice in the Lord,
I will be joyful in God my Savior.
The Sovereign Lord is my strength;
he makes my feet like the feet of a deer,
he enables me to go on the heights.

Not so strong yet, had not felt like running like a deer, and I was staying away from the heights. I did begin to rejoice occasionally. Joy was slowly returning. I worked on it. The many prayers of folks were gradually being answered. I had no trouble believing God is good. Just that I would have done things differently. Listening to a CD, the singer reminded me that someday we will have all our questions answered. For me these questions are fading. No point in keeping asking them when they have no present answers. So I carried on – thinking of things for which I could be thankful. If I knew all the answers today I would be God. Sure do not want that responsibility.

I practiced thankfulness – sometimes. Thanked him for the wonderful 48 years he gifted me with Betty. (See, I was on speaking terms with him.) I do thank him for discontinuing Betty's heartbreak and pain, although she so wanted to stay. I thanked him for the large and gracious Christian Community that had been extraordinarily helpful and encouraging. For our large family who had been so supportive. For neighbours to whom I could go anytime for hugs, chats and meals, and can mobile message anytime I need to talk to someone who cares. I must have been hugged a thousand times in the past three months. Loved every one of them! At home, at the neighbors, at family homes, friends' homes, at church, up town, at the hospital, post office, drug store, bank, Capital, IGA, in Calgary, Red Deer, Didsbury, Olds.

And maybe, I thought, in February or March or April. Possibly by next December, I will get my "feet of a deer" to enable "me to go on the heights"!

My neighbours and a friend had twisted both my arms to go to a dance. Had a wonderful time! Something like old fashioned square dancing. Thoroughly enjoyed being with lots of folks most of whom I did not know or knew only a bit. I am not a dancer but everyone was exceedingly patient and helpful. Most locals had not done this dancing either, so that helped me from being too embarrassed. It was nice to be able to touch lots of gals in such a "chaperoned" atmosphere, ages 3 to 70. Lovely folks, all. Touching and moving your feet, that's what you do when you dance.

What is it about touching a lady that at this stage in my life is so wonderful? For the first dance on the left I held the hand of my neighbour, Jerry; he had quite a rough one. But the young lady on my right had a very soft hand. I told her so and she smiled and said thank you. I always loved holding Betty's hand. Did when we drove, walked and sat together almost anywhere. Her hands were soft. So were her feet. She took real good care of herself, buying special lotion by mail from Rocky Mountain House that kept her skin soft. During her final days I applied to her skin Apricot Kernel Natural Skin Care Oil, and Shea Butter & Sesame Oil Body Balm to keep her skin from drying out. These half-filled bottles rested for months on her small bathroom counter off our bedroom. Soft skin is feminine, guess that's one reason why I enjoyed myself so much; I got to touch a lot of soft hands. It gave me a nice warm feeling inside, something I haven't had for weeks. That day, for a while, life was good. Thanks, Lord, for all the soft, feminine hands. Maybe for my neighbour's rough ones too.

On February it seemed like Betty was present. I had returned from taking six boxes of her clothing to the Tilly, Prairie's thrift store. Seemed like she was riding with me. I did keep some special items: a shawl she crocheted, the dress she wore at our son's wedding, a couple of my favourite tops and a few other items. Her blue jean jacket and slacks I may use to cover one of the chests I make. A great way to store some of her mementos.

Her clothes had gone to Calgary where her oldest niece, little sister, and daughter sorted them and each found some things to take home. Including several very old items that came from Betty's Mother and Grandmother. I brought the remaining clothes back home and just before re-packing them for the Tilly I invited my neighbours over for Tammy to find something to fit her. They have been special friends of Betty and me since they escaped from Ontario to move next door. Tammy was pleased to find a couple of tops that Betty had sewn and she looked real cute in Betty's tuque, long wrap-around pink scarf, and matching mittens. I am pleased that so many folks were able to make good use of Betty's fine clothes. This makes it easier to see them leave our house for the last time. I thought of warning folks who take home her clothes from the Tilly that I reserve the right to step up and give them a hug if I should see them walking down the street, or at church or wherever, wearing Betty's clothes! I did warn Tammy (hope it snows!).

For breakfast I ate the second last of her whole wheat cinnamon buns. For lunch had one of her sub buns with tomato and cucumber. Only two left, the last of her baking. For dessert I spread some of her apple butter (2010) on a piece of chocolate cake I made using her favourite recipe. Great apple butter; if you want the recipe look in the Appendix.

I should set things straight. My recent posts on FB had been somewhat troubling and perhaps a bit negative. I wrote those when I was remembering and briefly struggling again with a flashback to grief and sorrow. But most of the time I was finding ways to be happy and to begin to enjoy life again. Going dancing (I don't dance!), visiting folks and having a meal with them, having folks over for a meal (four or five times now), and getting out and about and back to joking around with whomever crosses my path. Today at the bank I had a humorous theological exchange with a bank clerk while she paid my bills. And chatted and laughed with a PO employee on the sidewalk. I talk to folks every day. In fact I am fast becoming a people person, I think. Normally I have preferred to stay home and read a book rather than try to make small talk at a party. But now being alone at home pushes me out the door to find company, and I am enjoying every minute.

Betty's thousands of snapshots now reside in Bragg Creek at our daughter's. I look forward to spending quite a bit of time there helping make scrapbooks and albums. This will honour Betty and preserve our larger family history that she faithfully recorded on camera for sixty years. And the history of the Gkids from the day each one of them arrived at the hospital. It will be a hugely memory packed endeavor; Betty will definitely be there.

Facebookers responded.

Joyce: Again let me say how well you articulate your grief experience and I applaud your facing things head-on, seeing people, in effect, getting back on the horse and living life. That does not in any way mean it is easy but you are an encouragement, I am sure, to anyone reading this who is having a similar experience. God's peace be yours.

Irene: Your stories bring back so many memories! And I also loved it when I found people who treasured and wore some of Virgil's clothes!

Merle: I am wearing a shirt of Betty's at the moment and think about her whenever I look down at it or look in the mirror. Shed a few tears too, of happiness and of sadness.

28

That's Not Fair – She's Not Finished

January 30 I substitute taught the Prairie Grade sixes. At noon I whipped a kid six times at X and Os. I thought, I'm going to have to tell Betty this! Of course then I got the shock again. Often when at work or away from Betty for any reason I would think during the day when something neat happened, "I'll remember to tell Betty that." To keep the record straight, the kid returned with his buddy, an expert gamer, who proceeded to beat me three games of six. Well, didn't have anybody to tell anything to when I got home.

February 3 Betty showed up. I had been using the large boxes we took bread to markets in to fill with stuff to take to the auction. Every time I picked up a box I shed another tear, realizing that never again would I be taking her bread to a market. It must have been at least 50 markets in the past two years. I enjoyed hauling her wonderful creations to various markets and bragging to people what great nutritious baking she produced. Multi-grain bread, with freshly ground flour and newly cracked wheat and rye. So many folks miss her baking, especially me.

Finished watching the movie, "P.S. I Love You," piecemeal for the past two days. A gal loses her father at 14 years old and determines to stay away from men. But much later Jerry shows up and she marries him. Sadly, he leaves after ten years; cancer of the brain takes him. She tries to find "a new normal" (my phrase), but struggles. Finally, she comes to her mother in tearful desperation. "This wonderful man happens to me and then he died. . . .I'm alone and it doesn't matter what I do or don't do, he's not here." "You are alone no matter what." Her mother responds, "Alone or not, you gotta walk ahead." He had sent her a letter to open after he was gone. It said, "Don't be afraid to fall in love again." Just as Betty had said to me.

In the movie, after a year she says to a friend, "It's been a year and Jerry's gone. I don't feel him around. He's gone. I don't think he's here anymore. I think Jerry's gone. He's really gone."

But for me, Betty is not gone. She is here every day. Everything I do, she shows up. That's not bad, that's good. When she shows up, I usually cry for a bit. I love her

137

still, and everything I touch around the house, she's there. That's not so bad. I love her and like when she shows up. But every time she shows up, I get shocked with the reality that she's not really here. She's gone. The movie closes with the song:

> She says I'm okay; I'm alright,
> Though you have gone from my life.
> You said that it would,
> Now everything should be all right.
> She says I'm okay, I'm alright,
> Though you have gone from my life.
> You said that it would,
> Now everything should be all right.
> Yeah, should be alright.

For me, everything is not yet all right. Maybe someday. Not today. Betty is not gone. She is here every day. I love her and kinda like when she shows up, but I cry, cuz I know she is gone. Not really. She is here but not here. She shows up, but not really.

I am alone but I gotta walk ahead.

Strangely, well, perhaps not, the movie was cathartic. Sitting an hour and a half watching someone who had experienced my story. I identified with her. Had a pretty good idea of what she was feeling. She helped me move ahead in processing my grief and sorrow.

Cherie responded to my movie story: You are doing great! You are talking and thinking, going out and coming home. You are golden, Arnold. You are mourning, but you honour your love of Betty by being brave and walking on in your life, missing her but not being impaired to the point of despair. She would be proud, probably telling everyone in heaven that she is so proud of her Arnold. He is just doing so great!

Dan echoed her comments: So well put! You are indeed my hero good Dr.

Jan: Wow oh wow! This sounds so familiar! I still sense Ray's presence and it is so wonderful. I had asked the Lord to let Ray appear to me sometime. I was at my daughter Carol's home and woke up early morning and looked up in the pitch dark. There was Ray so young and handsome, sitting there holding a baby in his arm and leaning down as though little ones were around him. I assumed they were his son Curtis and Jennifer's babies that didn't live. I was so excited and wanted to see the baby in his arms so started to get out of bed. As I did he just faded away. I will never, never forget the joy of seeing him again.

February 5, Sunday. This morning I turned to the Psalms for inspiration. Psalm 90, "A prayer of Moses the man of God": "Lord, you have been our dwelling place throughout all generations." Some time ago I had written beside this verse, "God is my permanent address."

Two verses down: "You turn men back to dust." Oh yeah, just what I need today! A reminder of God's curse of death upon mankind. "You sweep men away in the sleep of death." That's right, he stole away My Betty!

Then Moses says in verse 10: "The length of our days is seventy years – or eighty, if we have the strength." Betty was 70 – 25,550 days. Seventy plus 200 days, actually, so I guess she got a six and a half month bonus. A bonus of 0.0078%. This was my inspiration for the day?

I entered the church foyer and Karen hurried over to invite me to supper tomorrow. I was reminded of a discussion she and I had at the hospital the day before Betty left. I was sitting at the Y in the hallway doing my email and Facebook, where I usually sat at 10:00 in the evening. This was 15 feet from the door to a hospital room in which a 95 year old was dying, Karen's father-in-law. Each evening I heard his loud laboured breathing. But this day all was quiet, except for the whispers of family members that were gathering in the room. Realizing I was intruding on a private family event, I quickly moved down the hall to the foyer. In a few minutes Karen came to sit down and told me her father-in-law had gone to heaven. We chatted for a minute.

When she left I wanted to shout, "That's not fair!" He was 95 years old. My Betty was only 70. He wanted to go; "My chariot is ready," he had told folks. Betty's wasn't; she wanted to stay. She wasn't finished with me or her kids or her seven grandkids. And she wanted to teach her daughters how to make bread.

Following my morning "inspiration" I did not get much out of the sermon on Nehemiah except that he was a visionary who acted on his vision and got results. During the sermon I went back to my Psalm of inspiration and studied it a bit. Glad I did.

Moses: "Teach us to number our days aright, that we may gain a heart of wisdom. . . .Satisfy us in the morning with your unfailing love, that we may sing for joy and be glad all our day. Make us glad for as many days as you have afflicted us. . . .May the favour of the Lord our God rest upon us; establish the work of our hands for us – yes, establish the work of our hands."

Apparently I have some days left. I already decided to be happy because Betty would want me to be. So make me glad, Lord, for each of the days you still give to me, for I really do want to sing for joy and be glad all of these days. So I intend to number my days, whatever that means, deal with them one by one at a time, I suppose. Then God will give me wisdom. He still has work for my hands? I sure hope so, for every day I want to be meaningful in accomplishing the tasks God sets before me. Maybe I'll get to 95!

I snuck out of the sanctuary during the benediction; I'd had enough inspiration for one day, even Sunday.

Irene: I can identify! (Irene's husband, my brother Virgil, died in a car accident several years ago, just when he was planning his retirement.) Joanne: It is good to see you making progress towards healing – a step at a time. God bless. Dr. Reedyk: Hi Arnold: I have so appreciated your transparency and seeing your Christ like grieving. I have been very inspired. Dan so well put Dr. Reedyk. Arnold, you are such an inspiration to me as well! Louise: "Those who sow in tears will reap with songs of joy. He who goes out weeping, carrying seed to sow, will return with songs of joy, carrying sheaves with him." ~ Psalm 126:4-6.

Ann: Your documented journey of your grieving has touched the many family and friends around you. Your sharing has put into words what many have experienced and what we all will experience sometime. Thank you for your openness. God bless you, we love you and pray for you.

On February 9 I talked about soon shutting down the group. Several folks responded with their "story" of how the group had ministered to them.

This response came from Louise: Thank you so very much for this blog, Arnold. I have cried with you, our family has gotten to 'know' you, we've prayed for you. Your blog has been an EXTREME help to me personally as someone from our church was killed in a car accident last fall and his loving wife and kids were left behind. Reading your grief and 'experiencing' a bit of it through you has completely helped me in coming to terms with Glen's death and also helped me to see his wife with a new-found openness thanks to you! You have also really helped me grieve my dad's passing away when I was 20. I did not grieve properly; I didn't know how, and the memories and hurt were stuffed away. I now cry most every day, in a healthy way, for a relationship snatched away too early, and have resurrected long put away pictures, and am now openly living with his memory and celebrating his life and working through the sadness. God be praised!

I responded to her comments: Thanks so much for sharing this, Louise. I am so glad I was able to do this open journaling; your story alone has made it worthwhile. Serious grief and loneliness (the kind you experience when someone loved will never return) is so complicated, a path we walk probably only once or twice in our lifetime. For each of us it is a unique journey yet we can learn so much from each other. Community is a necessary contribution to surviving this difficult experience. We need to accept and own our strong emotions and sometimes share them with others to allow them to minister to us. And God is Good!

Cherie: So great that you are going to keep this going, we have learned so much, and I for one know you better for it. This is such a great group, times that are coming will have their ups and downs so this page will be nice to have cuz we all know the history of it, we will know exactly what you mean when you mention finding an old letter or knick knack that moved you to instant tears. We will see and hear and pray. And most of us have been in that place, so we will be great at cheering you up! Love and peace Arnold!

April: Dear Arnold, I can say that your journaling has blessed me so much. I am so thankful when someone can write with transparency and tug at my heart, because it reminds me to be kind every day, even when I don't feel like it. We never know what battles and sorrows people may be facing each day, and your ability to share it reminds me there are others who face what you speak of. I also know that someday I may have to face my own deep grieving, so I have taken all you have written to heart and I know it will help me some day. Truth be told, I needed it and I am so glad you allowed me to be part of your group. I have wanted to tell you for a while that you could take all this and write a book; you are an amazing writer! In my opinion, I think you should take up a new cause! I know I would buy a book with Arnold listed as the author! Rich blessings I wish you as you continue to discover a new you mixed with the best parts of the old one.

29

I Forgive God

I n the middle of an early February Sunday Sermon, the thought passed through my mind, "I forgive God for taking My Betty." It came unbidden; I hadn't thought that through at all. It had not occurred to me before this that I could or would or should forgive God. Me forgiving God! Thinking about that, I am somewhat dumbfounded that such a thought could cross my mind. I had to think about this. Take some time to sort this matter.

Can a guy, an ordinary human being, forgive the Superpower, the Ultimate Power of the Universe? Its Creator, Sustainer, and Father of the Saviour of this World? He through Jesus forgives our sins and waywardness. Our shortcomings, sinfulness and even our obnoxiousness. He forgives it all!

I decided to look up the word in "The Canadian Oxford Dictionary: The foremost authority on current Canadian English." What did I really do Sunday morning? I really do not know! Forgiving God?!

We do wrong. We are born in sin and choose to sin. Again and again and again. And God forgives. But where does scripture say anything about me forgiving God?

To forgive, says Oxford, is to "cease to feel angry or resentful towards." The word also means to pardon (an offender or an offense); to remit or let off (a debt or debtor). Of course God, in this case, or any case, is neither an offender nor debtor. He owes me nothing and by nature he cannot offend me. So the first definition must apply. It all hinges on me, in ending my anger and resentfulness. That has to be the nature of my forgiveness to God.

I guess some of my FB language had suggested God is guilty of something, like stealing away My Betty. Or taking her from me when I needed her a lot more than he does. Or absconding with her when she really wanted to stay. Of not keeping his scriptural promises to heal. There were probably more accusations that I had already forgotten. It is true. God cursed mankind with death after the original sin. As a result we all di e, the end of life here on this planet. Cancer, a part of that death curse, killed My Betty. But God did create the death sentence. Her death is his responsibility.

But you do not accuse a judge of a crime or misdemeanor when he orders a judgment to be carried out. It is the law, and his/her sworn responsibility to fulfill the law and carry it out. It was not Betty's sin that killed her, but the result of the sinfulness of mankind that had to be punished. The law must be carried out. God is just, and does not waver from his law.

So I was not really "forgiving" him, in our usual understanding of that word. I was dealing with a heart matter, my heart. No longer will I be angry or resentful to you God, for taking My Betty. Nor for taking her too early. So help me God to really forgive you, and to continue in this new state of my heart.

I have no idea where that thought came from that morning. God must have planted it. I must have somewhere somehow given him permission to do so. He knows my heart better than I do. I do not want to be angry or resentful. I told God, "Wherever that thought came from, thank you. Help me God, that when I am seriously missing My Betty, I just leave her in your arms of love. I do know that you love her and me and all of us. Gotta remember that most of all. I am going to need your help in keeping this commitment."

So I do forgive you, God. I hereby "cease to feel angry or resentful towards" you. I can't thank you, yet, but I do forgive you."

That day I finally crawl into bed and, as usual, read for a while. Soon I closed my book, turned out the light, and snuggled under the covers, closed my eyes. Immediately the sentence flashed through my head, "Thank you Lord for taking my Betty." I was totally surprised. Didn't plan that prayer, just as I did not plan that prayer flash during the sermon the day before. I thought for a few moments about what I surprised myself by saying. But I was tired so soon slept, after glancing at my bedside clock which said 12:02 AM, Just about exactly 12 hours after I forgave God.

I woke up before 5:00 AM. Usually do about then for a bathroom break. Thinking about what I had prayed five hours earlier. At 4:58 I decide to get up and talk to FB about this. When I word process my thoughts I usually can clarify them. Then I could go back to bed and get a few more hours of sleep.

I make some Postum. A hot drink is good, but not coffee; I want to sleep some more in a few minutes. It's not really Postum, but I like to call it that. They quit making real Postum several years ago. I saved my last glass container. I started drinking it about 60 years ago, long before I was allowed to drink coffee. This new stuff is called "Krakus", a "Product of Poland". Instant Coffee Substitute, which I get at the local Good Health Store. It contains: Extracts of roasted barley, rye, chicory, beet roots, a 100% natural product, it says. I use a rounded, almost heaping soup spoon full. It says "one rounded teaspoon" but I like lots of flavour. Added an individual packet of Splenda. Since then I've quit Splenda. It is pure poison. Now I use either Stevia or xylitol. The latter is very healthy. We now sell xylitol flavoured candy at our store, recommended by dentists. A friend said the other day that she uses Splenda to kill ants. So if you use the stuff, be thankful you are much bigger than them.

"Thank you Lord for taking My Betty!" I said it – to God, at 12:02 this AM. How could I be thankful to him for the death of my loving wife? I sat here amazed that I said that, almost unbidden. I sip my Postum. Doesn't taste too bad for a substitute. I know what you are thinking, that we are to thank God "in" everything, but not necessarily "for" everything. Well, look again as I just did. Ephesians 5:20: "Speak to one another with psalms, hymns and spiritual songs. Sing and make music in your heart to the Lord, always giving thanks to God the Father *for* everything, in the name of our Lord Jesus Christ."

Why would I want to thank God for the worst thing that ever happened to me in 70 years? (70 years and 15 days, to be exact) Then, besides that, thank him "FOR" it while I am making music in my heart to him? I guzzle the rest of my Postum before it gets cold. I'm not so sure, yet, about the music in my heart part. That's asking quite a bit.

Thanking God for a heavy duty disaster that breaks your heart does something significant in your heart. I think it goes a long way to improve the mending process. I doubt if my heart will ever be completely mended. Always a large scar. But I was recognizing in my thanks to God that he is sovereign. He does what he pleases because he is in charge. And he always acts in love; that's his nature. Love for Betty, love for me, for our kids and for our grandkids, and for everyone else who misses Betty, along with her multi-grain bread and sticky buns and corn chowder. By giving thanks I recognize that he did the right thing, even though that is not apparent to me and probably never will be while I reside on this planet. Sometimes a guy has to do something in the spiritual realm that doesn't make a lot of sense to your physical here and now very earthy physical mind. God sometimes does ask a whole lot of us – too much, sometimes!

Within 12 hours I forgive my God for coming and taking My Betty, and then took the huge step of thanking him for doing so. How could this possibly happen? The day previous I probably would have laughed if you would have said I was about to do either. The only explanation: so many folks had been praying for me. And deep deep in my heart I really do want a positive productive relationship with my Heavenly Father, today and for forever. He had honoured your prayers and my "secret" desires. In helping me forgive and be thankful "FOR".

I crawled back into bed. I need three more hours of sleep, so I hoped no one would phone till at least 9 AM. I really do have a quieted heart. And do I hear a wee bit of music?

The post of this "event" created more dialogue on Facebook.

Irene: I never cease to be amazed at the faithfulness of God's Holy Spirit to do exactly what's needed in our hearts – when we're ready! Shed lots of tears reading that one!

Duane: Just a thought – you refer to My Betty. Before she was your Betty, she was God's and even when she was yours, in a very real sense she was first and last – God's. About the duration of the sorrow and deep sense of loss. More than 30 years after my dad died at only 60 years someone asked my mom, "How long does it take to get over it?" She responded, "I have absolutely no idea!"

Arnold: Are you saying, Duane, that she is no longer Mine? We evangelicals like to say that we eagerly look forward to seeing again those who have gone before.

I am! Betty told me in the hospital (in writing – she asked for pencil and paper) that "I love you forever and ever, Amen." Me too!

Duane: No, I am not saying that. She is certainly yours to love and cherish in your heart forever. She was your wonderful mate. What I am saying is that even those that we love and care for and would die for are in God's hands. As their Creator he holds the right to work in their lives as he chooses. We are certainly part of that but in the end it is God to whom we all owe our first loyalty and in that sense she never was yours. We evangelicals may not have the final say on what heaven is like. I think we can certainly conclude that individuals will be recognizable to us and we will know each other, but can you imagine loving without a sense of ownership or prejudice? Where we will love everyone with the kind of love that God has loved us with? I remember an old couple at home who thought that God was preparing a mansion in heaven for them to enjoy as a couple. I don't think that is going to happen, but I am not the final authority on what heaven is like. The one thing I am pretty certain of is that it will be better than anything we can imagine. That includes the reunions with those who hold our heart.

An 8 inch wooden heart hangs on the entry hall wall. It says on it, "Our Father has many mansions; I hope mine is next to yours." This folk art picture I painted has two simple shacks behind a man who is handing his woman a flower. On the back I wrote, "Betty, It wouldn't be heaven without you and your hugs! I love you! Arnold Valentines 1985."

Joanne, one of my most faithful counselors, responded: Praise the Lord Arnold. That is such a huge step! I remember when I lost Cordell, the verse of scripture that came to me was, "In everything give thanks for this is the will of God in Christ Jesus concerning you." I cried out to God, "How can I be thankful for this? My Cordell is gone and now I have to face life alone." As I processed it all I decided that there had to be something I could thank God for so I started thanking him that Cordell was his child and now he was safely at home with him in Heaven where he was done with all the junk of earth: heartbreak, sadness, ill health, disappointments, disasters, wars, bills, worry, sleeplessness, growing old, etc. I found that my sadness turned to joy and I could hardly wait to also go Home. Heaven is so much more real when you have someone there that you love and want to be with. Until then though, I want to make both our Heavenly Father and Cordell proud of me by the way I grab on to life and live for God's glory. I hope I am fulfilling his purpose for me as I share what he has done in my life through this journey. Blessings fellow pilgrim. Joanne

Arnold: When we found out in the Foothills Hospital that Betty had incurable cancer, I said to her that "We are going to do this right." I tried to do that and did my best although at times fell short. No I have to do it for myself. I like the way you said it: Grab, Live, Fulfill. I'm going to remember those three words!

145

30

So Many Memories

February 9

Second trip to the Montgomery Auction house in Blackfalds. Items from almost every room in the house. I wished my FB friends you could have been there so that I could give them these things. That would have been more fun than selling them. So many memories. The big picture we bought from the painter we met in Ontario 40 years ago but haven't had it on the wall for 20. The smaller pic in front of it came from our Gospel Books and Music store in Red Deer we owned and managed for five years. Every item has a story. Betty is in every one! Now it is time to be like the younger generation and get rid of stuff we no longer use and lacks significant sentimental value! If you want some, come to the auction February 25.

Marg: Before moving out of my old home, I had a "garage sale with a twist – everything was free!" People came all day and took pretty much everything I had in the garage, including Matt's Elk horns his Auntie D gave him, and I forgot to take off the wall. He's since forgiven me.

Celeste: Hi Arnold, after my Grandma died my Grandpa got remarried fairly quickly. Both my Grandpa and my new step Grandma made it very clear that neither of them were replacing their previous spouses but that they were lonely and looking for companionship. Even we Grandchildren who were between the ages of 8-13 understood what was happening. A Bonus that came along with the marriage was a whole bunch of new cousins.

Arnold: Did they fall in love? Did you get a new Grandma? That's a question I have. My Gkids loved Gramma. Can they love a new one?

Celeste: We never felt the same about my step Grandma as we did for our Nana.

31

There's Not a Word for this Loneliness

February 10. I rolled over and looked at my bedside clock: 6:01 AM. As regularly happens I woke up thinking about stuff. Thinking awakens me, so that I probably would not go back to sleep. For several minutes I pondered whether or not I should discuss this matter with FB. It had been too personal to share, but I talked about it the day before with a couple who invited me for lunch and sent an email to my sister who has been a good counselor the past two months.

So I posted, "I can't help but wonder about finding another woman to be my wife. There, I've said it! I've just told a hundred relatives and friends. Wasn't going to tell anyone because even thinking about it was too uncomfortable. At least at first." I continued the post.

Betty has been gone not yet two months, although it seems so much longer. But I sit at home, alone and lonely. You really do not know loneliness. In the past being separated from Betty for a day made me feel like I was only half there. But that was not loneliness; I would see her again in a few hours. Loneliness is when she has left and is not coming back! The Inuit have 40 words for snow; there should be a special word for this kind of loneliness. It's kind of a burning ache in the gut that you know will not go away; there is no permanent remedy. You know that no matter how much time passes it will not entirely be gone.

So when I am lonely my mind wanders to the thought that I probably will someday need to think seriously about finding another wife. Just to write this makes gives me a twinge of guilt. Not yet two months and I am "betraying" the wife I've dearly loved for 48 years by even thinking about "replacing" her. Even though she told me I was to get married again. Then I did not want to think about it, but now I am. She knew me better than I did, methinks! I would get lonely and need someone. I am surprised it happened so soon. So I feel guilty. And I didn't dare say a word to anyone, too personal and private. I really didn't want anyone to know, until the past few days, that is.

So now I sit here drinking Postum (Krakus) and telling you. But everything I've told you the past three and a half months has been very personal. Folks don't usually talk about what I've been experiencing the past two months. Too emotionally laden and much too personal. But I inadvertently stumbled on to this path months ago and have told you almost everything. So I guess I should continue my story with the next "phase". I am attempting to turn another page and it is confusing. What should I or should not be thinking? I am looking for some dialogue here. I covet your advice today. Here's what I've been thinking and talking about.

I have been listening to other folks who have walked my path, looking for guidance. Here are their stories.

1. I met an old friend downtown a few days ago. His wife died eight years ago. He remarried last summer. I asked him how it was going. "Well, we come from different cultures and had to make some adjustments. But we are happy." He had known her for years but their new relationship was kicked off at a bowling event. She invited him for a gathering at her house.

2. A seventyish fellow whose wife died 19 months ago came by and told me his story. "I'm still married to her and have no interest in looking for another wife."

3. Had coffee downtown with a widower of three years. He is not interested in getting re-married. His adult daughter was living with them when his wife suddenly died. Since then she has cooked for him and looked after him in many ways. He has company. Does not live in an empty house and never has.

4. Had Sunday dinner with newlyweds a couple of weeks ago. Walked into the house and staring me in my face was a series of pictures of her and her previous husband's 25th anniversary. That surprised me. What would her new husband think of that? Visited them for several hours. They are happy together and answered a bunch of my questions, including some I didn't have the nerve to ask. Her husband died six years ago. She found her new man, from eastern Canada, through a Christian Internet find-a-mate site.

5. This Sunday I briefly chatted with a lady who is just engaged. Her husband died probably six or eight years ago. She found her new fiancé on an Internet matching site. A man out of province, similar to the above story.

6. A local man married his wife's sister less than two months after his wife died. Apparently his dying wife told him to marry her, someone he had known all his life. Apparently they are quite happy.

7. Yesterday I chatted with an old friend whose mother died of cancer 18 years ago. Her dad re-married in 15 months. She thinks her mother told her dad to marry this particular woman. This lady had not ever married and her mother had been trying to remedy that matter for years. They have been happily married for seventeen.

8. A lady told me just yesterday about an aunt that had remarried after only three months. Some guy came along and took advantage of her grieving and loneliness. She has been sorry ever since but strives at making this new relationship work.

Quite a variety of situations. From less than a year to several years. Marrying too soon, or getting hitched to a sister of your wife, getting to know a local lady while bowling, finding a spouse on the Internet, or not wanting or even thinking about getting married again. Everyone has their own story. Unique.

I told the old friend whose dad has been remarried for seventeen years that I was feeling a bit guilty about even thinking about another woman. She said something that has intrigued me. "Arnold, that fact that you are thinking about re-marriage says that you had a good marriage. If you had not had a good one you would not be even thinking about doing it again." Makes sense, right?

My serious grieving was done before Betty left. We had several intimate discussions about her dying and planning her good-bye service. Now it's the loneliness. And when it surfaces I cannot help but thinking of Betty's advice to re-marry.

I wasn't going to tell a soul, but now I have to tell you. I've had two brief interactions with a lovely blond gal. The first time I was mesmerized. But I spent a few hours repeatedly clicking on my "Self Control" button and got over it. Too much too soon. So the infatuation went away.

Several weeks ago I received a real nice sympathy card with a long note about this lady's fond memories of a relationship with Betty and me years ago. Another real nice gal. She separated from her husband at least ten years ago. I was seriously tempted to write her back to start a dialogue. I did search the Internet for her phone number but didn't find it. But I didn't write.

A couple of days ago I had a discussion with a lady whom Betty and I had gotten to know because of Betty's sickness. (That's all I can tell you now!). She is pretty and real nice. I'm a spontaneous guy and wrote out a sticky note that said: "Arnold. June 14. 5:30". I told her that I was going to pick her up that day and we were going to have supper together. Not a date, just a "social interaction". I said I was still crying every day so had to wait six months from the day Betty left. She surprised me by sticking the note on the wall and saying, "Well, maybe. We'll see." She had told me that she was going to do some traveling, alone. I asked, "Where is your husband?" He had left her three years ago. She was not over him yet, so wasn't thinking of a new relationship. Not yet. A divorce, I hear, can be as difficult and sometimes more so than having a spouse leave through death. Death brings certain closure, but a divorce does not. The spouse is still around.

There, I've let the cat out of the bag. I have been looking around. I admit it! Everybody I talk to about this echoes Betty's advice: Be cautious, give it time. Don't make a mistake you will regret for the rest of your life. Good advice.

So now it's your turn. I invite your response and your advice. Perhaps you have a story of someone you know whose spouse died that would help me understand my situation and where to go from here. Let's talk about this. Any of your thoughts are welcome. I've found over the years that when I have a difficult decision to make, I ask at least three people for advice. I do not necessarily take any one individual's advice, but the process helps me think it through to hopefully make the right decision.

This has been scary, nervously sitting here writing this into my computer, knowing you will soon read this. But I really do want to know what you are thinking? While y'alls are thinking about this I am going to go have some breakfast and maybe go lay back in my Lazyboy and have some more sleep. (If I can quit thinking about that pretty lady I am having supper with on June 14. I am smiling! Sometimes with all these mixed up emotions I am experiencing I feel like a teenage kid antsy about his first date. Now I am chuckling;-)

As usual, my Facebook friends found something good to say, a collage of insightful advice.

Louise: L♥VE! You have a great support network Arnold, and I know they'll give you good advice. I always wished my Mom would have taken longer to get remarried after my Dad died. We kids also needed time to get used to the idea that he was gone and when we'd go home he wouldn't be there. But Mom remarried quite quickly, within a couple of years, and it was tough. I'd say, let your kids in on the process every step of the way!

Arnold: How old were all the kids when your mom remarried?

Louise: I was 23, the only one married. I had an older sister, and two younger siblings, obviously different then your situation.

Arnold: My kids are pushing 40 and have seven Gkids altogether. But I agree about keeping them informed. Some surprises are unnecessary and unwise.

Tom: I have appreciated your journal over the past few months and have not responded here. I believe you have given yourself the best counseling and it would be difficult to add to it. It is a lonely time for someone who has had a wonderful marriage. You have said that you are looking. Isn't it strange that when we are married God says to keep our eyes on our spouse, but when our spouse it gone then our eyes can wander? This seems to be natural in God's plan. You have said, "make sure" or regret it. Once again great advice, but there is still a time when we "take a risk" and make a decision. However you have said that you want to take it slowly and give some time. Very wise as many times the quick decisions we come to regret. My only addition would be to "enjoy the journey" that you are now on. Enjoy the friendships, the excitement, the sharing, the "new life". Don't get tied up in what others "might" think for they have not followed the same path as you are on. This is God's path prepared especially for you and no-one has traveled it before or ever will. It can be similar but not the same. Love you brother. Have a wonderful journey.

Gabriela: Go ahead when you are really ready to put your mind and love 100% into a lovely woman. Even the Bible supports you, if you are a widower you can remarry. If it is God's desire, he even will take care of whom. Receive a big hug!

Richard: Live! Leave the rest up to God. Mary released me to remarry in the week she passed. What a wonderful gift. I had forgotten that until a dear friend reminded me. God brought a wonderful lady into my life. If you are sure it is God's will and choice then all is right and better yet perfect.

Marg: Well Arnold, its official. You're definitely moving on. Reading through your thoughts was an interesting, albeit a bit surprising journey. You are doing just fine, it sounds like, but more than anything, BE CAREFUL! I think of Bruce's Dad's last wife who made his life quite miserable, and ours as well. There's so much at stake here. Here's a list of things to ask any woman, some serious, some not.

1. Does she like redheads? You have a few in the clan! 2. Most important, does she have a growing and strong relationship with God? 3. What are her feelings on woodworking? 4. Does she like to garden? 5. Is she a good cook? 6. Does she have a genuine laugh and smile? Anyone else have questions to add for Arnold to ask a woman?

Richard: What is her love language?

Gert: "Guard your heart above all else, for it determines the course of your life." (Proverbs 4:23) And remember Betty's advice as well. I have heard too many stories where haste meets regret, my grandpa being one of them. Savor Betty for a while longer. By all accounts you had a wonderful marriage, savor the memories some more, and draw ever closer to the Lord during this time. He really does fill the lonely places. I know he does.

Tammy, from next door: Jerry says, can she handle snoring? Tammy says, will she like your neighbors?

Cherie: Arnold, please get to know yourself. Take time. Be careful. There is nothing wrong with a date and going out to do stuff; summer is coming there is plenty that will be going on. What do you love to do besides wood working? Do you truly love the garden? Would you go out on Blue Bronna riding adventures? Go to the tropics. Go on a mission trip? What do you like to talk about? What bores you? Have you gone to summer festivals like the Folk Festival in Calgary or the Blue Grass festival? Maybe you know everything about yourself (that would be amazing). Seek God; ask him to show you the undiscovered you and what would he like to do with you, not like a tool but like a friend. Who are you without Betty? It has been a long time since you were alone with yourself. Who is that Man in your Mirror? Love and Peace, Arnold.

Tammy: But really kidding aside I'm echoing the "take it slow" advice; you are a very passionate man and seem to take things head on. Take a step back and run with your own six months advice. If this is part of God's great plan for you he will send the right person and you will know beyond doubt that she's the right one.

Arnold: Mama Mia! You guys are amazing! Sure are giving me a bunch of things to think about. Knew I could count on you! Now I don't know why I was afraid to share this with you.

Joli: Sounds like Aunt Betty knew you the best and gave you the best blessing and the best advice before you even asked for it. Arnold: Betty had that gift! She had me figured all right – for 48 years.

32

Get a Nice Puppy

February 11. Lyle, my youngest brother suggested: Why not get a nice puppy? It would lower your stress level? Tammy: lol Lyle don't even ask.

I replied to Lyle: Tammy has been trying to foist a dog on me, so finally I sent her this note to set things straight: Having a dog would be as time consuming as a baby. What would I do with the critter when Jerry and I went to the city? Or went out for lunch? Or to church, or wherever? It would cost me $39 a month to feed em. It would smell up the house and leave hair all over. Every time I would sit I would get it sticking to my pants. Animals are a pain in the (several parts of the anatomy) so why would I want one?

If I am going to have a body around I want something with hands that I can hold, not paws that would scratch up the place. I prefer a face that will smile at me, and tender lips that would gently wrap around mine, not a slimy sloppy piece of flesh to slather foreign infested bacteria all over my face. I don't want a tail wagging when I come home, but a couple of arms to wrap around me, with a full body to snuggle up against mine. One that has a lovely feminine form that fits mine or that I can wiggle around until it does. Somebody to eat the same food as me, to sit next to me on the couch, shoulder to shoulder. Someone I can nuzzle behind the ear and experience the pleasant female fragrance, not a foul smelling creature that nuzzles me sometimes in unpleasant places. Whose hairy ears I'm supposed to scratch. Someone whose body is femininely soft almost anywhere I touch, not a creature hairy all over.

I want someone to stand on two legs and look me in both my eyes with love plus intelligence and tenderness. A body that could say much more than "ruff ruff", that would whisper sweetness in my ear and say a bunch of lovely things. A creature who speaks my language with whom I can carry on intelligent conversation, and maybe occasionally argue with. Someone who can go with me into any eating establishment. Or anywhere else.

My dog "treatise" created a bit of a storm from the dog lovers, but I did get a bit of sympathy.

Mahdieh: Just to let you know, dogs and cats are therapeutic. They love unconditionally. They really do! And if they are a rescue animal then you can feel very good about the decision. Ok, I've said my Save the Animals at the Pound Talk. Uncle Arnold, it may be a lovely time to get to know yourself as an individual again. I'm sure you are doing this now. So use this time to learn about yourself! Sorry! I don't want to tell you what to do. I agree with the others, when God knows you are ready and the person is ready he will send that person in your life to spend time with and get to know Arnold. We are all here to support you. My rescue dogs bring me a great deal of happiness making the hair in the house all worthwhile. I mean, "They LOVE unconditionally"!

Arnold: You dog lovers are ganging up on me!

Mahdieh: Who knows, a special lady friend in the future just may have a dog or a cat of her own!

Louise: We tried a dog once, but not a good idea for us go-getters. He really tied us down and we were looking for someone to look after it all the time. I spend a lot of time going to town for my daughters extra-curricular activities and that was not fair for our dog at all. He spent too much time alone and that created all sorts of other problems. Very time consuming if you want to do it right. Our cat is much easier; it doesn't matter if a cat has to spend a few hours alone every day. Cats just sleep and don't need to be trained, walked, loved, and socialized like a dog does. But oh my, the hair! If we didn't love our cat and have him for eight years I don't think I'd be able to put up with all this hair. Needless to say, I'm looking forward to being pet-free someday!

Arnold: OK, y'alls. Read Louise. Good thoughts. She wants desperately to be *pet free* someday! I already am. Why spoil a good thing? Thanks, Louise for giving some balance to this discussion.

Tammy: lol See Lyle, that's why I said, "don't ask." hehe.

Arnold: Tammy, are you actually backing off? That's not like you. Have you finally met your match?

154

33

Lots of Thyme and a Bit of Parsley

Mama Mia, did I open up a box of I don't know what – chocolates? I was going to say "Pandora's" Box, but that implies a bunch of troubles! I was not going to say a thing to anybody about what was swirling around in my head and infringing on the surface of my heart, nuzzling it to try to enter. FB handed me a bundle of thoughts that I was processing about looking for a wife, and I actually found some joy and fun in doing so. The burden of secrecy was gone. In addition to the Facebook responses, several emailed with more personal stories with significant meaning for me. I have found their stories and advice significant and thoughtful.

The previous evening I had taken a pot of freshly made veggie/bean/rice/ chicken soup over to Jerry, Tammy, and Reese's. They actually liked it. Nicely flavoured with lots of thyme and a bit of parsley. After supper (they had dinner, me supper as they are from Ontario and not yet true Albertans), I sat and conversed with Tammy about our recent FB dialogue, as she did dishes. It reminded me of when, as a teenager, I would sit on the stool by the chimney next to the wood stove, while Mom, a few feet away would hear my teenage problems and also tell me her story. (Now, everywhere I go, I find another Momma who wants to fix me up. Well, Betty did that too, so now I have to look to others, even to my neighbour!) Tammy is a wise person, and dangerous. She and Jerry have experienced a lot of life and she knows me so well that it makes me nervous. Betty and I became good friends with them the past 2½ years and the past three months they have become responsible for me: feeding, advising, hugging, advising, chatting, encouraging, advising. I am Reese's adopted Grampa. So she knows me too well, got me pretty much figured out. She is sticking to the six months. Not even a double date. Not even going to the restaurant for a coffee, with a lady. "I am going to hold you to this!" she emphatically tells me three or four times in our half hour conversation. She said I am too passionate a guy to do otherwise. She says that means that when I take on a "project" I barge in with all engines fully torqued, moving straight ahead (my interpretation of her words). Guess she thinks that in matters of the heart a guy, especially one in my vulnerable position, should use some peripheral vision and take an occasional look behind to check for unexpected or dangerous developments. (Don't tell her I said so, but she is right! It's so great to be loved by neighbours who really care! Am I blessed or what?)

Cherie said: "Please get to know yourself. Seek God; ask him to show you the undiscovered you and what he would like to do with you, like a friend. Who are you without Betty? It has been a long time since you were alone with yourself. Who is that Man in your Mirror?"

Now here is an idea that I have found novel and intriguing. Discover who I am! I've got to realize that I've been Betty's Husband for 48 years. This self-image has impregnated every aspect of me, physically, mentally, emotionally and spiritually. Most everything I have done in these almost five decades has encircled her. Is that the person I want to present to another lady? Not really. I cannot bring Betty along when I sit down to visit with another woman. I'd probably start crying every five minutes. That really did bring on a couple sobs. Guess more evidence I really do need the six months. So who am I? I really do not know. I could guess, but maybe it will take me six months to figure this one out. A good project for me on which to focus. Thanks Cherie, for this tip, coming from another wise lady!

On the other hand, being a husband or widower at my age is not going to make a huge difference in who I am. At 71 years my personality and character are firmly established. It's the teenagers who are supposed to find out the answer to "who am I?" The real me is pretty much set in stone. Obviously, however, my self image will change somewhat as I change in my relationship from husband to widower and perhaps again to husband. But I do know quite well the Man in my Mirror.

Several folks had commented to me that I was coming along quite well. Didn't quite know what they meant so I've tried to understand by looking in the mirror. Here is what I saw.

1. I don't cry much anymore. The loneliness is no longer a desperate ache. I am finding ways to cope. I am keeping busy and this really helps me re-focus. Even though Betty keeps showing up as I go through the house sorting stuff. That's okay; it gives me a chance to chat with her a bit, even though it means sometimes I cry again. Her pics around the house now more often bring warm memories than tears.

2. I am enjoying cooking. Made two kinds of soup yesterday and a bean salad (I make a mean one!). Baked a chocolate cake the other day, and maybe another one in the shape of a heart to take to my neighbours on Valentines.

3. Getting out every day to chat with folks, even if it is just to get the mail and a few groceries, or go next door. Always find somebody. No way am I going to be a hermit. I fear I am on my way to becoming a People Person! People have been having me over for a meal and a visit. I have started to joke around with folks again. That really pleases me cuz that is basically how I often have related to folks. Sort of a normal for me. And I occasionally once again have been giving someone a hard time. Guess that's kind of a gift I have! Another normal? Jerry has become my buddy. He hugs me every time I show up. When I am going to the dump, Red Deer or Calgary or wherever, if he is not previously occupied helping somebody else, he

comes. Or he goes somewhere and invites me. We stop at thrift stores; he buys books and I add to my LP collection. And look for neat Blue Jeans to cover my chests with.

4. I am sort of seriously thinking about the "possibility" of getting married again. The guilt I have felt about thinking "about another woman" you have helped to dispel, almost. Bev (an old friend from the Blackfalds Auction) says that is okay, a sign that I had a good marriage otherwise I would not want another. Interesting! And I found a lady to safely flirt with! She is three thousand miles away, too far to think seriously about and far enough away so she will not drop by to slap my face. Fun! Please do not tell Tammy about this or she may stop it, too.

You have helped me to commit to doing the six months (just over four left). I do promise not to have a "date" in that time. But, if some nice lady stumbles across my path, shouldn't I be polite and pick her up? What if I am camping and a nice single lady stops by to borrow some coffee? Shouldn't I offer a hot cup? Maybe God sent her?;-} What if a group goes bowling and some lady needs a partner? What do I do? Be rude and say "no"? I will be very careful. I know I am very vulnerable right now, and as Betty warned, "Take your time and make sure you wait for the right person!" Good advice. Very. Y'alls have helped me take this to heart.

5. I enjoy watching movies. Even by myself. My house has morphed from an empty Cavern to a Sanctuary. I now love to come Home. I decided a few weeks ago to be happy. Most of the time it works. When it doesn't, I just work it out. I have discovered that you really can "decide to be happy".

18. I am starting to feel positive about the future, and actually looking forward with a tiny tinge of excitement and joy, growing in the past two days because you have cared – that there is still good life and happiness for me. And, as my lovely sister said yesterday by email, "God gives us the desires of our hearts." I promise to guard my heart with due diligence. Gert noted, "Guard your heart above all else, for it determines the course of your life" (Proverbs 4:23).

34

Betty Came to Church

February 12, after attending Church, I told this story to Facebook.
I was not going to tell you this as you would for sure think I was going nutso! But I had to talk about it with somebody. So I emailed my sister, chatted with my daughter on the phone, and then my Pastor son-in-law, and my savvy neighbour. They didn't seem to think I'd gone off the beam, and there was some agreement about what all this meant. So here goes.

I got to church just as it was about to start, sitting next to a single guy. On my right was an empty chair. It has seemed right to have an empty chair next to me at church.

We stood up to sing our first song, which I didn't know so was not singing. Instead I found myself standing there holding the hand of this lovely lady I'd taken a shine to. I was really enjoying this; she was warming my innards! Lovely!

Then Betty showed up – seven feet in front of me, out of reach. She looked at me. For a half minute we just stood there looking into each other's eyes. I tried to make her smile or at least have a twinkle in her eye, but I realized I was attempting to force this. She just looked at me, seriously, but not condemningly. Then she slowly turned and was gone.

I started to cry, sobbing. It is very hard work crying unobtrusively in a crowd. Tears were running down my face and dripping on the floor. Now I'm crying again as I write. Betty was gone and now so was the other lady. Alone again. I cried for the next half hour. Another sermon about Nehemiah, but not much in it for me.

What was I to make of this? You need to realize that I did not really see anybody; this happened in my imagination. But it was just as real as if these two ladies had actually been there. The four people I shared this with tended to agree with what I had concluded after coming home from church and pondering this crazy thing that had happened.

God was giving me a gentle tap on the shoulder. "Arnold, I have given you those Facebook Counselors for a reason. You need to listen to them. Wait. You are rushing into things. Wait; take your time. You have got lots of it! Just wait." Betty was reminding me of what she had said in the hospital: "Take your time. Don't rush."

True, I had committed to the six months – no dates, but realized I was plotting how to court a lady without actually having a formal "date". I have always been good at getting around the rules, when necessary, of course. So I did get this message, specially packaged for me. Next time it may be a whack on the side of the head. Don't want that. I am listening this time.

So no more plotting, no more strategizing, no more flirting with the 3,000 mile lady. I am going to concentrate on getting to know my Father better, and plan on getting acquainted with the Guy-in-the-Mirror.

Thank you Lord for being patient with me. Thank you Counselors for not making me out to have gone off the beam, completely whacko. For understanding that I am experiencing a bundle of mixed up emotions right now. And that's why I need to take time. Just cool it, Stauffer. Slow down the revs! Enjoy life with just your Father, your friend in the mirror, and all those good people out there that really do love and care for you. Oh man, am I a slow learner sometimes!

Facebook concurred with my conclusions on the matter.

Tom: You are one smart man. Have a great day in your decision.

Arnold: Guess I'll keep going to church. That's where God speaks to me, not in the songs or sermon, but in unusual and untried ways. He's the most creative personality in the universe, that's his privilege. Hey, I am becoming a New Man! New ways of doing things. It's started already yet.

Cherie: Thank goodness Arnold. Cool your jets and just sail for a while. Don't be so afraid of being alone with yourself and Jesus. Grab a pal and go bowling, or ice fishing, barn board hunting, whatever. Just stop trying to nest.

Louise: Have you ever read 'The Walk' and the sequel 'Miles to Go' by Richard Paul Evans. I'm thoroughly enjoying them. It's about a guy whose wife passed away and his subsequent unrelenting search for hope. I just went to his website and it looks like a third book in the sequel will be coming out soon: The Road to Grace.

Merle: So glad Betty stepped up and you listened. I thought I was going to have to make a long phone call to you for a one-to-one counseling session. My sister is so very wise.

Ann: You are being wise to take advice. In my past a friend lost his wife and showed interest in me. I was very interested but thought he was moving too quickly. As a result he married someone else shortly and the rest is history. God bless your "wait".

Cindy: Thank you so much for sharing, Arnold. Never think you're nutso, just very honest and real, pain and all. Waiting is wise, but I know not easy. Will be praying for courage and single-mindedness for you in waiting, as emotions sometimes have a way of taking over common-sense.

Arnold: Thanks! All you fine folks.

It was February 14, Valentine's Day, 2012. I wrote to FB: FREE, FREE, FREE! That's how I felt yesterday and today.

On the way to Blackfalds with my third and final downsizing load for the auction, my Buddy Jerry said, "Arnold, you are a Master Craftsman. You know how to have an excellent marriage. So you can pass those skills you have mastered in the past 48 years on to another marriage. A new woman will benefit from those skills." Now there's a new thought!

Echoes the same comment of the three different ladies. "The fact that you are even thinking about marriage again suggests that you and Betty did have a good one. Otherwise you would not be thinking about another marriage."

Now don't get your shirt in a sweat! This comment from Jerry was sparked by a ditty I was making up and singing loudly as we hurtled down the road. "Free, free, free, I am wonderfully free!" This is true. All encumbrances are gone. My mind and emotions are free of ladies. You guys have been advising me clearly and strongly to take time, but it took a gentle tap on the shoulder by My Lord Sunday to convince me to back off. Just thankful it was a gentle tap instead of the whack on the side of the head that I deserved. I am a visual guy, so I guess I also needed the picture. Jerry caught me with a sob on the way home as I remembered seeing Betty on Sunday. Love and marriage are not on my mind today. I told Jerry I was going to FB his comment, that's all.

So today, to celebrate Valentine's Day, the only ladies I have in mind are my daughter-in-law and my three lovely little granddaughters. I'm taking them chocolates and roses. And a chocolate heart cake with strawberries. And a half dozen roses to Tammy, the lady who has helped me so much during the past three months. And a chocolate heart cake for all the Roberges, also. With strawberries. Chocolate and strawberries go really well together. And Jerry gave his permission for me to take the red roses to his wife. Then on Friday my daughter is coming with my other four GKids, and we will have another chocolate heart cake with strawberries. And chocolates. What better way for a Grandpa to celebrate Valentines. Especially when there are absolutely no big ladies to complicate his life! I am free. Free to have an absolutely lady-free Valentine's Day. Just little ones; I am blessed with five beautiful Grand Daughters, and their Moms of course. That is more than good enough for me today.

Thank you, Lord, and y'alls for being patient with me.

HAPPY VALENTINES Y'ALLS!

Amanda: Boy, sure sounds like a lot of chocolate cakes! I'm almost jealous! As my three year old Asher said to me this morning "apple dinos day!" Lol. Happy Valentine's Day.

Lyle: I just wanted to comment the other day but I'll do it now. I think if you come to the point of being content spending quality time with the man in the mirror, women will be more content with you.

Tammy: Thanks Arnold. We Roberges are so thankful God blessed us with your love and friendship ♥ Our very special valentines treat from a very special person ♥ (Tammy posted this picture for the FB Group.)

I took a bunch of Valentine stuff to my three GGirls and their Mom & Dad. Chocolates, red roses, chocolate cake with strawberries, gifts.

What a bunch of lovelies! The only tough part was coming home. I had to leave without Gramma. She loved her kids and GKids so much. That was her one major regret when she got sick, that she would not be able to visit and look after them anymore. What a major loss for them! I cried half the way home.

But I have been faithful to my new commitment, not even thinking about Big Ladies. It has been very freeing, making life much less complicated so that I can get along doing the important things I am supposed to be doing.

Tomorrow Tara is coming with my other four GKids. I am feeding them home made mac n cheese with wieners, and broccoli salad which all of them like. Would you believe that all my grandkids like broccoli? And waffles for breakfast when all seven Gkids will be here along with three of their parents. The house will come alive for sure!

The valentine's event brought strong affirmation from Facebook.

Louise: Sounds wonderful and your Gkids have a real gift in you. Bless you for loving them in a way that is tangible and builds memories! Irene: So happy for you; the right thing to be doing especially on family day weekend! Jan: I love this Arnold. Once we can make a difference in other people's lives great healing is taking place. You are amazing! Cheryl: Hi Uncle Arnold! I thought about you and Auntie B today as I displayed the special dishes of hers that you passed on to me. Once again, thank you for sharing the treasures. OXO. Merle likes this.

I was so pleased in being able to pass Betty's special things on to people like Cheryl who would appreciate them. Because they came from Betty's family I thought it was the time to pass them to the next generation. So glad Cheryl and others enjoyed them.

By the end of February, I reported to FB that I was doing ok. I was learning to live alone and finding it is not so bad so long as I keep busy and get out every day. God is Good!

35

My Chance for an Oscar

February 20. Read Ephesians and then went for a walk. Taking a walk in the country has always been one of the best ways for me to talk to Father. I was wondering where all the power is that believers are supposed to have, as mentioned in this book.

February 21, 2012. Betty talked to me today. As I looked for our marriage certificate to copy and send with the Application for a Canada Pension Plan Survivor's Pension, I was flipping through her file, "Keepsakes". This 3½ x 5 card popped out, in her handwriting: "Every grief that strikes us is an invitation from the Father in Heaven to lean hard." Thanks Betty, for this wonderful reminder.

February 22, 2012. Sent off applications for The Canada Pension Plan Survivor's Pension and also The Canada Pension Plan Death Benefit. Documents and more documents. It is much easier to be born than to die. Went to the bank a couple of weeks ago to make the necessary changes and they kept me for over an hour and asked me come back again to sign more papers. Have to change names on all kinds of stuff as we had both of our names on everything.

You guys who want me to discover the Guy-in-the-Mirror, I told FB, would be pleased to know that I am going to Drumheller on Sunday to audition for the Badlands Passion Play. Maybe I will get to be a Roman Soldier! I've always wanted to be in drama, and even being part of a crowd with a non-speaking part will be a neat experience, just to be on the other side of the stage.

I was reading a chapter in Ephesians every day and meditating and praying on it; getting to know Father a bit better. And I stayed away from the ladies. I reported that I was pretty much behaving myself and attempting to do the right things, at least what they told me to do and not!

I resumed walking. Did very little when Betty was sick. Doc says to walk and lose 25 pounds. So I walked twice this week, sometimes to the post office, 25 minutes one way. One trip took me well over an hour and a half. Chatted with a friend at the post office, a husband of a Farmers' Market Vendor on a Main street sidewalk, and three Prairie folks as I sauntered through their turf. Walking is enjoyable. Scenery, good exercise and people. Don't want to be either a hermit or a couch potato. Had supper three times this week at the neighbour's who do a great job of tolerating and entertaining me. One day Reese and his Mom made delicious crepes. We filled them with peanut butter, cinnamon, fruit salad, cottage cheese, peach jam and cream cheese. Delicious! Reese had been campaigning to make them for Grampa – that's me!

On February 24, for brunch I ate Betty's last sub bun, a bacon and tomato. With sides of a dill pickle and slices of a portabella mushroom. Tasty! In the evening I found two of Betty's multi-grain buns in the freezer door of the fridge. Mama Mia! So I cut them in half and slathered them with mayo and placed a sardine on each. Yummy! If you want a delicious fruit salad, mix five or six fruits and berries together and add a can of peach and mango pie filling, which adds a thickener and lots of flavour. That's what I had for dessert. Orange chunks, strawberries, grapes, apple chunks, fresh pineapple chunks, banana slices, and whatever other fruit you have on hand.

The next day I attended the auction sale in Blackfalds. Jerry and Tammy came, and my brother Lyle and his stepson, Kyle, spent the day with us. Watched the Grand Caravan loads pass to new ownership under the auctioneer's hammer. A large original oil painting we had bought from the artist in St. Jacobs, Ontario, on our cross Canada trip 40 years ago. Paid $95, sold for $10. A ship's wheel obtained in Boston on the same trip; bought for $25, sold for $100. Four boxes of kitchen stuff (cake and pie tins, bowls, mugs, cake decorating paraphernalia, and much more) for $10. I had continued the downsizing process. It was sometimes difficult as Betty really was there as I decided what to do with each item I pulled out of a cupboard or off a shelf somewhere in our house. So many memories of our life together. Sometimes stuff we had not used for twenty or thirty years. The oil painting and the ship's wheel had been stored in the downstairs closet and the kitchen stuff in the bottom cupboard or hall closet. Seven huge tables at the auction covered with our items, much of it from our Barnboard Woodart business, which has taken a downturn the past four years. But we both are collectors and savers, not part of the throw-away generation. But the stuff had to go! Some of my antiques sold well: cream cans, wooden barrels, Prairie benches, etc., and my best woodart item sold for $75. One print I had intended to frame brought $160. It brought more than enough to pay for Lyle's 61st birthday supper that day in Red Deer, for the five of us, following the auction. Nostalgic but fun day for me, but also another part in the process of saying good-bye to Betty, and a lot of no-longer-needed this and that.

On February 26 I got the news that they are giving me a role at the Drumheller Passion Play. I may be even a small speaking role, says the Director. I've found a way to invest a large number of hours between now and July 20, the final performance. It took only ten minutes; they gave me two sentences of Caiaphas telling folks that it is better for one to die. I said it twice, Director Roule gave me some advice, and then a third time.

They probably take anybody they can get as they need 200 crowd people, but a small speaking role would be fun. Okay, FB folks, an interesting step in discovering the guy in the mirror! And in stepping out.

Merle was sure I would be up for an Oscar award next year! Arnold: Ok Merle, you will have to nominate me for the O, doubt if anyone else would. Well, who knows, maybe I will have found a new calling. Chris Plumber is over 80 and up for a big award tonight! Tara promised she would come even if I just had a part in a crowd scene. So who else will come?

36

I have to eat these @#$#%!&! tasteless things*

Shed some tears the morning of February 27, just a few, playing Wheel of Fortune. Betty and I played it almost every evening, about 10 pm when the new WF day started with a gift to us of 30 cyber gold pieces. We did quite well at it. Our personal experiences each added to solutions so that we got a lot more than either of us could have alone. Something neat we did together, with fun and laughs. I haven't been very keen on playing it since she left. But I am close to the 200 level so thought I would go up another that morning. Betty's pic is on my bookshelf; she's smiling at me! Just made it to level 199. Do 200 tomorrow.

The next day I was crying again. Will it ever stop? Going through some things on Betty's dresser and came across several pictures of her holding her Grandgirls. She was at her loveliest when with her GGirls, all smiles and charm, she loved them so much. I cried. Later, I opened Facebook and immediately saw the picture of her and me, taken last summer. And I cried. I shouldn't complain; everybody says that tears are God's gift to help the healing. I know that. Some people can't cry even if they wanted to. So I better be thankful for God's gift. Not a day has passed since Betty left without a sob and/or tears. Something said or Betty showing up at home as I handle or look at some object that has Betty written all over it. She is everywhere. But nowhere.

Next day. Man o man! Cried like a baby today. Haven't cried like that for weeks. Over some buns. A couple of days ago I noticed a package of six brown buns in the freezer. Aw, I thought, there are some of Betty's buns left! I was so happy. So today I decided to have a couple for lunch. I nuked em and then cut one in half. It was not Betty's bun but from a package I'd picked up at a grocery store. But I decided to eat it anyway. Sad looking colour, poor texture, and absolutely tasteless. How can people sell stuff like this and call it food? Then I remembered in the hospital a few hours before she left, Betty asking me, "Is it time for me to go?" Then I said yes, but today I realized I made a mistake. "It is not time for you to go! I have to sit here and eat these @#$#%!&*! tasteless things. You should have stayed!" Guess it wasn't really the store bun, but another shocking realization My Betty was gone and wasn't coming back. As I posted a note on FB I can't see the computer screen for tears. Guess it will be awhile before I can really say Goodbye. She baked our bread and tasty buns for 48 years. How will I get over that? I've seen her bake bread dozens, maybe hundreds, of times. I loved to sit at the kitchen table and watch her, a skilled artisan at work; maybe I will have to start making my own.

Sunday, March 4, I went to church. Met a nice lady at the door who joked with me for a bit, and then I went over to the coat rack and met a couple who have been good friends. We had some good laughs together. This was my best move through the church foyer so far. You know why I would come to the church just when it is time to start and try to sneak through the foyer into the sanctuary without getting caught? So somebody will not stop and ask, "Hi Arnold, how are you doing?" After I made initial arrangements with the undertaker to prepare Betty for burial, he phoned and the first thing he said was, "How are you doing, Arnold?" Immediately he backed off and apologized several times, saying he was not supposed to ask that question. When you ask that question I just might get choked up or burst into tears. I did not like doing that in the church foyer with 75 folks watching. At least that's the way I feel when it happens.

One of the first times I came to church after Betty left, an old friend made a joke and we had a good laugh. This was the best greeting I have had in two and a half months. Do not ask a grieving person in public how he is doing. Here are some alternatives. You don't have to ask the "how are you" question to show that person you really care. Just make conversation for a minute or two. The care from you will quickly be obvious. Start an easy non-threatening conversation and test the waters to see if the person wants to talk about how s/he is. Perhaps just say, "Hi!" and tell me you are praying for me. Then I can respond in whatever way is appropriate for me at that moment.

Here are some staple conversation starters that I have used. 1. Hi Fred, did you do some good this week? 2. Hi Sally, great to see you out and about. 3. Arnold, you are looking good. You must have eaten your veggies this week. Think of some good and safe, non-threatening conversation starters.

I started March 6 weeping again. I missed Betty so. Something real good happened yesterday; I was hired as the new Manager of the Three Hills Good Health Store. But I could not tell Betty. We shared everything. No secrets. And one of the best parts of the day was when we would come home from work and talk about the happenings of the day. Often when something neat occurred or I accomplished some little thing, the thought would pass through my mind, "I have to remember to tell Betty this." So today I texted my neighbour; had to tell somebody. I needed a focus as I established my new "normal" and this new job was a terrific one for me.

That day I was confused. How could I still miss Betty so, but at the same time yearn to be touched by someone else – by some other woman? Apparently God has created in us a deep desire for companionship, and the deepest measure of such a relationship takes place in the intimacy only possible between a man and a woman. So that most meaningful partnership possible between two human beings has been torn from me. That leaves a serious bleeding wound. I tried to bandage it every day, sometimes more than once, but the wound would not stop seeping.

One day I attended a meeting in which four ladies and a fellow sat around a table. One of the ladies whom I have known for years asked, "Arnold, have you been hugged yet today?" I had not, so before I left all five of them lined up to hug me. That was very comforting and meaningful. Walking home I thought, "I should have asked for another meeting tomorrow!" Smile. Several times during that period I said to ladies I was chatting with, "I try to talk with a pretty lady at least once a day so that I do not lose the touch!" This little joke always brought a chuckle.

I had supper at another friend's place. Afterwards the husband and wife and I sat at the table after their kids had gone to bed. I started getting choked up when talking about Betty. The lady reached over with both hands to grasp mine. For ten minutes we held hands a couple feet away from her husband while we all chatted. For me to touch soft feminine hands held so much meaning. When leaving I thanked the husband for allowing his wife to hold my hand. He replied, "That's okay." They both understood what I needed that day. My love language is touching; that's a basic part of who I am.

One more thing. This touching business had nothing to do with sex. It really is not even physical. I am still trying to understand this. For 48 years I could touch one lady any time I wanted to. Now I can't do that anymore. Why is touching so important to me? I think it has to do with, as much as anything, companionship. We are made to relate intimately to another human being. That relationship takes place between a husband and wife at various levels of intimacy. Even meeting in our hallway or while going up or down the stairs I would usually deliberately touch Betty on the way by. I would never do that with another woman, not even now. If Betty was still here I would not ever touch another woman, except for handshakes and legitimate hugs. It has something to do, methinks, with knowing that there is another person in my life that I can always reach out to and know that she will respond with a meaningful smile. The touch, a physical connection, though brief, is a significant reminder that we have a lot more going for us. It is symbolic of our deep deep caring and long history of loving for each other. Now, for me that's gone. It probably is something like losing a limb but the phantom pain tells you that the limb is still there. Your brain won't accept the reality of the amputation. Perhaps in touching another soft hand for just a moment that reality of my past experience returns, so I enjoy for a brief moment. Does that make sense?

On March 7, I reported to FB that I would not be holding any more hands. Time to move on. I'll stick to a brief hug, or handshake.

37

I Did Not Cry Today

March 8. I visited with Betty that morning. She was sitting across the room in our 25th Anniversary picture. Talked to her about my crying. "Betty, I know you are gone and won't be coming back. You did not choose to go, but wanted to stay with me. It was not your choice. Now I am alone. I miss you but I have to get along with the rest of my life. But I keep crying. Cried every day since you left. I want to quit, but can't. Everyday something reminds me that you are gone a n d n o t c o m i n g b a c k. What am I going to do?"

Sometimes it hits me with a shock like a slap in the face. An activity that we've always done together, but now I have to do alone. Picking up some object that has meaning for us both. Something neat happens but I cannot tell you. So many things. I opened my email and there was an ad for the latest Arts Academy play. We went together to them all. Now I have to go alone, if I go at all. Every day there is something, and activity or item that was important to us together when you were here but now it's gone. Cuz you're gone. You have been ripped out of my life, but so have a dozen things we do together every day. How can I get on with the rest of my life when you keep coming back this way every day? It's not that I do not want you, but you keep me held in the past when I have to move forward into my new future. I feel guilty talking like this to you, but I have to settle this matter.

I wanted to turn this page, like I have turned others in the past two and a half months. Can't cry forever. So what happens this afternoon? I go for coffee with a friend. We spend a couple of hours chatting, mostly talking about my situation. I get choked up a half dozen times. When will this stop?

March 9. I did not cry today. I determined to not. Almost a couple of times, like when I met a couple on the sidewalk I know from the Farmers' Market. Of course when I saw them coming I knew we would talk about Betty's bread and buns. We did, but I did not even get choked up. Instead we had some good laughs. Maybe at last I've started to turn this page. To stop crying all the time. Perhaps my chat with

168

Betty helped to take this small step forward. Thank you Betty for giving me this permission. I feel good about this. The first day since Betty left that I have not cried.

March 10. There's a dance tonight and I am not going. I was thrilled last month at a similar "community" dance. I got to touch the soft hands of a lot of ladies, ages three to 83. It was great fun and very meaningful to me. This interaction with the ladies filled a deep need for me. This time I really have not made a decision to not go I'm just not going. Don't have a need to do this anymore; it just disappeared. I am totally surprised about this because I enjoyed the last dance so much. It is the discussion I had the other day, attempting to understand why touch is so important to me, especially to touch a lady's soft hands. That chat pretty much cured me of the need for such a touch.

This development in my life, again, illustrates how important my journaling is to discovering things about myself. Once I understand my need then I can deal with it. I am an intuitive guy (as opposed to logical) and need to put my thoughts into writing or spoken words to clarify them for me, so I can understand them. This process oftentimes helps me to crystallize my sort of abstract ideas and enables me to understand myself or whatever I am grappling with. Thank you FB for allowing me to make you part of my ongoing discoveries about my new "normal". I am slowly getting there! I believe that I have turned another page in this touching business.

I've discovered something else. I can tell Betty things. That's one area that has caused me a tear or two, not having anybody to tell stuff to. I phoned Telus to see about getting TSN added to my basic satellite bundle so I could watch the national curling competition. They not only gave me this channel but added six complete bundles. I said to the lady, "I've got everything with Telus now so you guys should give me a good deal." She did: lowered my telephone charges also, then gave me 100 more minutes of long distance, and decreased the total bill to less than what I had originally signed up for with just the basic channel package. Now that is something you gotta tell somebody. So I told Betty – out loud. And then I laughed. It was so much fun telling her. Why, I wondered, did I not think about this before? Instead of shedding tears about her being gone forever, I can still talk to her and enjoy it! (Okay, so you think that's kind of strange. Well. . .you haven't had your spouse of 48 years leave, that's why!) If I keep making these kinds of discoveries every day I will soon have my new normal established and can get on with the rest of my life. And be mentally, emotionally and physically healthy! God is good. Thanks, guys for praying for me.

I didn't cry today. Day Two. Almost, but not.

March 11. Didn't cry today. Day Three. Had several chats with folks at church today and didn't get choked up once. As I look back on this week I am grateful for the progress I've made, for the two or three pages I have turned. Besides these new discoveries I got back into my shop. Two ladies showed up to ask me to create one of my camelback trunks for a wedding present. I did. It turned out to be one of my nicer ones. The recipient of the trunk stopped me at church later to enthusiastically express her gratitude for it. I also built a chair riser for an elderly man who lives in the Lodge, requested by a friend at Home Care. And helped my neighbour repair a bookshelf for a mutual friend. First time in almost six months I've done significant woodworking projects. I thoroughly enjoyed it. Going to spend more time in the shop.

You can view Betty's slide show on YouTube. This was shown at her Goodbye Service December 21. This is a private show but feel free to pass this YouTube connection to anyone whom you think might appreciate it. Thanks to Bob from clicthreehills for making this possible. http://youtu.be/oJVTmalrAvY www. youtube.com

Merle: Thank you, thank you so much! Amanda: Beautiful. Louise: Hard to say anything after that. God's Blessings are so evident through the years! Irene: Thank you so much I appreciate the opportunity to watch this!
Arnold: Irene, I have a copy of this for you along with an audio of Betty's Goodbye Service. I will bring it over soon. I'll swap it for a square meal.;-} Irene: Thanks Arnold – look forward to that! Just let me know the day!

I read Psalm 30, March 14, and again the next day. Thousands of years ago David wrote this Palm which has now become my story. Adapted.

I will exalt you, O Lord,
for you lifted me out of the depths.
O Lord my God, I and my Facebook friends
and many others around the globe called to you for help
and you are healing me.
Weeping may remain for many nights,*
but rejoicing always comes in the morning.
When I felt secure, I said,
"I will never be shaken."
O Lord, when you favored me,
you made my mountain stand firm;
but when you hid your face,
I was dismayed.
To you, O Lord, I called;
to the Lord I cried for mercy.
You turned my wailings into dancing;
you removed my sackcloth and clothed me with joy,
That my heart may sing to you and not be silent.
O Lord my God, I will give you thanks forever.

*I did not cry for three days. The last three days I did. It's too hard to try to not cry! Especially when I am working with Betty's pics and Goodbye Service CD. When I told a former widow that I was done crying, she replied, with a grin, "Good luck in that, Arnold!" She knew – been there done that. However, I was so grateful that I can make this post that day. God is good, always!

Joanne: Hi Arnold, I'm so glad you are turning to the Word and finding the comfort you need. It is a daily process and the healing is only gradual. Eight months from now when you are feeling much better, something may trigger a memory and you will find yourself weeping again. You will wonder, "Where did that come from. The storms do lessen in time. Right now the waves are still quite high and still sweep you off your feet, but in time you will come out into the sunshine again. It is a process that you have to go through and the only way to get over it is to go through it. It isn't pleasant but it is very healing Those who put it off, have to face it sometime and it is better sooner than later. We also enjoyed having dinner with you last Sunday. It must have been ordained of the Lord. We do it almost every Sunday so feel free to join us any time. Blessings, Joanne and Tom

Arnold: Joanne, your responses always add significant meaning to my journal postings. But then you've been there and that enables you to see between my lines. Thank you so much for the many times you have done so, in many ways!

Jan: This is so wonderful! Praise God for His faithfulness and healing power as we put our trust in Him. What a great psalm! The Lord inhabits our praise. Praying for you much.

Cheryl: Hi Unc Arn. I saw the picture of Auntie B's spinach lasagna. Would you send me that recipe please? I would love to have it. I have her saskatoon pie recipe and make it often – yummy.

Arnold: My verse this week has been Psalm 32:8: I will instruct you and teach you in the way you should go; I will counsel you and watch over you.

Bob: What a great verse to follow your last post. Blessings Arnold!

Louise: Check out: http://youtu.be/2SLHWFpSlq4, Thy Word – Maranatha Singers. A beautiful and inspiring song from the Maranatha Singers that talks about the word of God – the Bible. May we all be blessed by this music. Your word is a lamp to my feet. Arnold: Thanks, Louise! You blessed me largely!

38

Moving Ahead

M arch 22 through 29. Lots of exciting things happening. Interesting past few days! I posted it all on Facebook.

Would you believe that I spent six hours on Wednesday with a real nice lady? Watched a movie. Just in case you are wondering, we sat in separate chairs. Discovered we have a lot of common interests from photography to wood work and other things. We are both artsy and intuitive. We are going to church together in the city this Sunday and then for lunch. We had a long talk about the fact that I am not interested in looking for a wife, but just fun and companionship. She agreed that she was in a similar situation. So we are calling this a non-date. No romance, just a social get-together. It was so nice to have a lovely lady in my house for a while! We had some good laughs but some real serious discussion about my situation. We behaved really well!

March 22 I manned my woodart table at the Three Hills General Store for their Grand Opening and will do the next two days. Took a break and went for a haircut because I have to look good (or the best possible) for my non-date. Had an interesting chat with Betty's hair dresser of 18 years. She was divorced a number of years ago and later her former husband died. Now she is dating. I shared with her some of my thoughts about getting interested in and relating to other women. She gave me several pieces of advice but the one that stuck was about a young lady she heard talking with Dr. Ruth. The lady was very upset that her dad was dating a woman within only six months of her mother's death. Dr. Ruth said. "This is good. Your father had a real good relationship with your mother. If she had not he probably would not want to have a relationship with someone else. But he did, so he is seeking such a relationship with another woman. This is good!"

Then this afternoon a lady stopped by at the General Store and said much the same thing. She is 50 years old. Her husband died several years ago from Lou Gerig's disease. Now she has been married for several years to a man who is now 66, sixteen years older than her. She strongly encouraged me to not hesitate, if I feel ready, to start a social relationship with a lady, or several ladies. The General Store proved to be a Godsend. Sure a good place to meet folks. I've had dozens of great conversations and lots of laughs.

I have also talked with an older couple Betty and I were in a small group with. He was our leader and we met at our house. Also chatted with a couple of other gals who are close to my situation. Everyone did not hesitate to approve my getting involved socially with a lady or two at this time. I had chatted an hour and a half with my lovely daughter who said, "That's okay." And a couple of weeks ago my neighbor buddy said, "Arnold, you are a master craftsman. You had a great marriage – you know how to do it right. So you can be very successful if you have a second marriage." Wow! That was a thought. Maybe the same concept applies to Non-Dating.

So there you go, folks. I have been hiding this from my Facebook counselors because I was afraid you would rap my knuckles for going ahead with the ladies too soon. I had been committed to waiting six months. Well, I decided to talk only to folks who I was pretty sure would agree with my desire to step out (smile). I know the calendar says it is too soon. Betty left only three months ago. But remember that I was saying good-bye to her for two months before that.

I yearn for companionship. And I have thought and prayed about making right decisions. I know I am vulnerable and fear making bad decisions. So I am making thoughtful choices, receiving lots of advice, and praying that God will guide me always. So is the lady that I am planning on spending time with. When we are together it is a "threesome". I have talked with her about where I am in my grieving process and cried several times when talking about Betty. And this is okay with her. She shared some of her family struggles and also cried. We are both being very cautious, carefully nurturing only a social relationship.

I am happy again. Happy as much as I have been since Betty left. Mama Mia! Life is good. Actually, we feel like a couple of teenagers sneaking off together. Haven't dated for 50 years and neither has she for many years. This really is fun! I phoned her when I got home from the Store and we visited for a half hour. Sweet! And I think Betty is smiling.

The past few days have been very encouraging to me for another reason – and a bit scary. A couple weeks ago I was hired to manage the local health food store. Ever since when I go down town, which I do almost every day, one, two, or three folks stop me on the sidewalk or in the post office or grocery store and exclaim: "This is such exciting news about your new job!" Many of these people I do not personally know but we recognize each other from the Market. The store has remained "stable" for the past 15 years and everyone, it seems, is tickled that a guy with a creative vision and managing experience is taking on this job. One lady said, "Arnold, we expect you to work your magic in the Store!" They all know that the Farmers' Market has grown and prospered and become an increasingly significant item in our community over the past two years. Now they have oversized expectations that the same thing will happen to the Good Health Store. That's the scary part. I am really tickled with this new job, ten hours per week and the Board agreed I could work those hours on my own schedule, so long, of course, the store is managed properly. I do expect to invest many more "volunteer" hours than that, especially at the first, during my huge learning curve. I was looking for a new focus when I decided to not substitute teach anymore and to not manage the Farmers' Market this year. So this is right down my alley, and I feel supremely blessed. Betty was on the Good Health Board for three and a half years so I am carrying on her mission! God is so good!

Yesterday I took off my wedding ring. Quite a struggle. Had to use soap. Left quite an impression on my finger after wearing it for 48 and a half years. Maybe when the shrunken mark disappears that will be a sign start serious romantic dating! (smile) I looked at my hand a couple of weeks ago and was totally surprised that I was still wearing it. Had not even thought about it till then since Betty left. I realize, now that it's gone, that I used my thumb to often rub the underside of my ring. I keep doing it. Feels funny with it gone. One more thing gone – forever. But I have turned another page the past few days, turned to joy, happiness and excitement. At the moment life is wonderful.

I hope you guys are all excited for me!

Thank you to those who gave me permission to step out and move on. Although one family member said it was not her business, I replied, yes it is. I value my family and close friends who know me and my recent story. Their approval is important, although y'alls would also say that ultimately it is my decision. With yours and Betty's permission I have turned another page; you have gifted me with a new sense of freedom and joy and happiness. (Well, I am shaking in my boots, a bit!)

Cherie: Well, at least you are getting out there and figuring yourself out. Like the tin man, in the Wizard of Oz, you are moving in ways that you haven't for years! It's pretty great! Careful of the uneven ground though, it's easy to trip on things you are not used to seeing on your path, although, you will find that if you do trip and fall, you will have your friends around to help you back up.

Arnold: Tin man! Like that. Very rusty too. I am watching for quick sand, pot holes, ditches, etc. I know they are there. Scary but exciting. An adventure.

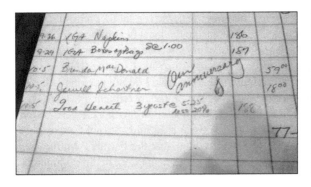 

March 29. Working on Income Tax today. Hunting for and finding all the pieces. Betty entered all the info in a ledger and added all the totals. Then I put all the rest

of the documents and info together to take to our Accountant. Betty was always so efficient and organized about money matters. This saved my hide many times. We always had money to pay our bills because she every month put away into savings one twelfth of every annual payment like insurance, vehicle licenses, business license, AMA and so on. That took a lot of consistent work but really paid off. Today I am filling out the ledger from very carefully noted income and expenses in her secretary's pad. Everything is there, neatly noted. Look what I found:

This was Betty's final entry on our 48th Anniversary. Her two final batches of bread for two of her best regular customers. Then we went to the Good Health Store where she purchased three packages of yeast. Ten days later the Doc said she had inoperable pancreatic/liver cancer. The tears flowed today.

I checked Betty's wallet for the record in her cheque book, every cheque we wrote was recorded. I had looked through her wallet before but this time I did a better job. Found this note in the bottom of the change section. Years ago I gave her this note. Sitting in church, I tore off this tiny piece of paper and wrote this love note and passed it to her: "Did u no I love you. I think ur the greatest!" A big fat exclamation mark at the end. I wonder how many times she pulled it out and read it. Nice warm feelings and another flood of tears.

Yesterday my neighbour wondered why I had taken off my wedding ring. So I asked what she thought I should do with it. "Put it on the other hand. Do you still wear your neck chain? Put it on the chain." So I did – around the cross. Tammy, you made me cry again! Now it's next to my heart.

Cherie: Brilliant! Wow! I just really like this Arnold! Arnold: Me too, Tammy is a wise woman. My sister told me the other day I should listen to the ladies cuz they know better the things of the heart. Glenna: Beautiful! I can just see Betty smiling!

Betty, it sure would have been much more fun if you would have been here to help with the IT. We made such a great team for this task. Tomorrow I am going out of town and meeting a lady friend for a day trip to two of our old haunts. But I wish it were you. I will be taking you along, I suppose. I won't tell her. I have to warn you though, when and if I ever seriously start looking for another wife, as you said I should, I won't be able to take you along then.

39

My New Jobs

M ay 18. Started my new job as Manager of the Three Hills Good Health Store. Everybody was very welcoming, knew most of the customers and have a great staff to work with. Gets me out of the house every day and off the street. Love every minute. Everybody is expecting great things. We plan to add a large bulk food section and double the product lines. It is a part time job but I am working full-time because of the huge learning curve. Drop by. Our goal is to keep you young, healthy and good looking!

My first day of my new job serving my first customers. Managing the Three Hills Good Health Store

Cheryl: Good for you Uncle Arnold!! Tom: Way to go! Thanks for sharing your new career.

Gluten free products, many great new products good for a variety of issues, Food section, Supplements

My Second Job

May 18 I travelled to the Drumheller Badlands Passion Play site for the first of a ten week stint. Always wanted to be in a play and now I had my chance. They gave me the role of Annus, the High Priest who offered the sacrifices. He had only a few sentences to say. No matter, this experience contributed greatly to my "coming out" and getting involved with people. Getting to know new folks, eating and worshiping together. Working close with a dozen guys, making new friends. We spent a lot of hours together on stage and behind it waiting for our many and mostly very brief appearances. Being an integral part of the Greatest Story Ever Told burned in my heart and mind forever a new depth of meaning to Jesus life, death and resurrection. A wonderful time. Here is a sampling of our activities.

Above, the High Priest is on the altar at the right. Everyone is bowing, not in reverence to Jesus in the blue at the top of the Temple, but because of the fearsome sound of the voice of the Heavenly Father affirming his Son.

On the left I am getting fitted with the High Priest's paraphernalia. The fellow who used the costume the year before must have been a little guy as the seamstress had to add a foot to the skirt and several inches to the sleeves. I am practicing my stern Teacher of the Law glare. And just getting started with the required beard.

To the right, the official photographer caught me with my natural smile. But this time I had my regulation length beard for the play.

During one of the early weekends we are practicing a temple ritual.

Below we are doing a "fill-in" part of the scene. The staging area is so large we had at one point we had several of these small teaching groups scattered across it.

Great fun hob-knobbing with the guys; above, coffee after dinner with the drummer and John who played Nicodemus.

Here the Teachers of the Law pose in front of the temple. Usually very hot and dry in the valley but this day it was raining. Hence, the windblown look and the rubber boots.

The boys, especially a couple who were divorced, were quite fascinated when I told them I had found my gal on the Internet who had agreed to marry me six days later. This happened the second and third weeks at the Passion Play practices.

179

Part Four

New Hope – to Love Again

40

My Love Letter to Betty

March 27 post to Facebook. I hesitated to post this as well as the previous one. But some of you have been with me almost five months now. This is an important new development in traveling the new road I've been sent down, so I decided to share these rather personal "social life" events. You have been so helpful to me that I feel I should be open about this latest page I am turning in discovering my new life. I am always grateful for your care and concern.

My Love Letter to Betty

Hi Betty! I have been having a wonderful time this week starting to open the precious gift you gave me before you left. I am crying right now, but with tears of joy, although mixed with a touch of sorrow. You told me I should get married again one day while we were sharing the palliative care room. I didn't accept your gift at the time, nor did I view it as a gift, but you caused me to begin thinking about this after you left much sooner that I would have guessed.

Twice this week I spent time with a lovely lady. Ok, this is not about marriage at all, but I guess your gift has allowed me to take the first steps. Can't get married without finding a lady who is willing to spend time so we can get to know each other. This is not about marriage, just companionship. And we do have plans for getting together again over the next few weeks. We seemed to hit it off and enjoyed each other's company.

This experience has me shaking in my boots! Mama Mia! I haven't dated in 50 years. I feel like a 14 year old on his very first date. I told the pretty lady sitting across from me at Boston Pizza yesterday to please not pinch me today for fear that I might wake up and discover that this was just a dream and the lovely person across the table would disappear into the mist! But she let me talk a bit about you; I asked her permission. She was very gracious in understanding that I am on a discovery mission and being with her is part of the process in unraveling my feelings and finding my way forward. She is willing to help me with that and recognizes that I am still in a grieving/healing mode. This means so much to me! She was divorced a few years ago and has her own struggles.

I really miss the times when we chatted about our day, shared our lives with each other, and I loved to go for walks with you, cuz I could hold your hand for a half hour. Remember, I told you that several times just before you left and were still able to walk. I miss the times we just sat together in the living room, both reading our books. The times we watched our favourite TV programs, and playing Wheel of Fortune on Facebook every evening. That was neat, with our varied experience together we could solve most of the puzzles. You were always sharp at it. Together visiting our kids and GKids. Buying our groceries and sometimes preparing our meals together. Sitting in church side by side, driving places with you nearby, close enough so I could reach out and hold your hand briefly. Sitting at the kitchen table watching you at work, the bread and bun artisan extraordinaire. And so much more. When you left all these wonderful experiences were torn from me. How I miss them!

So I've started the first step in opening your gift. You understood me much better than I could figure myself out. It has been an emotional roller coaster ride trying to travel this road. I have missed you and our companionship so much. At the same time I could not understand why, at the same time, I yearned so for female companionship with another person. But I've done a lot of talking the past two weeks with close family and friends, who have helped me understand. We have a fine son and daughter who are so understanding, and so many others. Two ladies this week, on the same day, told me that the reason why I yearn for female companionship is because you and I had such a satisfying, loving relationship. We were great companions and lovers. Especially the last four years, both retired, we loved our togetherness and were seldom apart. Guess I just cannot get along without this kind of sweet companionship. So I am going looking for it – with the permission you gave me.

You cautioned me to take my time. It seems early but after counsel from so many I have thoroughly enjoyed taking the first step. I have been cautious, prayerful, and seeking advice from people who know us and know our story and especially my story since you left.

You wrote a note to me in the hospital that said, "I love you forever and ever amen!" Remember, you asked for a piece of paper and you struggled to write out this special love note. I keep it now in a special place, with some of our other special treasures. And I will love you forever and ever amen! The 48 year old Grand Cathedral you built in my heart is locked. No one else will enter – ever. Guess another lady may have to build her own alongside, if this should ever happen. Don't know about that yet. Just between you and me, however, it could never be so grand. But thank you for the precious gift you left with me. A gift of joy and happiness and renewal. As I continue to unwrap it I will be forever grateful for your loving kindness in giving me this freedom. Well I've cried enough now, going to get the mail. Probably some more books on vegetarianism from Amazon at the post office. I'm working on being healthy. I want to be around a long time for our kids and GKids. For both of our sakes.

Today Betty, you still have all my love, Arnold

Jan: This is amazing! God is so good and is allowing you to begin another step of this journey. To just allow the Holy Spirit to guide your thoughts and those you encounter is so exciting. Your note to your Betty is precious and lets us know where you and the Lord are going with your friendships. This kind of friendship is so important and definitely fills a big need right now in your healing. Thanks so much for sharing. This is so helpful to all of us. My prayers continue to take you to the throne for God's amazing grace to be with you.

Danielle: Beautiful! Betty was a very Sweet lady! Glenna: So lovely, Arnold! You are such an expressive writer. Your love and commitment to Betty has been a great example. Ann: So glad for the update. You have given us all a lesson in realizing how we should treasure our/my spouse while we have them.

Over the next couple of months I spent lots of time on ChristianMingle and another Internet dating site. My good friend, Jerry, encouraged me to do so. After corresponding with a dozen different ladies, I was growing tired of finding mostly divorcees who all seemed to either have too much brokenness or not enough interests common with mine, or believing significantly different theologically. I chatted on line with gals from all over Alberta, in BC, Saskatchewan in in several states. One lady from Arizona seemed like a good prospect, but. . .

At the end of May I posted this note: Well, my supposed lady friend disappeared over the horizon without me. She decided as a divorcee on the basis of 1 Corinthians 7 that she could not remarry. I was already seeing some red flags pop up, so this new development was easy to receive. When I started looking for a mate, I had said that I would not go on dating sites, would not correspond with a divorcee, would not look far away, and would not go across the border. So what do I do? Go to Arizona on a dating site and found a divorcee. Well, it was kind of fun while it lasted. I'm busy with the Passion Play for the next two months anyhow. I found her on ChristianMingle; she should not have been on there.

Christine, a friend from the Passion Play responded: You are busy, Arnold! We need you! Besides, you never know what can happen in the Passion Pit! lol. Arnold: Oh yeah? There are lots of pretty girls (I would not have noticed them but one of the guys mentioned it;-} but they are all way too young. Where are the mature fun loving ladies? Christine: Lol. There are some older ones. You just have to look.

The second week I travelled to Drumheller for play practice, Friday through Sunday, I changed my "requirements" on ChristianMingle. Instead of being open to getting to know divorcees, singles and widows, from now on, from now on I wanted to hear only from widows. That was a fateful decision! My life changed instantly and dramatically.

Within minutes of this request, on May 26, 2012, I received a ChristianMingle message from gmtexas. This dating site, as do others, want you to use code names until you get to know each other. They want you to make sure you are confident enough in each other's story to share your personal information.

However, within 24 hours we introduced ourselves to each other on Facebook. Here is what happened next.

41

I Found Her! Love on the 'Net

J une 1. I decided to make my announcement on my regular FB page in a photo album of My Love, taken from her FB page.

Gloria Miller, My Sweetheart and Wife to Be

Gloria and I are supremely excited to share with you our love for each other and announce our upcoming marriage, date to be announced. Sometime between this August and January 1. (NOTE: We eventually decided on July 24, immediately after I completed my stint at Drumheller in the Passion Play.)

Arnold and Gloria are very happy to announce that we will be married July 24 in Dallas, Texas. We will travel to Three Hills where we will live for the next 30 years. Warm thanks to all who have encouraged and congratulated us. Gloria and I met on the dating/mating site, Christian Mingle, on May 26. Six days later I asked her to marry me and she replied, "YES!" The rest of this story appears below. She woke up the next morning in Grand Prairie, Texas, singing this Frank Sinatra song:

Young at Heart

Fairy tales can come true, it can happen to you
If you're young at heart.
For it's hard, you will find, to be narrow of mind
If you're young at heart.

You can go to extremes with impossible schemes.
You can laugh when your dreams fall apart at the seams.
And life gets more exciting with each passing day.
And love is either in your heart, or on its way.

My new family: Cynthia, Bridgette, Mark, My Love, Craig

Gloria has a daughter, grand daughter and two great granddaughters in Texas,
and two sons, a daughter and four grandkids in California.

I received a wide range of responses to the abrupt and rather spontaneous decision to end my search for new love.

Shannon: I'm happy for you and yet afraid for you all at the same time. I deeply
want you to be as happy as is possible on this earth and I want you to have someone
to share the joy with. I have always known you to be a thinking man in addition to
being artsy so I choose to trust your judgement. I encourage you to enjoy dating.

It can be a blast getting to know each other and something to savor. I realize it can be hard to be so far from someone you love but perhaps it is better to wait, be a little careful, and then shoot caution to the wind! As for internet dating, I used to be against it until some folks close to me found the love of their lives that way and have been incredibly happy ever since. Who really cares how it happened? It happened and brought joy! I would encourage you to pray lots, ask God, hold your plans and for that matter needs lightly. Ask him to give you loads of wisdom and be willing to change your plans if need be. Listen to those who love you but realize they may be still grieving and unable to see what you see. No matter how much you love another there will still be tons of grief. I am praying that you have indeed found a second love of your life and that she will bring you as much joy in life as you I know will bring her. Question to myself: Would I do what Arnold is doing? Probably not, but who knows! I haven't walked a mile in his shoes and I don't know what he knows. What I do know is that God and many many others love you and we are here to support you no matter what.

Michelle: O Arnold!

Richard: Been there done that, and we are blessed! Each day we are together is a treasure even with the bumps, learning and growing together. Wishing you much happiness.

Merle: I will give you one of Komie's favorite pieces of advice to his dad: measure twice, cut once! Moving too quickly with anything, usually leads to poor results, having to redo, undo, wishing we didn't do. Enjoy the time learning to get to know the new independent you and what you can do to better the world. When you have learned that, joining up as a team with someone else can lead to a wonderful, fulfilling experience. Does this sound like it could be coming from another lady's mouth, a lady that was closely related to me? Betty only wanted the very best for you. Not saying don't go there, just don't be a sprinter, do the long run and enjoy the scenery!

Arnold: Merle, I've already investigated my new independence. After surviving the sharp pain of loneliness after Betty left, it morphed into "aloneness". One day I thought, "Maybe I should remain single." There are advantages: go anywhere, wherever, however, whatever, without having consult anyone, depend on anyone, just do your thing. Don't even have to phone home. I even wondered if this thought had come from our Lord. After about ten days of this kind of thinking, I realized that this is exactly what I most enjoyed about being married. Someone to plan with, go and come with, someone to be there when I did not want to go somewhere alone.

I decided then that I wanted that loving companionship again and started to seriously consider looking for a wife. I sit here in my living room looking at a statue of Adam. God, with hands on each of Adam's arms is pulling him out of the dirt from which he was created. I identify often with him. He was alone and God soon saw that he needed a companion. And gave him one. I believe that God has just done that for me. Merle, I dearly loved your big sister, still do and always will. But she left. Before she did, she instructed me to get married again. She even specified what kind of person I am to marry. Merle, she ordered Gloria to be my new wife, and when I discovered her I really had no choice but to allow her into my heart. I understand the value of your advice of waiting and not hurrying, but for me, now, it is time to act, not wait. I have found it interesting that the individuals who have walked down my path, whose spouse has died and they have remarried, are wishing me well and congratulating me. Not one of them, and there have been several, have cautioned me about the timing. The Chair of the Elders from my church is very happy for me. I covet your blessing, too, Merle.

Jake, a long-time acquaintance, recently had married his wife's sister less than two months after his wife died. Before she died, his wife had had told him to do so. He phoned her up and they agreed to marry, just a couple of months after his wife's death. Jake said to me, "Arnold, you've been around a long time. You've learned to make many big decisions and obviously know how to make the right ones."

A lady my age was excited for us. She came into the store and I brought her up to date on our love story. I commented that it happened very suddenly. She responded, "Folks our age cannot wait till the sun goes down. Why we don't even buy green bananas anymore!"

My son said, "Dad, I knew you would get married again." Daughter Tara was initially devastated by the suddenness. I had been talking by telephone every week, keeping her updated on my dating site gals. But I had just a few days before commented briefly about gmtexas and suddenly I sent her a picture of Gloria and announced that we were getting married. Dumb move to introduce her so spontaneously and suddenly, but I was so excited I just had to tell her. Should have been a bit more cautious. But she soon got over the shock and quickly acted to make Gloria a friend on Facebook and gave her a warm welcome.

42

What is Love?

June 11. I had not posted much to the FB group for two months. This story filled in the gap, bringing the folks up to date on my "things of the heart." This group was drawing to a natural end, unless some of them wanted to volunteer as second marriage counselors.

What is Love?

A friend asked me yesterday, "How can you fall in love over the Internet?" Well, you can and you can't.

Six weeks ago as I substitute taught the Grade Sixes, I sat at the Teacher's desk while they worked, pondering the question, "What is love?" I knew what love was when I was married to Betty for 48 years. Then she left, but I still love her. How can you love a person who is gone and you will never see them again in this life?

I wondered, "Will I ever find love again? What will it be like? How will I know when I am in love?" Gloria showed up and answered these questions.

We have broken every rule in the book in our three weeks of getting to know each other. Some of my relatives and acquaintances think this is okay and trust me with my decision to ask Gloria to marry me. Others are deeply disturbed, believing that I am making a serious mistake in one of the most important decisions we can make. I understand this concern; I would be troubled too if this happened to someone else that I loved.

I broke all of society's rules about courting and falling in love and deciding to get married. We broke every Internet dating rule: be cautious, take your time, don't give out personal information until you know the person well, do not make serious decisions until you meet face to face. And I had decided – my personal rules: no way was I going to look for a wife on the 'Net'. I wanted to look in her eyes, into her soul and hold her hand. No one far away, especially not across the border, which would be too complicated. And she was not to be older than me. Guess what? Gloria, who is nine months older than me, lives 2,000 miles away in Texas. Her flight here will take almost six hours flying time. How do I explain all this?

When my son-in-law read this on FB he castigated me for bragging about breaking all the rules. Not so. But he did not believe me when I told him so. These events just happened that way. Gloria and I had carefully prayed for guidance. Young folks do not seem to understand that people over 70, with their seven decades, have broad based and sufficient life experiences. Having made hundreds of major decisions, they are capable of making their own rules for personal matters. We love our Lord and seek every day to be sensitive to his Spirit. Sometime you just gotta move quickly! When you know that you know.

Three recently married couples in our church found each other on a dating site. Sixty percent of marriages today start on the Internet. I had looked around locally and found no one that was interested in me. Several friends urged me to check out a Christian dating site, which I did. Found that most of the women were divorcees and in corresponding with a dozen of them found them to be mostly desperate and/or broken. So I changed my request to "widows only". Within minutes of making this request ChristianMingle had sent my picture and profile to Grand Prairie, Texas, near Dallas. Gloria happened to be on the site and checked out this new Match, as they call it. She instantly fell in love with my pictures and profile so contacted me. I read her profile, viewed her picture and knew immediately, "Here is my Dream Gal, the one I have been searching for." We began corresponding, usually three or four times a day, sometimes by IM, Instant Messaging where we chatted live. For both of us it was "Love at first profile reading on our computer!"

Gloria and I both are amateur word artists, poetic, artsy, diehard romantics. We were soon expressing our amazement that we had found each other. Words became tender and romantic expressions of affection, adoration and then love. She wrote to me, "Arnold, your words of love have opened the doors of my heart!" She said that ever since she had been widowed, her heart has been closed. She used to write songs but has not for nine years. Now I had helped her open her heart again. I was afraid I would never find love again, then Gloria slipped into my heart and warmed me all over. We first exchanged pictures and information, a bit about ourselves and what we liked to do and what we valued. Then we started to show appreciation for each other's talents and interests. We were so much alike, and that's why we were matched. Soon we were exchanging words of love. Last Friday, after returning from seeing "Ann of Green Gables" at Rosebud, I checked the site to see if she was there. She was! We chatted for an hour, then about 2:00 am her time I asked her to marry me. She said "YES!" You say, "Arnold, you caught her at a weak moment!" Probably (teehee).

Why can't you fall in love over the "Net? Over the centuries countless numbers of people have found love across oceans and continents, sometimes waiting three months for their love letters to cross. The power of the pen. Today it's the power of the Net's instant messaging. No more waiting three months. Now we can talk to each other across borders and over thousands of miles, getting love notes to each other in a fraction of a second.

I have been strongly urged to cool our engines and take our time. "This is too fast! You need to see each other, spend time courting – get to know each other before you make the final decision." I would say the same thing to someone I observed doing what we have done.

We both prayed that our Lord would guide us to the right person. She waited a lot longer than me. Almost ten years. Both of us continue to be amazed that we found each other, exactly the person we wanted to marry. We are astounded in our love and affection, that this could have happened to us. As we attempt to understand it, we can only attribute it to the hand of God acting on our behalf. Gloria's daughter Bridgette said, "God has just popped you two together!" and she is okay with that.

What is love? It is a mysterious exchange of some kind of electrical sparks that can travel over continents and oceans. It's magical. Filling one's heart and whole being with scintillating warmth and powerful and urgent desires and longings for the other person. "Well," you say, "that's infatuation." Probably.

Love is a many splendored thing. Hard to put into words. But it is so much more than feelings. True love cannot be experienced until you marry and commit to your life together. Real love is a decision and a commitment over time. This means that come hell or high water, I am there for you. Love is facing together all of life with its manifold troubles, its burdens, afflictions, sorrows, conflicts, heartaches and the multitude of issues. And enjoying together life's celebrations, joys, wonderments, walking together in the rain, wanting to spend most of my time with you, enjoying just being with you. Celebrating each other's successes as we encourage each other along life's pathways to be all we can be for God and others. But especially for each other.

Gloria and I are not naive about this wondrous event. We both experienced good marriages. If we had not we would be running the other way. We already know what it means to fall in love. Both our spouses were taken from us by the evil of cancer; they left long before we wanted them to. We still love them and talk to each other about them. After 48 years of loving, I will always love Betty. I will still cry sometimes when I remember her, probably always will. So does Gloria, occasionally, over her absent husband. As we have found love in each other we bring to our relationship also our love each for another person. That's understood. I cannot negate 48 years of love because I have loved again. Betty spent 50 years building a Grand Cathedral in my heart. But she left, and now it's padlocked. No one else besides me will ever go there. Now Gloria found her way into my heart and started to build her own house of love. And I have joyously welcomed her.

Can you fall in love on the Internet, without ever talking to or actually seeing the person? Gloria and I did.

Here is the prayer I sent to Gloria when she sent me her flight itinerary. She is coming to visit June 20 and staying for a week during which I will introduce her to most of my family and spend lots of time together.

WOW. PERFECT. Only 20 days till I hold you in my arms. Thank you Lord for this special gift you have reserved for me. I sure don't know how I managed to receive such a beautiful woman, beautiful in every way. I am so grateful and promise to love her forever. To be her protector and provider, best friend and lover, spiritual leader and soft shoulder for her landings, and care for her and respect and honour her always. She has slipped into my heart and begun to build a house of love. The love she placed there has warmed my whole being, helped me turn the page of my life to a new chapter. Together, Lord, with your help and love and wisdom we will, the three of us, write the rest of what is now "our" story. A story of complete joy, admiration, adoration and love, of love and honour and respect for each other. We have been surprised by joy and passionate love for each other. We searched far and wide for each other and you brought us together. Blessed be the name of the Lord. ♥♥♥

June 5 at 8:09am. God is Good!

43

100 Beautiful Women

June 11

I owe my life and happiness to 100 beautiful women. Maybe 200. Let me tell you why.

When Betty got sick and spent a month at home where I looked after her, at least eight wonderful ladies came from Home Care, one every day to help us. Then Betty and I were in the hospital for a month before she left, living together in palliative care. Possibly a couple dozen nurses helped me look after her, and they were very much concerned about my welfare, as well. Some hugged me and offered encouraging words. A couple of weeks after Betty left I dropped by when eight nurses were in meeting to thank them with a couple of huge boxes of chocolates. All of them lined up to give me hugs. (8 + 24 = 32)

From the start I journalled this pathway first that Betty and I travelled, and then by myself. To 153 caring, praying believing friends and relatives – most of them (let's say 95) wonderful ladies; so many of whom offered constant encouraging and loving responses to my sharing of sometimes very deep and personal matters. Merle was especially helpful in palliative care with her four years ministry in that area at the Foothills hospital. We talked for many hours by phone. Tammy, my lovely neighbor, was the woman in my life when I so badly needed a female friend to chat with regularly. She and I messaged on our cell phones daily for perhaps a couple months. I shared with her what was happening in my life and she advised me on lots of things – sometimes when I didn't ask for it!:-). Her husband, Jerry, gave us his blessing. She even held my hand once, for a very short time! They opened their house to me for countless meals and visits. Son Reese adopted me as his Grandfather.

Jan, Betty's step brother-in-law's wife, told me her story and regularly gave good advice, most recently saying, "Arnold, you have to go with your heart!" Niece Susan surprised me regularly with some very mature advice on matters of the hearts. So did Tammy when my interests turned to thinking about looking for another wife. Joanne, the prettiest lady at our church, was such a good friend. She visited at the hospital, bringing treats and books. Some about heaven for kids for Betty's grandkids, and later the best book I read on grieving. She advised me with private FB messages, and invited me for Sunday dinner with her and her new husband where they shared their newlywed stories with me for several hours. (32 + 95 = 137)

Several friends told me to check out dating sites on the "Net". I did not want to do that but I had already checked out three different divorcees in Three Hills, but they were not interested in me. So I signed up on ChristianMingle. Discovered a gorgeous 50 year old who thought our age difference was too great for getting serious but she said she would chat with me anyway. So we exchanged messages daily for a month and now talk occasionally on Facebook and by regular email. She was experienced at dating and especially on how the dating sites worked and gave me a lot of excellent advice on matters of the heart. Helped me see that one lady I initially was interested in was not so good as I first thought, so I parted ways with that one. And she assured me many times of God's care, direction and healing. (137 + 1 = 138)

An amazing thing happened during this period. Every time I went downtown I was stopped by one, two or three people who encouraged and often hugged me. Most assured me that they were praying for me. Many of these ladies knew Betty and I from the Farmer's Market where Betty's baking was so popular; some of their names I did not even know. (40) I went into my bank one day, boldly walked into the manager's office and told her I came for hugs. Her and the other lady in her office jumped up and hugged me. I stopped and Sears another day and the clerk ran around the counter and gave me an affectionate hug AND a kiss on the cheek. Mama Mia! The first time I met with the Health Club Board that owns the store I now manage, the six ladies lined up as I was leaving and I got a hug from each of them. (138 + 49 = 177)

I attended the Nicki Cruz Rally in Edmonton. The theme was on God's love, a message that God had been recently assuring me of. During the singing of a song about God loving me, I was raising both hands to heaven, tears were coursing down my cheeks and I was feeling literally showered in God's love. A beautiful young lady came up to me as I sat enjoying the atmosphere and the blessing at the end of the Rally. She said that she had never done this to a stranger before but she said God had given her a message for me. "God dearly loves you!" When I told her about Betty's passing she said that the emptiness I experienced when Betty left would not be filled by another woman. I needed to love God first and he would look after the finding of a wife for me. I assured her that the message was right on because I was already moving in this direction. She said, "God has taken your broken heart out, is kissing it and putting it back in place, new again." What a wonderful confirmation and assurance of God's care for me. She told me her name was Robin and we hugged. That's all I know about her. (177 + 1 =178)

Now I work with two lovely ladies at the Good Health Store. Energetic hard working gals who love their job, love their product and customers and love their team leader. One of them wears her faith on her sleeve and I kid her about my not having to go to church on Sunday anymore because she gives out a sermon every fifteen minutes. We have a lot of fun working together. (178 + 2 = 180)

The past four weekends I've spent at the Drumheller Passion Play. What a great experience of community, besides the unusual inspiration of participating in the greatest story ever told. We went through the first half of the play yesterday. I am the High Priest who offers the Passover sacrifice and later incites the crowd to call for Jesus to be crucified. Nine of us Teachers of the Law are on stage for quite a few of the scenes, without very many speaking parts. A lot of ladies in attendance. I met a pretty blue eyed blond, a student from Rosebud. Every day I tell her my latest news about Gloria and she reports on what she has read from a copy of the Message I gave her. We met the first Saturday at the coffee percolator and introduced ourselves to each other, as is the practice, and fell into conversation. I soon discovered that she was not a Believer nor had ever had a Bible in her hands. She has never been to a Christian Church. So we discussed the fact that the Passion Play was the central story of our faith. She asked what Jesus means to me. Wow! What an opening. So we have had several follow-up conversations. (180 + 8 = 188)

After Robin told me that God would provide me with a wife, I went home totally relaxed about this matter. It was a pleasant relief. I had wondered if I would ever love again. Three days later Gloria appeared on my computer screen. ChristianMingle sent her my picture and profile. She instantly fell in love with my picture (she thinks I am cute – tee hee!) and messaged me. The same thing happened to me – instantly in love. We had been looking for each other and God helped us find the other. She had been on the site for two years, chatting with several men, but was ready to give up because she could not find anyone interesting. We messaged several times a day, sometimes back and forth live. Two weeks later I asked her to marry me. We plan to marry in Grand Prairie, Texas, on July 28. We will then drive to Alberta in her Buick Sabre, pulling a U-Haul with her belongings. And live happily ever after at 614 – 8 Street North in Three Hills. We are both in a state of complete wonderment and see God's fingerprints all over our great togetherness adventure. (188 + 1 = 189)

Why am I counting? Just for fun; numbers are not important. What is important is the fact that God knows that I needed comfort. My love language is touching, so a hug means a lot. Always been a hugger, but at home I have not gotten any for six months. I told my sister Lil that I was getting good advice on matters of the heart form several ladies. She said, "That's good, Arnold. They know best about these matters." Lil has spent many hours reading my emails and responding with always good advice and cautions, and so much love and encouragement. (189 + 1 = 190)

God has sent so many wonderful lovely women to bring me encouragement after he took Betty home. Through them he demonstrated his wondrous unconditional love for me, for which I am forever grateful. There have been quite a few men who also ministered to me, but in these matters they mostly do not have the same touch as the ladies.

Most of all, my lovely caring daughter, Tara. She made several two hour trips from Bragg Creek, although very busy with four of my grandkids, to help out while we were in palliative care and since. We talk an hour or so on the phone every week, when she listens to my latest stories. She has been here for me. I love her so, the best daughter a father could ever ask for. Lovely in every way. (190 +1 = 191)

Frankly, it has been exciting and good for my ego to be loved and cared for by so my beautiful women. But most important has been the knowledge that this has been an important way in God has showered me with his abundant love through these caring wonderful people. I've kidded some of them, "I try to talk to a beautiful woman at least once a day just to keep up my skills." I've been "mothered" by quite a few and have joshed with several about that, "Do I look like I need some motherly care and advice?" with a smile, of course. Some of them seem to see me as a great big Teddy Bear needing to be smothered in love!

Gloria's and my love is sparked with electricity, driven by the mystery of wonderment and the deep magic that happens between a man and a woman. In ten days she will arrive and at last I can look into her lovely blue eyes and peer into her soul. I can hold her hand and snuggle on the chesterfield and the park bench at the end of our paved walking path. And watch the sun go down. I told her that it is good she is arriving at midafternoon as the sparks will fly so much that if it was at night someone might call the fire department. I plan to have someone standing by to pry us apart. I was a bit worried as she is 5 ft. 3 in and I am 6 ft. 2 in. I said, "Gloria, your lips are 11 inches lower than mine. How are we going to work that?" She replied. "Oh Arnold, I will show you how!" Ooooh! Do I love this marvelous gift from my Lord! God is Good. So Good! So loving.

44

I don't even buy green bananas!

June 14

I cried. It was six months ago today, on December 14, at 1:45 pm, that Betty left me, never to return. Not long before leaving we expressed our love for each other. Suddenly on May 26 my life was forever changed.

I kept my promise to FB to not date for six months. After several had encouraged me to check out dating sites, I did for six weeks. Then Gloria saw my picture and profile and fell in love with me. So did I when I saw hers. We had been looking for each other. She for two years, me for six weeks. She was on the verge of giving up her quest to find a husband. Now her friends are intrigued that she found a guy who manages a health food store as she has studied nutrition. We have a lot in common, love to make each other laugh and we write poems to one other. A wonderfully mature Christian Believer. We pray together on Facebook Skype.

Not long ago I was asking around, "Why are things of the heart so difficult?" Now I wonder how they can be so wonderfully mysterious and magical. Thank you Lord for the Wonderful Gift you have just given me, a new story just begun to be written, but already promising to be a marvelous one. A story that we have only written the Preface to and started on the Introduction. A fairy tale of wonder, affection, and magic. But also a tale of deep commitment come hell or high water, and I can imagine of drama interchanged with quietness. Of travel and relaxation. Of togetherness of all kinds every day all day. Of passion, compassion, and mutual admiration. Of building and creativity, writing, music and walking in the rain. Of holding hands, snuggling, kissing, hugging, touching. Of telling each other our story as we continue to write ours. Of encouraging and blessing each other every day. Of together walking with our Lord and loving him every day and serving him all the days every day. Of helping others along life's pathway, encouraging them to grow in every way and to keep their good health. Of a closeness and a wonderment that we have found in each other. Thank you Heavenly Father. I love you Gloria! Forever and always.

Next Wednesday Gloria will arrive in Calgary to stay a week. We will visit most of my siblings and other folks. Tammy and Jerry next door have graciously offered her a room for her stay. She is looking forward to moving away from the hot climate of Texas and the fast paced city life. She talks about fighting metal every time she leaves home in her car. Not so in Three Hills. Today I am heading for Calgary to apply for a passport. The day after we present our last Passion Play in Drumheller I plan to hop a plane and head for Grand Prairie, Texas, where we will be married. Then drive to Three Hills in her 2000 Buick Sabre, pulling a U-Haul with her belongings. She is coming to my house, soon to be "ours". (When went to pick up the trailer, it was obviously too small. So we rented a truck and pulled the car home.)

Of course this is sudden. Gloria and I are just as surprised as you are. Startled by sudden love that invaded our hearts without us even talking on the phone – just messaging on the dating site. We continually wonder at all this, fascinated, now as we visit on FB Skype. As we ponder this, Gloria and I have concluded that God's fingerprints are all over this amazing event that has already begun to change our lives forever. So many folks my age, some whose spouses have died and they re-married have encouraged me in this and are very happy for us. One lady to whom I mentioned that this happened awfully fast, replied, "Arnold, at our age we cannot wait around; I don't even buy green bananas!"

Jennifer: I hope the very best for you, too. Perry and I met on line and we are married now. God bless you!

Cherie: I have been watching, reading and trying to understand. I am the voice that you will not like Arnold, I am sorry but, uneasy. You do not know her. Neither do your friends or family. She hasn't visited, or met your church family. Your Mom would be freaking out right now and your dad would be checking her credentials! I have been tight lipped about this because we are not best pals, you and me, but I took the ride with you when you lost Betty. We exchanged ideas and thoughts. You were going to take a tour of yourself. That was not a tour, but a glimpse; like you peeked out from the hands over your eyes, but if you feel this is a gift from Jesus, then I guess I am in the wrong and I haven't been prayerful enough, not listening close enough. I guess I am not recognizing God's work. Sigh.

Irene: Arnold, you are a very special and unique person. Never have I known anyone who has been so daring as you have in the extent of your transparency to trust your loved ones so much with your sorting process. The speed of this relationship development is also rather unique. I pray God's continued blessing as you follow the Lord as best you know how in this development. I will enjoy meeting this lovely lady.

45

The Final Post

August 25. I've called this, "The Final Post". It is time to close "Betty Stauffer's Update Group". Y'alls have been so wonderful and helpful. When I badly needed someone you were here. I am so grateful. Now I've found a new wife and a new book is being written in my life. The Final Post attempts to update you about my new life and how I got here. It may seem like a new book in some ways, but it really is a continuation of the story that began last June when Betty started to get some new pains. She was pretty sure it was cancer, I think, although she did not say that. My story took several unexpected turns; thank you for being part of it. Some of what I include here has been said in previous chapters. I write this as a summary of our fifteen month odyssey.

I will leave this Group open for a couple of weeks should you wish to respond. I would love to see a final response from you. Thanks! Thanks! Thank you!

The Final Post

Gloria and I celebrated our first one month anniversary yesterday. Went out for Chinese food. So much has happened that it actually seems longer. The week-long trip from Dallas to Three Hills. Busy at the store catching up upon our arrival. Lots of work to make changes in the house, my moving over to make room for Gloria. I've found love again. A wonderful Southern Belle.

This Support Group started when Betty got sick. Originally I sent daily reports to about 50 relatives and a few close friends. Then it became a journaling of our experience with cancer, dying and death. And the struggle for me to say goodbye to the Lady of My Heart for 48 years. Eventually, as folks requested to participate in our then my story the number of this group reached 153.

Your responses surprised me. At the heaviest times, when I would write several pages in a day, I would check in several times to read the responses. Always they were helpful, comforting encouraging. You have been my Counselors who helped me survive a difficult experience over several months. Y'alls have been so wonderful.

So helpful. Several of you have expressed strong sentiment in how the sharing of my grief experience has helped you. One person said that after reading some of my thoughts she realized she had never grieved for her Dad who had died a couple of decades ago. So she retrieved his mementos and cried like a baby. Others have copied writings and passed them on to friends for their encouragement. Dozens of you have suggested I publish this journal, which I may do someday. I've wondered about all this response. Perhaps because few people have had the opportunity to walk intimately alongside a person who has gone through my experience. So we all find it very difficult finding something to say to a person whose spouse has died. For those of you who have been helped by sharing in my journey, I am so happy for this benefit to you.

But the benefit has been mostly mine. Every day I shared with you my struggles and issues with the most difficult series of "events" in my life. To write my feelings every day was a deeply meaningful therapy that helped me process each new phase and to turn the page to the next one. As my painful thoughts surfaced on the computer screen they translated from one language to another. They morphed from the abstractly difficult to understandable thoughts and concrete statements that I could better deal with. And to know that 153 friends and relatives cared for me in the midst of all this, and were daily praying for me, was so meaningful and encouraging. This journaling and your responses saved me, helping me to move along instead of wallowing in my disappointment, sorrow, loneliness and grief. Sometimes I hesitated to post some thoughts because they were so deep and so personal. But always I decided to do so because I wanted to tell you the whole story, not just parts.

My life is now three books: Before Betty, With Betty for 48 Years, now the third is titled, "Gloria and I".

A few of you have been upset with me, a couple very much so, for re-marrying so soon after Betty left. But you are partly responsible for this decision.

You gave me the special gift of caring and counseling. Your ongoing support through my difficult period helped me effectively deal with tough issues and to turn the pages. Without this journaling and your responses I would still have a lot of pages to turn. I've also gone out of my way to receive wisdom from several folks who have already been where I am. They have given me the valuable counsel because they could best understand my experiences and the decisions I was making. I have several friends whose spouse died and they have re-married. Their stories have helped me tremendously. Recently I sat in an office with Richard, an old friend whose wife had died of cancer and who had recently re-married. Tears were running down his and my cheeks as we shared in wonderment how a person could still deeply love a woman who is gone and never will return, while at the same time seriously love and marry another.

If you have not been in my boots, you cannot understand my situation. My feelings. My new love. My choices. People my age are better able to, and have been very encouraging and congratulatory about my marriage. Many younger folks, clearly, have difficulty with re-marriage, as noted in my previous essay about falling in love on the Internet.

Gloria's family has been very welcoming. I am friends with many of them on Facebook. My siblings and nephews and nieces have already made her part of the family. Life goes on. After all, life is for the living. I still cry occasionally for Betty, especially the past few days as I have had to make more decisions about some of her precious possessions.

Glory and I started out in a fairy tale of infatuation and love. Our word art shot cupid arrows deep into each other's hearts and souls. Love was magical and exciting as we both had suddenly found the dream person for which we had been searching. But the fairytale dream bubble has burst on the plain of reality. The rubber has hit the road and we are busy making the necessary adjustments. She was single for nine years and now is part of a two-member team. We live in a house in which I've been ensconced for twenty years, and where Betty is still in evidence. I absconded with Gloria from her closest daughter, grand daughter and two great grandkids. She left a different country and culture. We share many common gifts, values and interests but also run headlong into differences. So we are making the adjustments necessary for our love and joy in each other to continue to prosper. We are finding, with pleasure, that our deep love and commitment to each other covers these difficulties and allows us to make satisfying decisions, compromises and adjustments. We brought a truck-load of her belongings from Texas and now have to make very practical decisions about which ones to keep and what to put on the garage sale pile, or take to the thrift store. Her steam iron is new, as is her crock pot. Mine is several decades old, a wedding gift, so mine goes to the garage sale. My coffee perk (only a year or so old) and grinder (Kitchen Aid) are fancier so we keep them. Gloria's very colorful dinner set goes into the cupboard and my plain set goes into somebody else's home.

So there you have it, a snippet of my new life. Gloria and I believe that God's fingerprints are all over our brand new story. We both prayed for guidance in the search for a mate, and that we would not make a mistake. When we met on the ChristianMingle site we instantly fell in love and knew that we had found God's choice. We both were so sure that I asked her to marry me on the sixth day. Almost instantly she responded, "That's where my heart is, Arnold. YES!" Gloria's oldest daughter says, "God popped you two together." We know that God brought us together for a purpose. She is a beautiful mature Believer. When she was ten years old attending a Catholic church she wondered why she had to deal with all the paraphernalia, like beads and crucifixes. Her heart's desire was simply to have her own personal relationship with Jesus, without middle men or statues. At this early age God was speaking to her.

Now both of us seek together to draw closer to our Lord and listen for the special ministry he has for us. We want to write poetry, songs and a book. We are both artsy and love to work with wood. Our plan is to make funky birdhouses and clocks, and I will continue with cedar post vases and jean chests. All kinds of ideas. Looking forward to where our passions and interests and love for the Lord will take us. We've embarked on an exciting new adventure. We've discovered that we cannot out guess God. He answers in his way, in his timing. His unconventional plan for us has been a beautiful surprise. His ways are beyond our tracing out.

"For my thoughts are not your thoughts, neither are your ways my ways," declares the Lord. (Isaiah 55:8)

Oh, the depths of the riches of the wisdom and knowledge of God!
How unsearchable his judgments,
and his paths beyond tracing out!
Who has known the mind of the Lord?
Or who has been his counselor?
Who has ever given to God,
that God should repay him?
For from him and through him and to him are all things.
To him be the glory forever! Amen. (Romans 11:33-36)

A poem I wrote to Gloria the day after we decided to marry. . .

A few hours ago methinks I had a dream.
In the middle of the night I clicked on Facebook
And there I saw the most beautiful lady I'd seen.
I fear I've fallen deeply in love and she took
My heart.

She stole my heart and soul,
But I've never felt so whole.
She gave me back my life
When she promised to be my wife.
I gave her my heart.

Was this a dream or was it real?
My heart is full and bursting still.
How could it not be real
With the wonderful way I feel?
We gave each other our hearts.

Bubbling and bursting with joy,
Where are the words I can employ
To share with you my wonderment,
And the life we're about to enjoy?
Our hearts entwined in love,
Forever, and blessed by Father above.

A final note, written August 25.

I was determined – no bride from the 'Net.
Nor marry one I'd never met.
No one far way or across a border
Nor older. That was my order.

Now Father and Son above they chuckle,
"We sure fooled him and made him buckle.
He should have long ago learned
Never say no and get yourself burned."

My kingdom has no long borders.
Age and distance should not be orders.
A Southern Beauty I've set aside,
For all time to love you at your side.

Joyce: Once again, Arnold you have expressed yourself so eloquently. I have appreciated your sharing so openly and honestly and know it has been cathartic, even though painful, for you. Also it has doubtless helped many others. Vulnerability is difficult but it is really the only way to honestly reach out and it helped you in your healing process. I applaud you and I certainly wish you and Gloria every happiness. Personally, I have never been one to condemn when or if someone remarries after being widowed. Thank God, I have not walked that road so I have no idea of the pain and loneliness that brings. I believe we all have to follow our own path. Blessings to you and Gloria as you follow yours together.

Ann: Congratulations! We have been awaiting the next chapter in your life and glad that the silence meant you were too busy making history to record it. Blessings on your marriage, thanks again for sharing your life.

Joanne: Dear Arnold and Gloria, we have enjoyed reading about your journey and your transparency in your trials. It is always good to recognize the hand of God and what he is teaching us through the difficulties in life. Sometimes God gets blamed for things he did not do. He has given us a free will and he always allows us to exercise it. I'm glad that you and Gloria feel that you married in his will because that will help you through the difficult times if you stay true to those commitments. As you both know, it takes more that passion and romance to make a strong marriage. That can wear thin and even be taken away with one good illness. A deep love for each other, mutual respect, not taking each other for granted, putting the other's interest ahead of your own, these are the required building blocks. It is only right that you should be closing the curtains now. After all, marriage is a private affair and may the Lord be with you both and bless you abundantly so you can finish the race well. That 'great cloud of witnesses' would say that the prize is worth the struggle. We all want to leave a good heritage for our children to follow. You can be sure that they are listening and watching to see how it all pans out. With Love and Prayers from fellow pilgrims, Joanne and Tom.

Joli: I have appreciated your honesty (challenging!) throughout. I am sure you can understand everyone's initial reservation over an internet relationship, but it was only out of concern for you! Your continued openness has helped greatly to bring understanding. By all reports, Gloria, you sound like such a lovely woman and I look forward to meeting you someday. God bless you both in all these adjustments you will be making together. How special to experience falling in love together twice in a lifetime! The added maturity must make it an amazing experience. I look forward to seeing the book.

Jan: This is so awesome. It makes my heart leap as I look back to your brother and me, how we found each other in such a miraculous way. I had to laugh when you were saying how you had to make decisions about what to keep and what must go. Ray was so easy and as we talked it always just seemed right. I sensed that in your decisions. Again, thank you for sharing your hearts just as you did through those months after Betty made her journey to Glory. I love this and the poem you wrote. My son Stephen and Katarina who met on the Internet are now in her home country, Sweden. Stephen was getting a glimpse of Katarina through the past years. Before Stephen got to Sweden churches and friends wanted to hear Katarina's story of how they met and who Stephen is. I am so blessed how God is working in my children and grandchildren. My love and trust grow deeper and deeper as I learn to know God more than I could have ever imagined. Love you two! I pray that you will continue in your love for each other and the Lord. Jan

Suzan: Hey Unc. You touched so many lives with your honesty, hurt, triumphs, joys and sorrow. You have taught us all much about leaning on God for your *every* need and want. It will help many of us when some day we lose our spouse in old age or for a different reason maybe. I pray God will bless you immensely for sharing your heart with us. You allowed us to get to know you in a way that we might never had if you had not been so willing to open up your heart to reach someone else's soul. You are a true testament of the saving grace of God and his forever love for us all. May he bless you richly in your new life with Gloria. Love to both of you.

Lyle: Thank you for the way you have shared your thoughts so frankly and intimately. It took courage to do that and many times you spoke to my spirit.

Colleen: Arnold, I hope you already know from our communications how much we love having gotten to know you and Betty, how much we enjoyed, laughed and cried through all your postings, and how happy we are for your new found love. Hope to continue to hear more from you and will be one of the first to buy your book when you get it done.

Richard: We are still lovin the dance and the new adventure. Thank you Arnold. You have expressed much that has been/is on my heart and in my mind for so long. A book perhaps? I look forward to meeting "your" Gloria and introducing her to "my" Lana. Much respect for your journey. Just a thought: as far as getting married "too soon," when God is leading the time is perfect.

Arnold: Thank y'alls. Thanks so much for your continuing care and friendship.

46

From Infatuation to True Love

December 14

December 14, 1:45 pm. That is the time Betty left, one year ago. Christmas approaches, with all its traditions, and this year with many changes.

A few days ago Gloria and I decorated for the season. Two large boxes of tinsel and bobbles and candles Betty and I have had for years came out of storage. And a couple of Betty's special Christmassy cross stitch pieces: a welcome with a bear and another with three carolers. This year most of these items did not fit our new decor so I've put the best in a box for Tara and the rest for the Tilly. Gloria and I went downtown and picked out all new tree decorations. We needed to make this Christmas "ours" so we have a totally new look in our living room. I kept the seven foot tree, the large Nativity scene, though, and the old fashioned cardboard one. It was identical to the one we had when I was a child. And some of Gloria's decorations grace the room.

I hope that you can understand the "ours" thing. You should be able to grasp the fact that I cannot allow Betty to interfere with my new relationship; she would not want that. The past six months have been a big adjustment since she and I lived in this house for almost twenty years. She was still much more here than I realized until I brought Gloria home; her handiwork remained throughout the house. But now we have mostly new furniture in the living room, and Gloria and I fixed up a main floor room for her "office", which looks quite nice. She has some of her furniture in our bedroom as well as in her room. This had been the GBoys' room, which is now moved to Betty's former basement sewing room, and Tara gets her sewing machine. I took it to the Sewing Centre in Red Deer and had it souped up!

Gloria and I, before we married, discussed that fact that because both of us had long and good marriages, we cannot come together without bringing our missing spouses. They will always be part of our lives. We cannot share our stories with each other without reference to them, and we do so occasionally. My Betty and Gloria's

Bob are an integral part of our separate lives and always will be. We sometimes share anecdotes about them, and do that freely. That's our life together.

Gloria has been a wonderful support. Her husband died ten years ago at home with colon and liver cancer. She knows about the first anniversary of a death of a loving spouse. We share our stories and she encourages me. She said recently, "We are creating a new life together and saying good-bye to another." She also believes that God brought her into my life so soon to help me walk through this first anniversary of Betty's passing. Life is for the living. Our months together have brought Gloria renewal. She says, "Things that had died inside me are slowly coming alive again." Together we are experiencing a growing tenderness and affection for each other. The first three months of our relationship were filled with difficulties in adjusting to each other's values, habits, and idiosyncrasies. We still, occasionally, have to deal with issues. Like they say, we fell in love with a personality but discovered we had married a "Character"! Our strong commitment to our marriage vows, even though they were made before a Dallas Judge, and our initial infatuation (untried love) with each other, kept us together until we are now experiencing a growing depth of love and care and the wonderment of discovery. We have now become best friends, something we did not have time or the space to develop before our marriage, being 2,000 miles apart, and only six days of courting. We love doing things together, whether enjoying a movie, preparing a meal, or shopping for groceries or Christmas presents, whatever. The companionship we both sought has now become a satisfying reality.

A few younger folks felt very strongly that I remarried too soon, but I've never felt so. Being married too soon means that Betty would be interfering with Gloria's and my relationship because of my too strong an emotional attachment to Betty. She hasn't. But I don't understand, still, how I can still love her so and sometimes seriously miss her while my love for Gloria is steadily growing. Well, I don't try anymore; love is a matter for the heart. Not the head. Heart stuff sometimes has no logic and cannot be explained. Thank you, Betty, for blessing me for 48 years. Thank you Gloria for filling my aloneness and blessing my final years with a new friendship and companionship. God has richly blessed me with two wonderful women! I am grateful.

The next chapters tell Gloria's and my story, just about exactly as it happened. First, you will read of our ChristianMingle meeting. Then twenty-four hours later we switched to Facebook where we were able to meet each other's family in pictures of events from the past several years. It is presented here almost word-for-word as it happened.

As I have read it recently, over a year since we fell in love, it sounded very much like a couple of teenagers falling in love for the first time. That's the nature of love; it has never had boundaries for age, or for space in today's world. Enjoy our love story. We sure did!

47

How to Fall in Love via the Internet: Getting Acquainted

From: ChristianMingle <Cara@mail.christianmingle.com>
   Subject: Someone's Trying to Get in Touch With You!
   Date: 26 May, 2012 6:29:32 PM MDT
   To: Arnold Stauffer <astauff@telus.net>
   Reply-To: ChristianMingle.6hfz30bpz9.f-w6@mail.christianmingle.com

You just received an email!

Hey,
I just sent you an email! Go to your inbox to read it.
Hope to hear back from you soon!
- gmtexas

READ NOW!

My **first contact with Gloria**. As I write this February 16, 2013, she is out in our kitchen making herself a cup of coffee with the fancy machine my daughter and her husband gave us for Christmas. Almost nine months have passed since the "fateful" date, May 26, 2012. We just celebrated our first Valentine's Day with dark chocolates, a pen, and a stuffed puppy from me, and a fine elk leather wallet from Gloria. But to get back to our origins, here is what Gloria saw on Christian Mingle. I had been corresponding with a dozen divorcees but didn't find one with whom I wanted to spend the rest of my life. So I changed my request on ChristianMingle to send me only widows. I thought perhaps I could find someone who would not require serious mending. Within minutes of my request I received the above notice. Gloria had seen my picture and profile, shown below, and instantly was caught in my trap!

For the profile, Christian Mingle asks questions or gives you leading statements for you to complete. This helps you to provide a variety of ideas about yourself for a potential "Mingler". This helps her decide if you are the kind of person she would like to contact, with the idea of getting to know you better. I saw the above note on May 26, read her profile (which has since been lost), and quickly responded. What I saw on her page was an exciting read. Here was the kind of gal I was looking for. When she had seen my picture and profile, she had thought something similar.

My profile picture.

Being originally from Oklahoma and recently Texas, Gloria was immediately taken in by my western hat and shirt. She loved the twinkle in my eye and the warm smile and rugged moustache. I had set the perfect trap to catch this lovely lady from Grand Prairie, Texas, situated between Dallas and Fort Worth.

My Profile Information

INTRODUCTION

I am somewhat of a teaser and joker, like to make folks laugh. Enjoy gardening, reading, watching movies, creating woodart in my shop, hiking, traveling, and cooking. Sometimes a quiet guy but do enjoy people – love to laugh and have fun. A good listener and conversationalist. An affectionate, unrepentant romantic Country Guy. I am looking for an affectionate lady to whom I can be devoted to and who will be the same to me. A person who enjoys doing, going, and loving – together.

BASIC INFORMATION
Male, Three Hills, Alberta, Canada, Age 70

ABOUT ME
Height: 6' 2" (187 cm); Build: I should maybe lose a few; Hair: Dark Brown; Eyes: Blue
Relationship Status: Widowed, with 2 children, not at home
Smoking: Never: Drinking: On occasion

Church I was raised Evangelical and now attend the Evangelical Free Church every week.

Education: Doctoral degree; Field of Work: Educator – Retired

Ethnicity: Caucasian; Languages Spoken: English

FUN FACTS

Self-description: A friendly guy who is affectionate to the one I love. Unrepentant romantic, fun loving teaser.

Music: Country/Western, Praise & Worship, Religious Music, Southern Gospel, Traditional Gospel. Favorite bands and musicians: none

Movies: Action/Adventure, Drama, Romance; Favorite movies and actors: Morgan Freeman; Favorite TV shows: cop shows

Outdoor activity: Basketball, Camping, Gardening, Photography

Indoor activity: Cooking/Culinary arts, Games, Movies/TV, Reading

My idea of a great trip: Just take off and see where you end up, although I'd like a cruise to Alaska

Food: Cajun/Southern, Chinese, Vegetarian sometimes; Favorite restaurants: Moxies, Milestones

Politics: Conservative

Schools attended: Asbury Theological Seminary, University of Calgary, Mountain View Bible College

Timeliness: I am usually early; as for fashion, I dress to be comfortable

MATCH PREFERENCES (the kind of person I would like to meet)

Age: Between 50 and 65 years old

Distance: Within 300 miles of Three Hills, Alberta, Canada

Height: Between 5' 0" (152 cm) and 6' 0" (182 cm); Body Type: Average

Relationship Status: Widowed

Church Attendance: every week

Smoking: Never. Drinking: On occasion

ESSAYS

What I'd like to do on a first date: Coffee (not really). Let's go to a nice quiet restaurant. Maybe for a walk in the park. Or how about checking out some garage sales, buy a couple of antiques and then coffee. Talk, walk and eat. If you let me I might hold your soft hand for a little while. Really – let's decide together.

My past relationships have taught me: To be a good listener. To be sensitive and really care for the concerns and needs of the other person. To say "I'm sorry!" sooner than later. I love to be affectionate and romantic. Love is as much a decision and commitment as an emotion. To take the initiative when things go wrong. Touching is my love language.

To me, being a Christian means: Loving Jesus as my Personal Saviour. Following him in complete obedience.

I've been a Christian All my life. I invited Jesus into my heart when I was four years old.

In five years, I see myself keeping healthy by continuing to explore what makes good health. Keep close to my kids and GKids. Create a large vision for the local Good Health Store that I manage part-time and lead the staff in fulfilling that vision. Help folks in need.

My favorite Bible passage is Psalm 32:8. I will instruct you and teach you in the way you should go; I will counsel you and watch over you. Psalm 25:14. The Lord confides in those who fear him, he makes his covenant known to them. It is not so difficult to follow someone that promises to teach and counsel and confide in me.

One final thing I'd like to mention: I've landed a very small role in the Drumheller, Alberta, Passion Play, which will keep me busy on weekends for 2½ months.

ChristianMingle analysis says I am blue: 32%, white: 25%, red: 23%, yellow: 20%. Blues Are: Analytical, Committed, Compassionate, Dedicated, Deliberate, Dependable, Emotional, Loyal, Nurturing, Seek Quality, Respectful, Sincere, Thoughtful, Well-Mannered.

On ChristianMingle you do not initially give your name or any other personal information. CM warns you to wait several weeks to become acquainted before you share how to contact each other outside their site. Gloria introduced herself as gmtexas; I was Woodartisan. Here is her first message to me, and the ensuing dialogue. Some of the references in our dialogue refer to comments we made about ourselves that are available to anyone on the site, if they happen to find us.

From: gmtexas
Sent: Saturday, 26 May 2012, 11:59 AM
Subject: A comment about your profile

Gee whiz. . .wish you didn't live so far away! You have a really nice profile and pic's. Great smile. My late hubby was Canadian. They make 'um really good in up your way! gmtexas

Woodartisan wrote:
Hi gm, you must have been sitting by your computer waiting for my reply! Aren't there any good looking guys in Texas? You'd get a lot more hugs with a guy much closer. Or are you not into that touchy feely stuff?

I have a shop – you can come and build clocks in it any time. You can see some of the stuff I make on my website: www.masterwoodcrafts.com

If you are on Facebook you can meet my family and see a maple table I made for my daughter. She thinks just cuz I own a hammer and saw that I can make anything out of wood. But she wanted a table 73 x 46, out of hardwood. Took me a year cuz each step I had to check out how to do what next. I normally work only with barn board so this project was a toughie. Got it done finally.

My wife died last Dec 14 after being diagnosed with inoperable pancreatic/liver cancer only two months previously. She told me a couple of weeks before she left that I was to get married again. I said, Betty, I don't even want to think about it (now I'm crying) but I have come to see it as a gift from her, which I am now starting to unwrap. I was not going to go to the dating sites, but after several folks encouraged me to do so here I am. My counselors have strongly urged me to date several ladies, but wait till the six months, which is June 14, not far away. I've got a date for about then with a lady who wants to come and see the Play. I am corresponding with several others I've met here, and a gal I work with is attempting to set me up with her Aunt. This activity has been real good for me as it has helped me turn a page. From being in the sad past to the present to hope and the future. So I am having great fun chatting with a bunch of pretty ladies! Now one faraway in Texas. Mama Mia!

Just thought u should know all that up front. So let's have some fun chatting.

Do you like holding hands? Arnold

gmtexas wrote:
Sent: Saturday, 26 May 2012, 07:20 PM
Subject: RE: A comment about your profile

No I wasn't sitting by my computer waiting. I was reading emails and answering. Ahem! Thanks for the heads-up about all the gals you have lined up waiting for you. As cute as you are you shouldn't have any problems on that score. Wished I lived closer.

Yes, as I stated in my profile, I am very affectionate. Hugs, kisses, holding hands. (big on hugs) Nothing too good for my baby. There's a little bit of country gal in me. I love the country/outdoors/ animals/birds etc. etc. Don't much like city dwelling which I'm doing right now. You were widowed not too long ago, but it really depends on how you feel and your personal makeup. Some people wait months, some years.

I've dated some. . .but nothing ever got serious. Still waiting for that very special man to love and be loved. I am receiving attention on this dating site. Some have been wolves in sheep's clothing which I've had to even turn in. Men's profiles get stolen, which I found out the hard way. Be careful. I enjoy the chat rooms. Mostly 50's and 60's chatting and making jokes. It can get pretty funny sometimes which gives me a few laughs. You can find me on Facebook too. I will give you my full name. . .and yours to me. . .maybe when we are comfortable. OK? (you can't access my FB unless you have my name) Bye for now, gm

Woodartisan wrote:
So what's this comment on your profile "somewhat fashionable" person mean? I thought all the ladies in Texas were Cow Girls! And I don't see Country/Western and Southern Gospel in your profile!;-} Sorry, my spiritual gift is giving people a hard time – a modern version of the gift of encouragement. Ok, GM, it's your move. You started this conversation, so what do we do next? It's too hot in Texas for to go there today – probably 110 in the shade, huh? Do you want to chat? Arnold

gmtexas wrote:
Arnold, (see I picked up your name all by myself) Yes, it's kinda hot already here even though it's only May. Going to be around 90 degrees today and the weekend.

212

I like your "spiritual gift!" You have a good sense of humor. . .which if you read my profile you will have noticed that's big in my book. I would like to chat. You definitely have a very fun-loving look on your face. Or maybe it's more impish?

Woodworking. . .hmmmm. I love the smell of wood. I used to dabble in making stuff. Once made a pendulum clock. Really liked it. (I like clocks for some reason) Always wanted a shop so I could go in and putter around with woods etc. I've been widowed for almost nine years. My husband passed away right after we moved here to Texas, fortunately my youngest daughter lived here. Would like to hear back from you and more of your "gift." Gloria (is that better?)

P.S. Oh BTW Arnold, "somewhat fashionable" means I can dress not to embarrass anyone, but totally enjoy casual dress all the time. I'm originally from Oklahoma. Moved away to California in my 30's. Gloria

Woodartisan wrote:
Good morning, Gloria, On my way to work. Real busy yesterday. Just wanted to say Hi and let you know I will talk to you this evening. Now don't go running off with some better looking guy in the meantime! Saw you on FB. Interesting! Arnold

From: gmtexas
Sent: Monday, 28 May 2012, 10:25 AM
Subject: RE: A comment about your profile

Good morning Arnold, Yesterday I spent the day at my daughters. They have a pool so I made like a dolphin, or maybe a small whale. Two great grandchildren there. So cute five and seven. I had to get out of the pool as they got pretty frisky and I didn't particularly want to be drowned at that time.

I'll send you messages on FB also (private ones). . . . I don't plan on running off with anyone today. Maybe tomorrow? Where do you work? Do you chop down trees!? For the wood!? bye, bye Arnold! Gloria

48

Switching from ChristianMingle to Facebook

A fter the first couple of days corresponding on ChristianMingle we agreed to be friends on Facebook. This was an excellent move, although it is strongly discouraged by the CM people. They know there are some scams and fraudulent characters on their site so they do not want you to give out personal contact information until you are sure you can trust the other person. We were immediately "taken in" and trusted by the other, and decided quickly to get acquainted on Facebook. A good idea, because we both had several years of family and fun pictures which told us a whole lot about each other and our families. We trusted each other from the first day. Here is Gloria's Facebook request to be my friend, the first step in contact another person on FB. Of course I clicked on "Confirm Request" and now we had access to each other in much more detail.

From: "Facebook" <notification+z=yt9f09@facebookmail.com>
Subject: Gloria Miller wants to be friends on Facebook
Date: 27 May, 2012 11:06:20 PM MDT
To: Arnold Stauffer <astauff@telus.net>
Confirm Request

Arnold. 2:39pm May 28
  I took a quick look on FB cuz I wanted to view your pretty pics before going back to work.
  I have your pic from FB. You have always been one gorgeous lady!

Gloria. 2:41pm May 28

Wow. . .thanks kiddo.

Arnold. 2:41pm May 28

Trouble is I can't see the colour of your eyes. Guess I will have to drop by after all.

Arnold. 8:54pm May 28

Originally when I signed on CM I intended to avoid ladies a long way off, divorcees and any one south of the border – too many complications. So what do I do? Find a divorcee in AZ. She turned out after a month to be a shyster: lied about her age, repeatedly avoided answering simple questions about herself and turned out to be living in the same house as her divorced husband. So we parted company.

Immediately I got back on CM and this time I asked for widows only. So what happens? This lovely Texas Sweet Lady steps into my life and immediately, without mercy, attempts to steal my heart. 2,000 miles away, south of the border.

We should talk about some serious stuff. We both went on CM to find a mate, so maybe we should get some serious talk underway before I get totally swept off my feet!

Let's assume for this discussion that we really do fall in love and start thinking seriously about getting hitched. Several matters immediately come to my attention. You have GGKids as old as my GKids! I have seven GKids, my son's and his wife's three are 20 minutes away and my daughter and her pastor husband live almost two hours away towards the mountains and have four of my Gkids. All just as fine kids as anyone could order.

I am not excited about living in hot and humid Texas and I doubt with your history you would want to be in Alberta in January. So what about us living in Texas November to say April and in Alberta the rest of the year?

It seems a bit strange talking about this, and it is not a proposal but if we continue to chat. . . I might be enticed into your web!

So, Pretty Lady, you started this interaction so what do you think about this? Well, I suppose I have to take some responsibility cuz I set the trap by asking CM to find me a widow! Do you think our Lord is playing a joke on us? and having a good laugh about our new predicament.

What would your kids think? Mine are probably ok with whatever I decide as I have kept very close to them through the past six months and updated them on my "things of the heart".

Looking forward to some very wise words to come from you.

I find this matter between us very interesting – it already seems like we have known each other for a while. Maybe that's because we immediately hit it off.

Arnold

Gloria. 12:08pm May 29

Good afternoon Arnold. I was married to a Canuck and he loved the cold but it seems we lived in so many places had to adapt to whatever. . .even Guam! You talk about hot!

I have only lived here ten years, my hubby passed almost nine years ago. I'm still here coz didn't see any place else to head off by myself. One daughter here, four kids in Calif.

My life doesn't revolve around my grandkids. They love me and are interested in me and I them. I don't have to be in their pockets so to speak.

I had to sell the only piece of real estate I owned when hubby died. It all happened so suddenly after moving here to TX that in order to get into an apartment, buy work clothes etc. I had to sell the mobile home we purchased quickly so I could take care of him. So sorry, I live in an apartment. . .in the city, which I hate. I'm rather hot natured so don't need the HEAT all the time.

Unfortunately Arnold I'm not one of the "well fixed" widows.

I long to be with my mate. . .enjoying each other. . .loving each other and enjoying life, nature, the simple things. I'm not high maintenance.

I have no idea if God's orchestrating our meeting.

My kids would like to see me happy and in love again. No problem there.

I appreciate your honesty. Do you think you're ready for something serious? It's only been months since you were widowed.

Pray about all this and I will too. Gloria

Gloria. 12:10pm May 29

P.S. I started this interaction because CM sent me your match info and pic and I thought "he's cute" so why not.:)

Arnold. 4:00pm May 29

Oh Gloria, why are things of the heart so difficult? For 48 years I had it all figured out. Now I am back to square one again.

I am ready for something serious – a long story. Includes two months of saying good-bye to Betty, the last living together in palliative care. From Oct on I started a support group on FB, first to keep relatives and a few close friends updated with her, at that time, prospective surgery. The surgery soon turned into inoperative pancreatic/liver cancer. Every day I journalled the trail we have traveled for this group (now I am crying), which gradually increased to 153 people. I cannot put into words how meaningful this was for me – to put my thoughts and emotions into concrete words for them, knowing all these folks were praying for me and many responded regularly with encouragement and counsel. Not long before she left, Betty told me to get married again. I said, "Betty, I don't want to even think about it." She said, "Well sometime you will." She knew me better than I. Now I see it as a gift from her and I am gradually opening it. Someday I will tell you about her Good-bye Service and the coffin my brothers and I built for her. And there is a lot more. I started saying good-bye to her during the two months I spent with her before she left. My FB counselors have been pretty hard on me at times when they thought I was thinking about "girling" too soon. I promised to not date for six months – till June 14. Not far away now. But I did not promise to not go on dating sites, which several friends recommended that I do.

I should get back to work as I am sorta taking a lunch break. I will continue this story later, but I am, in case you didn't pick up on it, answering your question, "Am I ready to get serious?"

For the next six weeks I am very busy and can't do any serious courting. One of my most experienced counselors whom I met on CM, says I should date several ladies for a while. I think that is good. Sometimes I get confused about all this. I HAVE NOT DATED FOR FIVE DECADES!! You're the sweetest gal I've met on the Internet so I really want to continue our conversation. Who knows what might happen? I have been praying very seriously all along, as have others, that I make the right decision about getting married again. A bad marriage would be worse than being alone. I'll talk to you sometime this evening. Probably will work late again. Arnold

Gloria. 5:40pm May 29

Do whatever you need to do Arnold. I understand. Date away and if you come up empty handed look me up. Who knows I may still be around. You deserve someone special who doesn't have empty pockets. I'm currently looking for another job and so will hopefully be busy myself. God Bless. . . . Gloria

Arnold. 8:44pm May 29

Gloria! You sound like you are walking away. Notice that I said, "You're the sweetest gal I've met on the Internet so I really want to continue our conversation." That's what I need to do. To be quite open and frank, I could very easily fall in love with you. But I need a couple of months to play it cool. Just keep looking around. I chose a couple of months ago to be very busy during this time – seven days a week. Good therapy. Helps me turn the pages from being sad and alone to being out and about with a whole bunch of wonderful folk. That's just till July 22, the last performance of the Passion Play.

Please do not think that I was looking for a rich widow. I don't recall that such a thought entered my mind. I have noticed that many women on the sites love to travel and are seeking a man to do so with them. Not me. Like you, I really am a home body. My dream cruise is to Alaska, and I've had a life-long desire to visit Switzerland where the Stauffer's and Betty's ancestors came from to the US in the early 1700s. Then to Ontario in the early 1800s and then to Alberta in early 1900s. I'd like to visit the Stauffer castle that still stands in Switzerland.

Betty and I were living on our government Old Age and Old Age security pension. We had a bit of extra income from her baking and my few days a month of substitute teaching and managing the Farmer's Market. We have RRSPs but not a large amount. When our cash ran out we expected to move into a Seniors Lodge. My house is paid for so that is my old age security when I need to move into an old geezers' home. After working in ministry most of my adult life I have not stashed very much money. There you have it. We are both poor folks who would have to live on love – mostly. It really does not cost much to live when you do not run around a lot.

So here is the deal. Can we continue to chat for the next say six weeks, at least till I am not so busy? If we continue to hit it off and the other ladies I date (If I find any, well there may be one in Calgary.) get boring or run, then maybe – maybe – I should drop down to Grand Prairie to look into your pretty blue eyes and hold your soft hands and cuddle while we watch a movie, and laugh a lot and find some nice air conditioned places to have some fun. Maybe sit on a park bench in the evening, go for a swim with your GGKids, and see what entertainment Grand Prairie has to offer. (Did you know that Alberta has a Grand Prairie?)

Gloria, can we continue our visit for the next eight weeks, till July 22, and then have another discussion about what we might want to do for the rest of our lives? (But you probably in this time will run across some rich good looking Believer who will whisk you off into the sunset – that would be your gain and my loss!) Arnold

Gloria. 9:16pm May 29

Yes, I'm interested in staying in touch with you, of course. You're correct in cooling it and snooping others out, you may be giving me much more credit than I deserve.

I receive Social Security Pension (rather small) but it adds up when I work it makes all the difference. Plus I receive Medicare (health) that is taken from my SS benefits. As you probably are aware of when I turned 65 became eligible for Medicare that is taken out of my SS monthly benefit. Clear as mud?

I feel very drawn to you and can't explain it. I need to cool it too. I've been a widow for nine years this August. I want to be a couple again. Tired of dating, looking etc. Want to belong just one last time. I will be happy to keep chatting with you cute one. Love your happy smiling face. I copied it from FB so I can have it in my photos to look at.

Please remember me in your prayers as I'm looking very earnestly for work. So many have been out of work. I received unemployment $$ for 18 months until May 12th. . .then poof. It was a God send to have it so will not complain. God will not leave me or forsake me. Now I have to walk off the ten pounds I put on while not working.:(

Well, I'm going to sign off for now.

God bless, Gloria

Arnold. 11:53pm May 29

Gloria, I feel honoured that you are drawn to me. And I am to you. I do have a fear though, that because of the distance and family and border complications that we will get attached to one another but will not be able to do anything about it. My fear is that you may be hurt and I do not want that to happen. As I mentioned I think I need to take the advice of my pen pal in dating several ladies. That sorta sounds like more trouble than fun. It would be so easy for me to climb in my Grand Caravan and whistle down to GP and abscond with you back to Three Hills. Maybe it is good I signed up for my two jobs, keeping me busy 24/7. To keep me from doing anything

218

irrational. But there are dangers. What if three people fell in love with me during the next two or three months of dating? If I remember our laws correctly a guy is allowed only one wife – at a time. So two would get hurt – or perhaps just wait for their turn. Well, I am making light of what could be serious. So, Gloria, continue to help me sort this out. Ooooooh! I so do not want to hurt you or make mistakes in all this!

You are so much fun to chat with. But let me check on other stuff. Please put a check mark beside each of the following statements if they apply to you.

___ I am pretty
___ I like to make people laugh
___ I like to be around a guy who makes me laugh
___ I am a warm, congenial person
___ I am bubbly and effervescent a lot of the time
___ I love when my honey brings me chocolates and flowers
___ Some of my best times are when I can snuggle with him on the chesterfield watching a chic flic or just carrying on intimate conversation.
___ I love to hold hands while we go for walks
___ I want a guy with a warm and large shoulder for me to cry on when I need to
___ I love warm intimate hugs
___ I love to chat so need a guy who is a great listener
___ But I am an expert listener as well
___ He needs to love kids
___ Companionship – that is what I think marital bliss is mostly about
___ If I found my Dream Guy, someone who I would deeply want to spend the rest of my life with, I would go anywhere in this universe to live with him.

I am praying for your job.
Waiting for your answers, A

Gloria. 11:18am May 30
1. Matter of opinion. . .no to 6, yes to all others.

Remember, I was married to a Canadian. We had no problems on this side of border. I do understand about the distance as far as you're concerned. You haven't even begun to "go fishing". . .so why be looking down this way at all. I get it.

Besides I'm not sure you are ready after such a short grieving time. I've passed up opportunities with widowers who have less than at least a year. Preferably two years. It should be same with widows. Your pic caught my attention and only later did I find out it's just been months.:(

I do have a gentleman in AZ who is interested in me. So far it's stalled. My fault, I had him cool his jets for a while – seeking God.

God bless in all your searching. Gloria

Arnold. 3:49pm May 30
You don't like chocolates and flowers? How about just flowers?

Gloria, Gloria, Gloria! I know what you are doing – giving me the opportunity to head down the road. Please don't. All I am asking for is two months. The primary reason is that I am too busy till July 22 to do serious courting. But when I get into high gear. . .! Without question, you are at the top of my list. If it wasn't for the Passion Play I would come down tomorrow (except I do not have an updated passport). You passed my test with flying colours. You are my Dream Gal. I want a lover/hugger/laughing/make me laugh/loyal/attractive wife who will want to be with me most of the time. Well. . . I might be able to deal with you going to a ladies' meeting or the bath room by yourself. But I need to look into your eyes and hold your hand and go for a walk and snuggle and visit and see your life in GP. Can't do all that right now. Can you give me two months?

And if it doesn't work out would you be okay with us walking our own ways then? Don't want to take a chance of hurting you in any way. My counselors are not holding me back. Some are saying take your time. So I am – two months' time.

I have been fishing. Chatted with an AZ lady for a month but she turned out to be a shyster. Actually I did date a local gal for several weeks six or seven weeks ago (broke my promise and got my knuckles severely whacked by my FB counselors). I have done my grieving. That doesn't mean I do not still cry occasionally. A widow just remarried, on my FB support group, says I will always cry. I am happy, Gloria. These two jobs I have are getting me good times, great friends and lots to do. I did cry when I drove the Motor Home to the camp site on Saturday cuz it was the first time I had driven it without Betty.

So please do not run off. Just be patient for two months. That's not very long. Rub cheeks with your AZ man but don't get too cozy till I have a chance to gaze into your soul and hold your hand. And hug you to myself. Maybe you have got it figured out by now – my love language is touching. I have a suspicion that yours is too. A

Gloria. 5:10pm May 30

Oh Arnold you are so sweet and honest. Thanks. Unless the AZ friend comes here for a visit I will only be doing phone hugs. I've not met him yet. He's had several health issues etc. that have gotten in his way. He has a motor home and wants to travel this way. I'm a motor home fan! My nick name was "the bye-bye kid" by my hubby, Bob. Sometimes I do get a tear in my eye when something comes up that I know he would enjoy. It's human nature. My kids too. They adored him. Big ole Canadian with a big heart.

Maybe you Canadians just pop out of heaven that way! Big, loving and fun.:) It would be my luck to have you fall all over yourself for a gal nearer you. But if the Lord's will. . .it just would be. I need to work anyway and save some shekels, just in case you do ever make it here.:)

P.S. Not so much flowers, as I would love something carved or made from sweet smelling wood. Hand crafted. It wouldn't drop dead in a week. Savvy?

Bye my big Canadian cutie, Gloria

Gloria. 5:38pm May 30

P.P.S. Your messages are wonderful and two months should go by pretty fast. I'm very glad you have a support group (may I call you Arnie?) should have asked. Advice is good, but keep your main line open for God's voice. Me too.

49

I Know I Love You!

Arnold. 8:22pm May 30

I am working on my "main line" as you call it. I should tell you how the Lord recently showered me with his love and encouraged me to love him first over my search for a woman to love. A marvelous ten day story. I will tell you one of these days.

Actually I am looking forward to the day when you call me: Honey, Hey My Love, Yoohoo Wonderful Guy, Come to me Baby! But for now I guess I will have to settle for Arnie. Long ago there was another Arnold in our youth group whom everyone called Arnie and I was jealous.

Okay, Gloria you beautiful wonderful humorous Texas doll, I am tired of this mincing around. I plan to date mostly cuz my most respected advisor says I should and maybe she's right. You need to know I am serious. I talked an hour on the phone with a gal I have been chatting with, but the phone call didn't do anything romantic for me. She happens to come from the same background as me and we know a lot of folks, and she knows some of my family. In fact my daughter was friends with her daughter when they were at summer camp when they were 11 or 12. I will date her a couple of times and then shut down. She said on CM she was widow. On the phone she said they were divorced 20 some years ago. They did reconcile later after he had a heart attack and came back to the Lord. Then he was diagnosed with Parkinson's and came to live with her and their son in a platonic relationship. They looked after him. Weird.

Anyway, in support of an open and frank relationship with you I hope you will allow me to talk about my heart matters even when it involves others. Is that OK?

About the end of mincing around. I want to set sort of a date to come visit you. I am thinking sometime in August. I would love to be with you and your family on July 4, but I am up to my ears in The Play. Are there any exciting things going on in Grand Prairie or the area any time in August that we might like to be a part of?

Okay, no more mincing. If things go well in August I am going to ask you to marry me. We could get married twice, once there and then in Alberta. My extended family has Christmas get-together between Christmas and New Year's. How about at our celebration? The family would be together. When would it be a good time down there?

Gloria, I know you love me. It springs off the page in all your notes. So let's quit this little game we are playing and get on with it. And I know I love you. But really, I guess I don't know what falling in love means. I knew what love was for 48 years, but I guess now I need your help to find out again. Would you do that for me? Help me know and understand what it means to love again? (now I'm crying) So I am going to get bold and quit this nonsensical fooling around and get to the point. I love you, Gloria. And in August something or other I am going to ask you, if you don't ask me first.

Oh WOW! Can't believe I said all that. I guess my telephone conversation last evening convinced me. I think I now understand what is in my heart.

We will have some financial issues to work out, but if neither of us are spend thrifts we can make it. When I have been raising these matters the last couple of days, it wasn't because I had doubts (which is what you thought), but because they are matters we need to have serious conversations about. So my love, I have bared my heart. I have so badly wanted to tell you that I love you, now I feel so happy that I have. Watch it, now I might get pretty flirty at times and lovey dovey. That okay with you? I enjoy the romantic part of a relationship so much!

I have prayed from the beginning that I would not make a mistake. It seems strange that God would allow this to happen between us, or perhaps he had a hand in making it happen. Perhaps someday we will know the special reason why. I think I know – there just aint nobody in and around here who is so sweet, loving, passionate, humorous and attractive, and touchy feely. God knows I need you!! I can't believe I am saying all this. I didn't really intend to. Gloria it's been pent up inside and so I am just letting it flow.

So, my sweet lovely, what do you think? Are you ready to unveil your sweet thoughts? I know they are just below the surface of your pretty skin, so I am all ears.

A ♥ ♥ ♥ ♥

Arnold. 8:35pm May 30

I just found your earlier message and copied it here to reply. I am inserting my replies.

G: Unless the AZ friend comes here for a visit I will only be doing phone hugs. I've not met him yet. He's had several health issues etc. that have gotten in his way. He has a motor home and wants to travel this way. I'm a motor home fan! My nick name was "the bye-bye kid" by my hubby (Bob) Sometimes I do get a tear in my eye when something comes up that I know he would enjoy. It's human nature. My kids too. They adored him. Big ole Canadian with a big heart. Maybe you Canadians just pop out of heaven that way! Big, loving and fun.

A: I HAVE A MOTOR HOME AND IT'S BIGGER THAN HIS. AND I AM NOT SICK.

G: It would be my luck to have you fall all over yourself for a gal nearer you. But if it's the Lord's will. . .it just would be.

A: NOPE. NOT GONNA HAPPEN. I NOW KNOW THAT YOU HAVE MY HEART. AND THE REST OF ME WHENEVER IT IS APPROPRIATE.

G: I need to work anyway and save some shekels, just in case you do ever make it here.

A: It doesn't cost much to snuggle on the couch or go for walks or swim with your GGKids. Or eat at McDonalds.

G: P.S. Not so much flowers, as I would love something carved or made from sweet smelling wood. Hand crafted. It wouldn't drop dead in a week. Savvy?

A: Okay I will make something for you. I don't carve though. Have you seen my website? Would you prefer something from new wood or barn wood?

A ♥♥♥♥♥

Arnold. 5:05am May 31

Gloria, I woke up at 3:30 so decided to check in. I've spent the last hour and a half admiring all the handsome people in your family. I tried to figure out who they were. You have a daughter Bridgette, her daughter is Erin. Craig's your son? And you have a friend Mary? You are such a beautiful person in every way. How could I be so privileged that you would even consider coming 2000 miles north to be with me? What a wonderful thought! ♥

Arnold. 8:15am May 31

It's 8:11 am and I am making fruit salad for my lunch: strawberries, navel orange, grapes and maybe an apple, and a half can of peach/mango pie filling for sauce. Mmmm! The sky is a bit overcast. I've had tulips in my front garden for a week. Will you come to my house someday soon? ♥

Gloria. 1:50pm May 31

Arnie! You adorable man!!!♥ I'm sitting here looking at everything you wrote! I don't understand it but I feel the same for you.

Bridgette is my youngest daughter that lives here in Texas. Her daughter is Erin and 29 years old. Elle is my son Mark's daughter, my youngest gdaughter. The two little people you may see are my two greatgrands. They are so sweet! They will love you! My oldest daughter Cynthia lives in CA, my son Craig is out there too. So Cynthia, Mark and Craig are all in No. CA.

Mary is my childhood friend. Been friends since about 3rd grade. I spoke to her this morning and when I talked about you she really picked up on that. She said, "Gloria, he sounds so similar to you." You have so much in common. I replied: yes, and I'm a touchy, feely person and he is too! Ha. I'm going to send her the pic of you in that cowboy hat. That precious face is just adorable. You have a twinkle in your eyes.

Truthfully, I don't particularly like the idea of you "fishing" but hey, I have no control over it. I also spoke with my AZ friend last night who called me. He's a retired preacher, very nice man, but we've had some issues. I'm into nutrition and he is NOT. I took a nutrition course in college back in 1985. Didn't agree with what all they taught. Fluoride is BIG business here and poison. We can talk about that later sometime.

Most guys who get in touch with me are boring. They want much younger mostly, Betty Grable, Lana Turner, Julia Roberts all rolled into one. While they look like (I better not say what).

I'm still interested in nature, travel (sometimes) or motor-homing, loving whatever together. (big shoulders):)

If I lived in CAN at least once a year reunion with my kiddos. We always have a blast together. They buy my ticket to CA at Christmas time and we have so much fun. My jaws hurt from smiling and laughing. (I don't like flying at Christmas time but that's what has happened so far.)

You are adorable my sweet man. I went onto your FB profile too and admired your pic's and information. I just pray to God you are Real! ♥

Bye for now you cutie pie. Gloria

2:06pm. P.S. Yes, it would be very very easy for me to say, Arnie my sweet man. . .I do love you. That's what's in my heart now. How do you see so much with me? No one has ever noticed what you notice. Thank you so much for expressing to me what you feel. There's always stuff going on in Grand Prairie and surrounding areas. I'm between Dallas and Fort Worth. August is very good, but you have time to reconsider what you said. I laughed out loud at some of the cute things you said. I've kept a cork in my mouth with others, but feel like I can say what is in my heart with you. Yea God!! ♥

Big kiss for you, ♥

2:08pm. P.S. I would love to come see your place, but can't do any travel now. Oh BTW my passport is up to date!;)

2:47pm. I posted some pics of little ones so you can get a better idea on FB page.

2:50pm. P.P.S. Regarding matters of the heart between you and another woman, I'm not so much wanting to hear it, unless you tell me they struck out or something negative.:p

Arnold. 12:47am Jun 1.

I feel exactly the same way. I cannot wait till August so I am going to ask you now. I know this is not the most romantic setting for this question, and I only expect a tentative answer now, to be confirmed in August.

Gloria. 12:49am Jun 1.

On one of my Facebook pics you will see me floating in the water and I was looking down into the water. I feel like that's exactly what I've been doing these last eight months, floating and waiting. . .

Arnold. 12:49am Jun 1. (NOTE: It was 1:49 am in Texas. The posted times are according to Facebook in Alberta.)

Here's my question. . . .

GLORIA, MY LOVE ♥ AND JOY! ♥ WILL YOU MARRY ME? ♥

No more floating, waiting. . .

Gloria. 12:52am Jun 1.

Arnold, my heart is saying yes. I'm excited. I haven't been excited about anybody before. . .except you. Isn't that amazing?? YES ♥ ♥

Arnold. 12:54am Jun 1.

Oh Gloria! I am speechless.

Gloria. 12:55am Jun 1.

Oh cute one you just can't be! I think you're Italian or French of something!! ♥

Arnold. 12:55am Jun 1.

Swiss German. Miller is English. Anything else?

Gloria. 12:57am Jun 1.

I'm a Heinz variety. Miller is my married name. My maiden name is Peterson. Dad was Cherokee and either Swiss or Norwegian. Mother's side German, English, Dutch, Irish etc. etc. etc.:)

Arnold. 12:59am

Jun 1. So, my love! I just feel warm all over and in a dazy hazy lovey dovey bubbly wonderment! How could I be so blessed to have this beautiful, wonderful lady so far away agree to come and be my wife?

Gloria. 1:02am Jun 1.

Just like picking out of a catalog! That's what we basically have done. God has a sense of humor. Yes??? I feel very blessed sweetie to have your love. It's amazing me. But, we both probably need to go to bed now. You have to work don't you? You need some rest big guy. ♥

Gloria. 1:04am Jun 1.

You are the sweetest man I have ever met. Truly sweet and lovable. Wow! I'm the lucky one.♥

Arnold. 1:05am Jun 1.

I think that we are so blessed in finding each other. In God's Kingdom there are no borders. So maybe it is not so unusual as it seems to us right now.

Gloria. 1:07am Jun 1.

Good night my Canadian sweetheart. ♥

Arnold. 1:08am Jun 1.

By the way, I discovered yesterday on your site that you are trained in nutrition. I just got rid of all animal protein in my house and quit eating wheat. Plan to live to 101.

Gloria. 1:09am Jun 1.

You better live to be 101 cuz I do too.;p

Arnold. 1:09am Jun 1.

Nite Pretty Lady. Tomorrow I am heading to the PP right after work hope to chat with you in the evening perhaps 9 or 10. What time is it there now? 1:10 here

Gloria. 1:10am Jun 1.

It is 2:10 a.m.

Arnold. 1:11am Jun 1.

OOOOOH! Sorry I kept you up so late. I promised my Mom I would get you home on time!

Gloria. 1:11am Jun 1.

Big smooch to you to hold us until tomorrow.

Arnold. 1:11am Jun 1.

Same. Nite.
♥♥♥♥♥♥♥♥♥♥♥♥

Arnold. 7:29am Jun 1.

It's 7:13 AM.

A few hours ago methinks I had a dream.
In the middle of the night I clicked on Facebook
And there I saw the most beautiful lady I've seen.
I fear I've fallen deeply in love and she took
My heart. ♥

She stole my heart and soul
But I've never felt so whole
She gave me back my life
When she promised to be my wife
I gave her my heart. ♥

227

Was this a dream or was it real?
My heart is full and bursting still.
How could it not be real
With the wonderful way I feel?
We gave each other our hearts! ♥

Bubbling and bursting with joy
Where are the words I can employ
To share with you my wonderment
And the life we're about to enjoy?
Our hearts entwined in love ♥
Forever, and blessed by Father above.

Arnold. 8:09am Jun 1.

Good Morning my Sweet Love. Oh how I yearn to be at your side and hold your soft hands! To hold you in my arms and kiss your warm lips. To snuggle and cuddle. To share our life and dreams. To plan and come and go together. For a while six weeks ago I pondered if I should remain single. This thought came to mind that maybe my Lord was asking me to do this. I could come and go whenever, whatever, wherever, however. Some advantages perhaps, I thought. Ten days later I concluded: those are exactly the things in my life I want to share with some lovely lady – to live every moment in companionship, to plan our lives together moment by moment; we would go together wherever. Everywhere! Whatever I would do so would she, whatever she would do so would I. Whenever. Whatever. Wherever. However. Then out of a faraway place this precious wonderful beautiful gift of God gives me her heart in the middle of last night and promises come to my house and home to be my Whenever Whatever and Wherever and However. My Lord is blessing me beyond my fondest dreams.

Arnold. 8:52am Jun 1.

When are we getting married Gloria? Why don't you come up either for the 1st of August weekend when our family has a campout and have the ceremony in some forest? Or if that's too soon (not for me!) how about the labour holiday weekend the first weekend in September. Then we could go to California at Christmas and have a great shindig with your family and friends.

Gloria. 11:29am Jun 1.

Good Morning you big lovable poet, planner and player of my heart strings. ♥ You wrote me a poem. I loved it!! I've been smiling all the way through these beautiful bird songs coming from your very own heart. God is truly wonderful!! I feel so full. Of what? Feelings that have been untapped and dormant until now. You have the key to my heart. ♥

Did you see on my profile that I also write poetry? Nothing has inspired me for years since widowhood. But now you are opening up the doors to my heart. They are swinging open to your love calls. You are truly amazing! I have also written songs. I think you will open that back up for me also. Everything was frozen in time until now.

I like your idea of August weekend, forest, with your family and campout ceremony. A dream come true. September is ok too, but the selfish part of me is wanting sooner. Crazy. . .yes??

God seems to be orchestrating something here Arnie darling. You big wonderful Canadian man! You waltz in and take my heart. You are welcome to it. ♥

I love you sweet man. I L O V E you, Arnold Stauffer.

Bye for now. . . ♥

Arnold. 4:12pm Jun 1.

Gloria! Gloria! Gloria! Just got home to get ready to go be the Bad Guy at Passion Play. I just read this and I'm at a loss for words. Your words just overwhelmed me. You are so sweet and willing and eager. First I laughed with excited joy. Then I cried like a baby – for JOY, when I suddenly realized that I was now starting to realize that I am experiencing what it means to fall in love again. I wondered about this. I knew what real love was for 48 years but have never walked my present path before, so wondered. Know I am beginning to know and understand, Gloria, because you are teaching me. What a teacher! Mama Mia. With love like ours we will live forever.

Arnold. 4:14pm Jun 1.

I realized today that we do not have each other's address or telephone. I need to hear your voice. Maybe when I get back Sunday evening. (Here I gave her my phone number and mailing address.)

4:17pm Jun 1. I pulled a half dozen pics off your FB and sent them to my daughter, and took my laptop to work and showed the gal there and my Boss, the President of the Good Health Club that owns the store. They were very impressed. Gloria, I feel like a country boy who just got a date for the big event with the Prom Queen.

4:21pm Jun 1. I so love the words you wrote today. I will guard forever the key to your heart – the greatest treasure I could have right now! My love calls are opening the door to your heart? Oooooooooohhh! Sweet. Oh how I love you! ♥

I will tell my daughter and sister to start getting ready for our August wedding. Some folks are going to say this is too soon. My "Boss" who is also the Chair of our Elders Board whom I been on the Board with for years, said, "It does not matter what others think, Arnold!" Jan, who knows my story well, told me, "Arnold, listen to others, but you are the one who has to decide. Follow your heart!" I followed my heart. When I sat down to my computer the other day, I did not intend to say all those loving things. But I was challenged to "open my heart" (Was that our Lord?) and it just tumbled out! Talk to you later today before I head for the Motor Home. ♥

Arnold. 6:48pm Jun 1.

Gloria! You've no idea what you've done to me! Just got to PP and had a bite to eat. On the way here I become so overwhelmed with joy and gratitude I cried. I was giving thanks to my Lord for bringing us together; that's the only explanation for it. Two "kindred spirits" – Anne's favourite phrase in Green Gables – who found each other. Do you realize August is only two months away? Are you an organized person and can get a plan together? I am wondering, because we have done this before if we should go for plain and simple. What would you think of us shopping together for some real nice designer jeans and tops? And do a real country look. I also have an idea for a ring. Instead of a formal engagement ring how about more of a "friendship" ring? There is a local lady who makes some real nice jewelry with silver and gold wire, very creative. We could get her to put on it a stylize initials G and A. Would you like to wear something like that? If so, what else would you want on it, maybe surrounded with a hcart. If you would rather have something else please do not hesitate to say so. This is just a suggestion. If we liked it maybe she could also make us matching wedding rings. Whatever your heart desires, my lovely Texan Bride. Wow! was that ever nice to say!! ♥ ♥ ♥ ♥ ♥ ♥

Oh yes, thanks for numbers + your mailing address. (She gave me hers.)

I also have a web cam I've never used. It can be hooked up to chat. Do you have a built in one on your computer?

Love and hugs my Arnie man. Now I will be thinking of you all the time. Gloria

We discovered Skype on Facebook and for the rest of June and til July 22 we chatted live via our computers. Very exciting to be able to communicate while looking at each other. It was so much fun beginning to get to know each other, and to make each other laugh. We would spend an hour, often longer, every day. This was a wonderful means of getting acquainted and becoming good friends. Thought it was a great idea to develop a friendship if we were going to get married!

July the 23 I hopped on a plane and arrived at Gloria's in Grande Prairie, Texas, that evening. The next day we applied for a marriage license and spent three minutes before a Texas Judge exchanging vows.

He was in the middle of a court case, directing the choosing of jury members. During a break he came to his office to tie our knot. As we walked out of his office, we kissed. Then I noticed about 50 folks in the hallway, prospective jurors waiting to be interviewed. I threw up both hands and shouted, "Yahoo! We just got married!" The whole crowd erupted in applause and joined in congratulating us. Our Texas reception.

50

Gloria's Story: From Widowhood to Wonderment

The sparkle in his eyes. The warm smile – a bit impish. He wore a neat western hat and matching shirt. "Who is this cute guy?" I wondered. I opened my email May 26th, 2012 and there he was – sent by ChristianMingle for my inspection. Immediately after admiring his picture I went to his profile. Everything I read there made me wonder, "Is this The Man God had promised me?"

I had spent several years visiting various Christian dating sites for someone who was "interesting" whom I could love, and who would love me – for the rest of my life. Most guys I found on these sites emphasized what they liked doing – riding horses, golfing, traveling, snorkeling, climbing mountains and sailing. But they were boring. I found much to my dismay that most could not spell or use decent grammar much less put a complete sentence together. Often they would say something off color, suggesting their designs on getting a woman were not highly moral.

Ready to give up on ever finding "Mr. Right," I was planning on shutting down my site. Then this wonderful western guy from Alberta, Canada popped up on my computer screen. I was very ready to check this man out!

In 2003 my life had abruptly changed. My husband, who had been the center of my life for 25 years, was called to heaven after struggling for a year with cancer. I was forced back into the work force, this time as a widow. The sudden aloneness was dramatic and very heavy.

Through the ten years following my husband's passing, I had dated some gentlemen. No one I found proved to be anything I wanted to get very serious about. I did make some friends but that was all, no one ever proved to be what I wanted until I spotted Arnold, the Canuck. At first sight his profile and smile really grabbed my attention – with his Western style hat and such a delightful smile. Earlier a gal on the Christian Mingle blog site had told us how she got her dates: "flirt, flirt, flirt!" So that's what I decided to do. Fortunately he responded to my initial flirtatious hello.

Although we were 2,000 miles apart, distance didn't really matter to me. That's what airplanes are for after all.

I had stopped communicating with divorced men; they carried way too much baggage. Widowers and I at least had some common ground to start a dialogue with. Some men just needed a listening ear and perhaps a bit of counseling from a woman's perspective. None played tunes on my heart strings, until this 6'2" Canadian started sending me love poems and messages every day. My kind of music! Although we lived a long way apart, if God was definitely in this, I was confident that he could make it happen.

Looking back I know it was God, because I was about to throw in the towel as far as wanting a mate again. I considered that I had possibly missed God's will for my life. Suddenly my spirit revived and my heart and mind came alive. As our relationship progressed for the next couple of days on Christian Mingle and then quickly moved to Facebook, we both began to see God's fingerprints all over our newfound blossoming relationship.

Arnie quickly agreed to my suggestion to meet on Facebook to get better acquainted and to meet family members. This proved to be a smart move. I wanted to ensure that he was not some guy cloned by some unscrupulous person who stole his identity, which had happened to me on more than one occasion. This fraudulent activity is rampant on the dating sites. We learned lots about each other from the several years of family and personal events on both our sites.

We discovered that we both loved our families and were loved in return. That was most important for both of us. Pictures of Christmas, Easter and other family get-togethers introduced us to each other's kids, grandkids, my great grandkids and some of our friends. We both liked what we found.

Arnie's first phone call quickly followed and was quite a shock. When I heard his voice it seemed so familiar to me, as if I had heard it before. We talked for 1.5 hours. I was either floating on air or bumping into walls for the next several days. The warmth of new love started quickly melting the iced over parts of my heart. Almost forgotten feelings began to flow again, swiftly releasing the dam that had held back my love for so long.

We began communicating on Facebook's private chat area, sometimes in real-time. Then we discovered Skyping, which allowed us to see each other while chatting. Our world quickly moved to fast-forward. I liked what I saw and heard and so did he. With his busy schedule managing the health food store, and being a part of the Canadian Passion Play, his time on-line was scarce, but we managed to keep in touch daily, often visiting for an hour and a half. Sometimes I wouldn't get to chat with him until after midnight, my time in Dallas. We were an hour apart.

He would be up early, leave me a message, or poem on our private Facebook chat place before heading to work. That's when my heart really came alive. Arnie could write poetry and love letters like no one else could or ever did. He was a Word Artisan. We found that we both had writing in our blood and hearts. After my husband passed away I had stopped writing poetry and songs, but suddenly my heart was flowing with lovely words and feelings that I thought long dead within me. I told him, "Arnie, your words of love have opened the doors of my heart!"

After so many years of being alone I now knew that someone had love for me and I him. I had almost given up asking God for that special someone to come into my life. God never once discouraged me from praying for another mate. My faith had always remained strong until just before I met Arnie. I began to grow weary from waiting on God. However, God brought this new found love about very quickly. Although Arnie hadn't been a widower very long he seemed very prepared to love again. He had had a long happy marriage which had ended sadly like mine. God is in the business of answering prayers, even when in my case took nine years and Arnie only eight months. God did indeed answer our prayers, even though circumstances seem to deny the truth of it.

Astonishingly, I had a dream about Arnie just months before we met on the Internet. He was standing beside me in an empty classroom. Soon after I arrived at his house I actually saw hanging in his closet the shirt he wore in that dream. Was that why his voice sounded familiar to me when we first spoke on the phone? We did talk some in my dream. Interestingly, Arnie is very familiar with classrooms since he was an educator for many years. So a year after the dream it finally made sense why I should first meet him on his familiar turf. I didn't even like school and yet I was to marry a teacher. God certainly does have a sense of humor!

At this writing we have been married for seven months. We still love to make each other laugh. We cook and clean up together, and come and go with each other. You perhaps can imagine that two people who have experienced life for seven decades have pretty much established their values, habits and patterns for every aspect of living. Often we bumped head-on into each other, sometimes with a crash! For the first several months we had lots of differences to sort out as we worked to establish our life together. Sometimes it was troubling, but always our mutual love covered our disagreements. We took it to the Lord for his Counseling. He has been showing us how this will and does work with "his" help.

We look forward to the Alberta Spring and Summer to plant a small garden and work in Arnie's Barnboard Woodart Studio. We plan on doing traveling and exploring Canada.

As always, we plan to have the warmth of summer in our hearts and spring in our steps.

God is good! God answers our prayers but on his time table! Patience pays off.

Conclusion

51

Learnings, Affirmations, Conclusions and Advice

D ifficult experiences teach us. Hopefully. If they do not, we are doomed to have to learn the same principles and lessons later. Rick Warren, blogging after his son committed suicide, summed it up this way. We have three choices; you decide which will happen to you. "When difficult things happen they either destroy, define, or develop you." This chapter attempts to summarize what dying and death and finding new love taught me. I like to think that there has been more development than destruction.

As I shared my inner most thought, hurts, struggles and conclusions day after day on Facebook, people responded with encouragement. By sharing I opened myself up for their encouragement and counsel. But so many spoke about how my journaling had encouraged them, and helped them deal with issues in their lives. Dozens suggested I put all this in a book. For a long time I could not go back, but now twenty months after Betty left, I've completed the first rough draft and edited it a dozen times. My hope that this story – really the story of dozens of folks who were part of my odyssey – will encourage many. May you be drawn to a deeper relationship, not only with folks who care about you, but especially with our Lord and Saviour, Jesus. He is our real hope and strength, our comfort, grace and wisdom to maintain victory when defeat looms.

Here are some conclusions for the lessons of these past twenty months.

Lesson One: When the going gets tough, people of faith go to God

Shortly after we heard the devastating news that Betty had untreatable pancreatic /liver cancer I had lunch with my Pastor. After eating and talking about our situation, he leaned back in his chair and said, "Arnold, this is going to be a tough test of your faith."

I stared at him for a moment, wondering why he would say that. Does he know something that I do not? Has God told him about something that is going to happen that I am not aware of?

Thinking back over the years, Betty and I experienced a few severe setbacks and disappointments: a house that would not sell for many months, causing us to lose a bundle of cash. Later I had a good job going bad and lost it, and so on. But each of those heavy duty events turned into faith training sessions.

It was at the bottom of a deep valley of disappointment that I learned to praise God. Praise re-focuses my mind and spirit from my troubles on to the Ruler of the Universe to make any difficulty I am experiencing seem much smaller. In fact, miniscule – in the face of an all-powerful but loving God.

When everything was falling down around me then I would turn to the last chapter in Habakkuk. Mountains were tumbling, waters rising, warriors were attacking, farm animals had disappeared from the barn, fields were empty of crops and pantry shelves were absolutely bare. Could there be a list of events more devastating in an agricultural community? But what was Habakkuk's response? Though the worst possible situations are before me, he said:

I will rejoice in the Lord,
I will be joyful in God my Savior.
The Sovereign Lord is my strength;
he makes my feet like the feet of a deer,
he enable me to go on the height.

Was my faith "tested"? Not the right word. Life's lessons taught me to run toward my God, not away. Getting the boot from my only pastorate was the most grievous loss I had suffered to this point. During the next few months Betty and I listened a thousand times to a cassette titled, "Joy comes in the morning." A song of faith and hope. A chance to get our hearts and minds off the past to focus on God's hand in the present and future. It is too easy to revel in our misery at the bottom of the pit. Sometimes we want to, in a distorted sense of self-worth, continue to slosh around in the mud and slop of self-pity. Why should this be happening to us? Why are we being punished? We struggled out of that mess by practicing praise to our Father even though we did not always "feel" that sentiment.

My unspoken plan was to keep my eyes upon my Lord, to continue to praise him whatever, whenever. To drive myself passionately toward him – NOT away from him. If our faith is worth anything, bad things should turn us to God, not in any other direction.

Sure, I was unhappy with what God did to Betty. I told him so. But I learned long ago from studying the Psalms that God does not stomp us down when we are angry with him and tell him so. When we heatedly tell him what he has done wrong he never blasts us into oblivion with a bolt of lightning. His shoulder is very large. Big enough to handle a million such expressions from every spot in the planet. He created us and knows our frame, understands our deepest emotions – and offers his warm and comforting breast to cry on. In the midst of my deepest hurts I have imagined myself snuggled in the arms of Jesus. Just like an infant, I sought his warmth and desired to receive his succor.

For the two months that I watched Betty slowly starve to death, I could not imagine a more cruel thing for God to do to her – and to me. In an earlier essay in this book I explain why I take the view that "God did this to Betty. I came to believe it was God who did it, but not because she deserved it or knowingly did anything to bring it upon herself. It was the sin of mankind that brought his curse upon all of us – the curse of pain, suffering, dying and death. That was an amazing revelation to me to understand sin and suffering from this perspective. It helped to ease the burden. Human beings suffer, each one of us – somehow, sometime – but always.

On the back of the paper cover of Randy Alcorn's book, *If God is Good: Faith in the Midst of Suffering and Evil*, he asks, "What if suffering is God's invitation to trust him? And to hope for a better world?" This was Jesus' provision when he died on the cross, after hours of extraordinarily painful suffering. His provision is the final release from all suffering, forever. That's the hope and promise. True faith directs our minds and hearts toward Father. A solid relationship with him hopes in him for a new future, if not now, when we enter into the final phase of our eternal life.

I've learned to fix my "eyes on Jesus, the author and perfecter of our faith" (Hebrews 12:2). As this verse also says, "For the joy before him (he) endured the cross". Erwin McManus, in *Seizing Your Divine Moment,* says that "The journey through divine moments is not an escape route from personal suffering. In fact it strengthens our resolve to suffer in the now for the greater good that can be accomplished." (p. 140) McManus points out that whenever God is involved, the story is not mysterious. He wins. If I am on his side I also win and share in the celebration. Because we know that our story ends in a guaranteed glorious victory we sometimes think that every chapter should highlight a series of smaller victories. "In fact," McManus says, "it is better described as a roller-coaster ride with nauseating ups and downs." If my life, and the life of my loved one, is part of God's great story, death has significance and becomes part of the great final victory.

Lesson Two: God is good; he is good all the time.

God is good. He is good all the time.
Is he? Really?
We sometimes find this difficult to understand when struggling in despair at the foot of the mountain. The wonderful peaks on which we used to dwell now look so far away that we may never get back up there. And we feel that way about getting back to God – he's so far away.

When Betty was gone and I had severely grieved, endured supreme loneliness, I began to look around for another wife. Betty told me to, and this helped me get past the guiltiness I felt when I started thinking about looking. It felt like I was betraying her. But then this looking became a bit exciting as it helped pull me out of my agony. Hope stirred within me. And I started to smile again. I knew Betty wanted me to be happy, so I made a deliberate decision to be so. In this beginning recovery mode as I struggled toward the mountain top, I started saying again, "God is good; he is good all the time"

But I had said this also when I was grappling with the horror of cancer's devastation and the slow death of My Love. I have to admit that I took some pride at that time as I remembered I was able to say that when trouble was all around and in me. Now I could say it also when God's hand of good was more clearly seen.

Is God always Good? We say that he is, but why do we? Is he? Always? Hard to answer in the midst of supreme difficulty. I did say that at the bottom of the mountain, but did so from a strong faith and experience that had taught me that from past events.

Alcorn makes the point that the real matter is our dis-functioning hearing device. Or perhaps our seeing apparatus. We always want to *know* the "why". Why is this happening to me? What did we do to deserve this? As rational beings we want to know and think we do have the right to know.

The truth is that God's ways are beyond finding out. Who can fathom what goes on in the mind of the Almighty God of the Universe? Acorn quotes from one of Charles Spurgeon's sermons, who said,

> Providence is wonderfully intricate. Ah! you want always to see through Providence, do you not? You never will, I assure you. You have not eyes good enough. You want to see what good that affliction was to you; you must believe it. You want to see how it can bring good to the soul; you may be enabled in a little time; but you cannot see it now; you must believe it. Honor God by trusting him.

I really do not want to know the mind of God. If I did, that would put me his level of understanding and that would blow me away. Couldn't handle such a level of knowledge – it would destroy me. But why can't he at least let me know how come I am in this fix? But who am I to demand reasons from the Almighty?

Philip Yancy, in *Reaching for the Invisible God* (p. 57), notes that "The Bible supplies no systematic answers to the 'Why?' questions and often avoids them entirely." Sometimes even minor difficulty provokes a trust crisis, but "we dare not tread into areas God has sealed off as his domain. Divine providence is a mystery that only God understands. . .for a simple reason: no time-bound human, living on a rebellious planet, blind to the realities of the unseen world, has the ability to comprehend such answers." This, he writes, was in a nutshell God's reply to Job.

In the midst of his agony Job demanded reasons from God, but later, at the end of his long saga of sorrow he had to repent. God asked him, "Who is this that obscures my counsel without knowledge?" Job then admitted, "Surely I spoke of things I did not understand, things too wonderful for me to know. . . .My ears had heard of you but now my eyes have seen you. Therefore I despise myself and repent in dust and ashes." (Job 42:1-6)

At the end Job had gained a higher understanding about God's ways, but admitted there was a lot he did not know. Did he now believe that God is always Good? Probably.

240

Ask the "Why?" questions, but do not expect to always receive an answer.

Faith believes in God's ultimate unfailing Goodness. As Betty starved to death before my eyes over a sixty day period I don't think I ever disbelieved in God's goodness. When 120 of us prayed for Betty's healing and the heavens were totally silent, I had to submit to his sovereignty. You bet I was angry with him at times and told him so. I asked "why?" but heard no answer. But seven decades of life and faith helped me know and believe in his goodness. If I cannot trust God in the valley then I don't want him around on the mountain top either. King David wrote, "Good and upright is the Lord. . . .All the ways of the Lord are loving and faithful." (Psalm 25:8, 10)

In Psalm 34 David speaks of affliction, fears, shame, poverty, a broken heart and crushed spirit, and troubles. But he extols the Lord at all times and praise is always on his lips. He rejoices in affliction and glorifies his Lord. "Taste and see," he says, "that the Lord is good." I knew that before I started down this path with Betty.

Moses said, "Lord, you have been our dwelling place." (Psalm 90:1) He also speaks of trouble and sorrow and death, "The length of our days is seventy years – or eighty, if we have the strength; yet their span is but trouble and sorrow." But he turns to "God's "unfailing love". Betty was 70, so she had a "biblical span" of years. And her share of pain and trouble. But throughout, together, we found the Lord has been our address – the address of our dwelling place. Years ago I wrote this beside verse one: "God is my permanent address." I have experienced his unfailing love. With Moses I want to "sing for joy and be glad all (my) days. . . .for as many days as (I) have seen trouble." (Psalm 90:10-15) Trouble or otherwise, God is Good.

Lesson Three: God sometimes is frightingly silent. Now what do I do?

Why do I keep the faith when I slowly watch my Love of 48 years slowly ravaged by the evil of cancer? All the time knowing that it was because of God's curse on mankind's sin that causes her sufferingly slow death? Hundreds of people prayed for her, many in faith believing she would be healed. In response to James' instructions, we called for a healing service. One hundred folks showed up and the Elders prayed for Betty's healing. Six weeks later she died. Why didn't I walk away from God when he did not keep his promises?

When the disciples found Jesus' teaching hard to accept and many left. He asked the remaining Twelve, "Are you leaving too?" Simon Peter, the usual spokesman, replied, "Lord, to whom shall we go?"

I agree with Yancey (p. 39) that there is a definite lack of alternatives. "The only thing more difficult than having a relationship with an invisible God," he notes, "is having no such relationship." We all can identify with the demoniac's father in Mark 9 who said to Jesus, "Lord, I believe. Help my unbelief."

Why did God not heal Betty when so many believing folks asked him? I don't know.

Why were the heavens silent? I have absolutely no idea.

Yancey reminds us that many of our Biblical heroes, Job, Abraham, Habakkuk and other prophets, along with many on the Hebrews 11 list, "endured long droughts when miracles did not happen, when urgent prayers dropped back to earth unanswered, when God seemed not just invisible but wholly absent. . . .We may also experience times when God stays silent and all the Bible's promises seem glaringly false." (53)

We forget so often that the Bible never promises us life without trials. Rather, we are told out time here on earth will often be plagued with difficulties. God does faithfully promise to be present in the bad times.

I learned long ago that true faith is only authentic when it stays strong when the world is falling down around us and God seems to be off in Timbuktu. If I cannot trust my God in the depths of the mud in the valley, then I don't want to hang out with him on the mountain top. A capricious god could not create and rule a universe, nor could he earn the trust and faithfulness of his creation.

James (1:2) tells us to, "Consider it pure joy, my brothers, whenever you face trials of many kinds, because you know that the testing of your faith develops perseverance." Gerald Mann (*When the Bad Times are over for Good: Transforming Trouble into Triumph*, p. 21) points out that trouble can trigger tough faith, which is not unexamined faith. "Tough faith is not fair weather faith, where we believe because it's comfortable to do so. Tough faith is when you keep believing without supportive evidence." You cannot have tough faith – the kind that causes you to grow – until you have met God at the bottom of the valley, shoulder deep in the muck. James says (1:4) that if you persevere in this faith effort you will reach a completeness or maturity. Then you will lack nothing, that is, be satisfied with your status and state of life.

In the Western world we attempt to wish away the reality of pain and tragedy. When it comes we seek a pill or program or a self-help book to cure it and make it go away. We look for magic medicines and miracles. As Mann (2) says, "The Christian approach to suffering keeps getting lost in our frantic attempts to avoid pain. What is the 'Christian Approach'? To *metabolize* suffering – to accept it, embrace it, ingest it, digest it, and transform it into strength." Jesus endured suffering; he did not run from it. He hung on, and "ingested, digested and transformed the Cross into the Resurrection." In the real world we find a way to use our pain instead of denying it or avoiding it (4).

Of course the ultimate prize of tough faith is eternal life. "Blessed is the man who perseveres under trial," says James (1:12), "because when he has stood the test, he will receive the crown of life that God has promised to those who love him."

Again I return to Habakkuk. He had this mystery figured. He introduced his oracle by haranguing God for his silence and his do-nothing posture. Near the end his heart was pounding and his lip quivered in fear, decay crept into his bones, and his legs trembled. He was starving: no crops, figs, grapes, olives, sheep or cattle. Yet his final decision on the matter was to rejoice in the Lord, be joyful in God his Savior, and depend on the Sovereign Lord to be his strength. He is my hero in trouble; I seek to rejoice and be joyful because I serve a Sovereign God who knows what is best for me and mine. Habakkuk asked the "Why?" question, as we all do when in despair. But he ended up realizing that all there was left for him to do was be joyful in praise of his God.

Some Practical Advice: A Summary

1. Expect difficult times in life. Keep your faith strong in the good and happy times. This will help you keep strong when the world falls down around you.

2. Get out of the "woe is me", "why did this happen to me?" mode as quickly as possible. Why should it not happen to you? The Bible promises that our time on this earth will be filled with many difficulties. Jesus said, "In this world you will have trouble" (John 16:33). But God promised to be with us in their midst. "Take heart," Jesus continues, "I have overcome the world." Count on it, even though for the present you cannot see, touch or feel him. In him we may have peace. Why you? You may never know the answer. Our understanding of the mystery of suffering is limited. "The secret things belong to the Lord" (Deuteronomy 29:29). The answer to suffering: endure, seek God's comfort, learn your lessons, become strong. Thank God for this opportunity to develop your spiritual endurance, strength and maturity.

3. "Its' not fair!" I shouted at God when Betty was slowly starving to death. Doris Dougherty said that "No greater tragedy can be found than that of a soul crying out 'It's not fair!' and allowing the cold waters of cynicism to overflow and to drown him." (Quoted by Charles Stanley, *When Tragedy Strikes*, 22). She then points out "that there is no greater victory than to plunge into these waters where the bottom cannot be felt, but the strong person will 'swim until I can!'" You got to swim until your toes touch the bottom.

4. When you are at the bottom of the valley the only direction to look is up. Look around for God's touches, his fingerprints. Listen for his footsteps. You may not see or hear him today, or this week or next. Sooner or later, you will. Don't give up. He may speak to you through a friend, a sermon, a song, a movie, during the night in a dream, or from his Word. He has not deserted you. He may be quiet for a time, but he did not really take a hike. He is nearby watching, collecting your tears, waiting for an appropriate moment. When David was in great trouble and distressed (Psalm 56:8), he asked God to put his tears in a bottle (KJV), to be preserved and looked upon. He knew that God was recording his lament, keeping a record of his tears. Therefore he trusted God to keep him from stumbling, and to help him walk in the light of life.

5. Over the years I have learned to ask God, "What is it you want me to learn in and from this difficulty?" I am fearful that if I do not learn the current lesson, I might have to face another "event" intended to sharpen my learning device. Don't want that! So I look for evidence of what God

243

expects of me. Where he wants me to grow and mature in my faith. And I also look for the good that God is accomplishing, for he works good out of evil.

6. Do not keep mum. The Christian Community exists for you. Go to it. Talk. Share your difficulties with a listening, caring person or group. I heard several stories of some who did not do so when a loved one died. They became angry when someone mentioned the person's name. An individual who bottles up grief becomes sullen, sad, and eventually ill. Talk about your struggles. Ask your "why" questions. Share even you most personal issues with a trusting friend. Do not bottle them up and thereby poison your soul and mind. Our immune system is strengthened when we express our emotions.

7. Happiness is a decision. Decide to be. Keep busy. Listen to uplifting and inspirational music. Be with people. Avoid prescriptive chemicals; there are other ways to maintain a positive outlook.

8. Maintain good health. During tense and fearful times you will likely have to increase your intake of vitamins and food supplements. Avoid, if possible, prescriptive chemicals, which always have negative side effects. Eat lots of fresh, raw vegetables and fruit. Learn about superfoods.

9. Maintain a strong spiritual life. Search your Bible for answers to your questions. Draw deeply from your believing friends and pastor. Talk to God. Lay on his broad shoulders your feelings, not matter how harsh they seem. He knows about them anyway and completely understands their nature and what you need to rise up and be healed. Do not be afraid to express to God your toughest questions. If you are angry with him, tell him. The prophets did, so did David. Not small minded or petty, he tolerates our questions, doubts and even outrageous anger. Rather, he is standing by and welcomes them. He is hurting along with you. He understands and will not abandon you.

10. Cry. Weep. In our culture men are not supposed to. I was often embarrassed when tears would burst unbidden when I talked about Betty, sometimes months after she left. So many folk knew better, encouraging me to let them flow. Tears have a function. They not only help release tension, but they carry away poisons that build up in times of emotional stress. As Mitsch and Brookside say, "they wash our wounds" (67). Jesus wept, so did David, Abraham and Elijah. Tears are an integral part of grieving; without them we cannot heal. David wrote, "weeping may remain for a night, but rejoicing comes in the morning" (Psalm 30:5).

11. Be patient with folks who attempt to offer you comfort but who have no idea what you are experiencing. They sincerely want to offer you succor, but have only clichés that seem empty and fall on you like a bucket of ice. Many people simply do not have the experience or knowledge to know what to say or do. You can help them. Sometimes the best thing to do is offer them a smile, if you can muster one, and a thank you. Suggest to them something specific for which they can pray. If there is even some small thing they can do for you, tell them so. This will bless them for finding a way to bless you. Forgive them for their lack of insight and knowledge.

12. Search out those who have gone before you, in a similar experience. They will have some understanding, and are in the best position to encourage you and offer hope. Listen to their stories and their advice.

13. Get some help with practical stuff. When Betty left so did the dreams we shared about the rest of our life together. We were creating woodart and great bread for the markets. That ended. But my back yard was full of huge piles of cedar posts, ancient windows and all kinds of odds and ends I intended to use in my Barnboard Woodart Studio. Betty joked that I had collected enough material for the next fifty years! It had to be cleaned up, but I was so devastated I did not know where to start. Just recently my brother, Lyle, came along and helped paint our house. While here he suggested we also clean up the back yard. I knew it all had to go, somewhere. However, after 20 months of dithering, I did not have the energy to do anything about it by myself. He jumped in and we began hauling truck loads to the dump, and cedar posts to the neighbors for firewood. I picked and chose a few things to store for my woodart. Now it's almost clean and I can start building the planned deck. He did me a wonderful favour in getting me out of my lethargy. I should have gotten help long before.

14. Remember, *nothing* can separate you from God's love that is in Christ Jesus our Lord. Nothing in all creation (Romans 8:38-39). "You wonder how long my love will last? Find your answer on a splintered cross, on a craggy hill. That's me you see up there, your maker, your God, nail-stabbed and bleeding. Covered with spit and sin-soaked. That's your sin I'm feeling. That's your death I'm dying. That's your resurrection I'm living. That's how much I love you." (Lucado, *In the Grip of Grace*, 180)

15. "Now choose life, so that you and your children may live and that you may love the Lord your God, listen to his voice, and hold fast to him. For the Lord is your life" (Deuteronomy 30:20). This is your place of safety, holding fast, clinging to the Lord every hour of every day. For Jim Cymbala (*God's Grace from Ground Zero*, p.45) this clinging brings to mind the image "of a mother who is filled with joy as she nurses and cherishes her clinging infant, who in turn finds satisfaction and security in her." The Lord

245

is your life; cling to him for nurture as the infant does to its mother. "Come near to God," wrote James, "and he will come near to you" (4:8). Christ is your life (Colossians 3:4).

Appendices

Appendix One

Henderson's Six-Part Cancer Cure Protocol

Adapted by Arnold from chapter 5,
Cancer-Free: Your Guide to Gentle, Non-Toxic Healing, Bill Henderson
www.Beating-Cancer-Gently

1. Immune System Stimulation: Beta-1,3D Glucan. No cancer survives if the person's immune system is strong. This product gives it a boost. An insoluble fibre-like substance, it passes through the small intestine into the lymphatic system and into the blood stream and then into all the body's organs and bone marrow. It is carried by immune cells (phagocytes) that gobble things. It "primes" the neutrophil immune cells to recognize cancer cells and kill them. These cells normally do not "see" the cancer cells but Beta-1,3D Glucan binds to the cancer cells causing the immune cells to recognize cancer cells as fungus. This is the "single most effective immune modulator known." Obtainable from: www.AboutBertaGlucan.com/bspecial. 678-560-1808. (Take one 500 mg capsule per 50 pounds before eating or drinking anything.) IMMUNE SYSTEM BOOSTING IS PRIORITY ONE for cancer patients.

1a. Alkalizing, ionizing water filter for drinking water (from same source). Provides pure water while helping your body become more alkaline and get rid of free radicals. (www.BetterWayHealth.com)

2. Cottage Cheese/Flaxseed Oil Smoothie (The Budwig Diet). This mix uniquely kills cancer cells by the billions and makes every other cell in our body healthier at the same time. The cottage cheese is a perfect carrier for the oil. Once the flaxseed oil with its high concentration of Omega 3 oil gets to the cell wall or membrane it surrounds it with little magnets that "suck in" oxygen – which cancer cell hate. Simply mix two-thirds cup of organic cottage cheese (no preservatives), 1% or 2% fat, with 6 tablespoons of flaxseed oil. To make the mix more edible add Stevia as a sweetener and some almonds, walnuts, strawberries or blueberries. First,

mix the oil and cottage cheese in a blender and then add other items. (When cottage cheese is blended with the oil it loses all its dairy properties [casein, lactose, etc.], so people who are lactose intolerant can take this mixture.) Eat as soon as possible as it oxidizes. Use cold pressed flaxseed oil, available at most health food stores. Order Barleans (the best and freshest) from 800-445-3529.

3. Heart Plus & Green Tea Extract (Vitamin C & Lysine/Proline). The latter two are amino acids. Some folks strengthen this compound by adding green tea extract. A first priority for the cancer person is to slow down or stop the process of metastasis of the cancer cells. This treatment is gentle, non-toxic and readily available. It also gives a bonus of protection from or treatment of heart inflammation. A good source: Our Health Co-op, which sells it as "Heart Plus". This product includes rose hips. Order Green Tea extract separately. Take six capsules HP + 3 caplets GTE, daily, with food or between meals. Order this product from www.ourhealthcoop.com/product_p/gp.htm

4. Barley Power. Almost every malady can be traced to an enzyme deficiency of some kind. In this product there are over 3,000 different enzymes – all of the 3,000 that are in our bodies. Take 20 tablets per day, 6 or 7 – 15 minutes before each meal. If not doing three meals a day, take two hours after eating. Source: 800-358-0777 or 724-946-9057. www.GreenSupreme.net. You can also order this product (called Greens Plus) from www.ourhealthcoop.com/product_p/gp.htm

5. A Cancer-Fighting Diet. MAXIMIZE: raw whole vegetables. EAT: gluten-free, sprouted breads, flaxseed crackers, cereals (millet, quinoa, amaranth, buckwheat, etc.) without gluten and with unsweetened almond milk – not soy milk), lentils, seeds, nuts (no peanuts), fruit (except for berries and pineapple – a good cancer fighting fruit – limit fruit to one piece a day as it blasts your pancreas with fruit sugar). TOTALLY AVOID: sugar in any form (use Stevia or Agave), processed foods – in any form (If it is not in the form God made it, don't eat it.); animal protein (including red meat, fish, chicken, seafood, shellfish, eggs – all are difficult for the body to digest); dairy (also hard for body to digest): includes ice cream, cheese, butter (remember that cottage cheese is okay blended with the flax seed oil); gluten: bread, cereal, etc. – gluten rapidly turns into glucose which cancer cells love; other: drinking sodas (pop), alcoholic drinks, caffeine (well maybe one cup a day). Avoid vegetable juice as it lacks fibre – of which cancer people need lots.

6. Vitamin/Mineral Supplement. See your doctor for a recommendation regarding this item. The product Bill recommends is not available in Canada. (You can check out this product on: www.DrDavidWilliams.com)

Bill says: "If you follow this regimen diligently every day for about 6 to eight weeks you will not just improve your condition, you will probably be cancer free."

Appendix Two

Betty's Favourite Recipes

Introduction

I often told Betty that she has beautiful hands. Although in her 50s and 60s they became a bit gnarled with arthritis, I saw them as wonderfully attractive. With them she sewed dozens of cute dresses, tops, shirts and slacks when our children were little. As they grew she made all kinds of clothes for them and for me – even stretch pants and blue jeans. When double knit arrived she took a course in how to sew with this stretchy material. And another course in how to make blue jeans. The kids loved her blue jeans until as young teenagers they saw that their friends had special labels on theirs that were missing on Mom's homemade editions. She also knitted and crocheted, and for many years cross-stitched. Her cross-stitch art graces many homes as she often gave them as special occasion gifts. That is, until the kids and I complained that we had none of her great art on our walls. In a few months she stitched more than one for each of us.

All our married life she baked our bread, something she could do like nobody else. Everyone who was blessed enough to taste her dinner buns raved about them. This was one of our Son-in-law's favourite topics when he came for Easter, Thanksgiving or Christmas dinner. Sitting at our kitchen table, I often watched her punch down a batch of bread dough or roll out dough for sticky buns or whole wheat cinnamon buns. And then roll them up and cut them, then place them in baking pans.

I have often wondered how she was able to add her extra touch of flavour and goodness. Finally, one day not so long ago while watching her skillfully prepare a batch of dough, and talking with her about this, I concluded it had very much to do with her touch. She, from expertise gained over many years of baking, could tell by the touch of her beautiful hands when the dough had reached just the right stickiness. She read with her hands whether the dough needed a bit more water, oil or flour and always seemed to get it just right.

For years I've occasionally suggested that if she would let me word process her stack of recipes she could find the one she or I needed so much quicker. But she seemed to enjoy paging through her six inch stack of hand written recipes and others cut out from magazines and newspapers on cards of all shapes. She always found the needed one. Some were yellowed with age, probably 40 or 50 years old. You saw in an earlier chapter a picture of one of several she used most – Todd's favourite as a teenager – lasagna made with spinach. Tattered and stained, it was used probably hundreds of times.

Betty was a "foody". On our shelves and in drawers are dozens of recipe books, some over 60 years old. Cooking and baking was her occupation and hobby. For several years she read the Calgary Herald and reviewed several food newsletters from which she occasionally found another item she wanted to try. Some she then added to her pile, others went into the trash bucket if the finished product did not meet our expectations. Everywhere we lived she exchanged recipes with friends and we usually purchased the locally produced book full of everyone's favourite recipes. She gives the bride-to-be a big fat recipe book at her bridal shower.

– Written December 2011, when I started word processing these recipes while we lived together in palliative care. Since Betty left, I have edited into the past tense.

(FM) indicates this item was a specialty at the local Farmers' Market.

Bread, Buns, Loaves and Waffles

White Bread (FM)

In a large bowl dissolve 1 cup of sugar in 6 cups of warm water. Add 1 cup milk and one egg (optional). All at once add 8 cups flour, 2 tbsp salt and ½ cup melted shortening. Mix quickly and then add 2 tbsp yeast. Whip up thoroughly. Now add 6 cups more flour and mix with wooden spoon. With hands add 1 to 1½ cups flour until dough doesn't stick to bowl. Put 1 tbsp oil or shortening in bowl and knead dough just until a nice round ball is formed. Cover with plastic and place in a non-drafty area, to rise. (A *slightly* warmed oven is best for this.) Let rise to double in size twice, and punch it down each time. When it rises the third time cut into 7 equal parts – makes 7 loaves.

Multi-Grain Bread (FM)

Betty's Multi-Grain bread has made her an icon in Three Hills and community – and from Rocky Mountain House to Calgary. She chose this specialty for the Farmers' Market because other vendors were selling white bread. She also wanted a very healthy product, a criteria which this bread very much meets. It is packed with both nutrition and flavour. She adapted this recipe from one given her by her Sister-in-Law, Mary.

Item	5 loaves	4 loves
skim milk	2½ cups	2 cups
water	¾ cup	$^2/_3$ cup
canola oil	$^2/_3$ cup	½ cup
molasses	$^1/_3$ cup	¼ cup
sugar	½ cup	$^1/_3$ cup
salt	1 tbsp + ¾ tsp	1 tbsp
water	3¼ cup	2 $^2/_3$ cup
cracked wheat & rye	$^7/_8$ cup	¾ cup
oatmeal	$^2/_3$ cup	½ cup
sunflower seeds	$^2/_3$ cup	½ cup
oat bran, flax, ground flax	$^1/_3$ cup each	½ cup each
yeast ~ Fermipan	2 tbsp	1½ tbsp
whole wheat flour	7½ cups	6 cups
unbleached flour	about 5 cups	4 cups

Raisin Bread (FM)

½ cup canola oil
½ cup sugar
<2 tsp salt
<2 tsp cinnamon
1¼ cups milk
¾ cup water

2 to 3 eggs
1½ tbsp yeast
2 cups washed raisins
7 cups flour (4 white, 3 unbleached)
Makes 4 loaves

White Dinner Buns (FM)

Makes 4 dozen
4¾ cups water
$7/_8$ cup sugar
$2/_3$ cup oil
$1^1/_3$ tbsp salt
3 eggs (or 2 large)
$2^2/_3$ tbsp yeast
7 cups Robin Hood white flour
The remainder, use unbleached

Dinner (FM)

Makes 4 dozen
4¾ cups water
$2/_3$ cup sugar
$2/_3$ cup oil
$1^1/_3$ tbsp salt
3 eggs (or 2 large)
$2^2/_3$ tbsp yeast
$1/_3$ cup molasses
8 cups whole wheat flour

	Two Dozen Buns	One Dozen Buns	Two Dozen WW Buns
Water	$2^1/_3$ cups	$1^1/_6$ cup	$2/_3$ cups
Sugar	under ½ cup	> ¼ cup	$1/_3$ cup
Molasses	—	—	¼ cup
Oil	$1/_3$ cup	$1/_6$ cup	$1/_3$ cup
Salt	> 1tbsp	½ tbsp	1 tbsp
Eggs	1 large	1 small	1 large
Yeast	1½ tbsp	¾ tbsp	1½ tbsp
Flour	3½ cups	1¾ cups	4 cups whole wheat

Multi-Grain Buns (FM)

	Four Dozen	Two Dozen
Water	3¼ cups	$1^2/_3$ cups
skim milk	1½ cups	¾ cup
Sugar	$2/_3$ cup	½ cup
Molasses	$1/_3$ cup	$1/_6$ cup
Oil	$2/_3$ cup	$1/_3$ cup
Salt	$1^1/_3$ tbsp	$2/_3$ tbsp
Eggs	3	1 lge or 2 small
Yeast	$2^2/_3$ tbsp	$1^1/_3$ tbsp
whole wheat flour	7 cups	3½ cups
unbleached flour	about 5 cups	2½
Oatmeal	1 cup	½ cup
ground flax	¼ cup	$1/_8$ cup

Flax	$^{1}/_{6}$ cup	$1^{1}/_{3}$ cup
sunflower seeds	½ cup	¼ cup

Buns (Two Hour)

3 cups water
8 tbsp sugar
6 tbsp oil
1 tbsp salt
2 tbsp Fermipan instant yeast

2 eggs
7 to 8 cups flour – enough to make a workable dough
Mix yeast and 4 cups flour

In a separate bowl, mix eggs, sugar, salt, oil and water. Add flour/yeast mixture. Blend, add remaining flour and let rise 15 minutes two times. Punch down but do not knead. After the second time form into buns and put them into greased baking pans, cover, and let rise for one hour. Bake at 350° for 15 to 18 minutes. Makes 4 to 5 dozen buns.

Cinnamon Buns

Using the above bun recipe: Divide the dough in half and roll into rectangles.

Combine the following *for each rectangle*: ¼ cup melted butter, ½ cup brown sugar, ½ cup raisins, 1½ tsp cinnamon. Spread the mix on the dough rectangle, roll up, cut into 16 buns. Put in 9 x 9 pan and let rise for 1 hour. Bake at 375° for 20 to 25 minutes

Bun or Cinnamon Bun Dough (FM)

Betty's earliest recipe. She keeps this one on top of the microwave with all her Farmers' Market recipes.

In a large bowl dissolve 1½ cups sugar in 4 cups warm water. Add 3 beaten eggs and 1½ half cups milk. All at once add 8 cups flour, ½ cup melted shortening and 2 tbsp salt. Mix quickly. Add 1 tbsp yeast and whip us thoroughly. Add 5 cups flour and stir with wooden spoon. With hands mix in another 1½ cups flour – until dough does not stick to bowl. Put 1 tbsp oil or shortening in bowl and knead dough just until a nice round ball is formed. Cover with plastic and place in a non-drafty area to rise. A *slightly* warmed oven is best. Lest rise to double its size twice, then punch down each time. When raised the third time roll it out.

Syrup for Cinnamon Buns. Use a good amount of margarine, heavy on the brown sugar and cinnamon. 2 cups white sugar, 2 cups brown sugar, 3 cups hot water and a sprinkle of salt. Dissolve, let cool and cover bottom of well margarined pans. Don't butter sides of pans.

Moisten underside edge of roll with water and stretch – so it sticks to the table. Bake at 340°. Watch closely so they do not get too brown – probably about ten minutes for each side. It is a good idea to turn them 180° about half way through.

Whole Wheat Cinnamon Buns (FM)

2¹/₃ cups water
½ cup oil
½ cup sugar
2 tsp salt

2 eggs 1½ tbsp yeast
5 cups whole wheat flour
About 1 cup of white flour

Mix and let rise for 20 minutes. Cut in half. Roll out thin – about 12 inches square, spread with Becel (margarine) and ¾ cup brown sugar and a generous sprinkle of cinnamon. Roll loosely. Cut in eight pieces. Put in pans and pour sauce over them. Let rise for 20 minutes. Bake just under 350° for 13 minutes, turn and bake another 13 minutes.

Sauce: ¾ cup brown sugar, ¾ cup whipping cream, ½ cup butter.

Gingerbread (whole wheat)

½ cup butter
2 tbsp sugar
¾ cup light molasses
1 cup flour
1 cup whole wheat flour
1 tsp ginger
¾ tsp soda
½ tsp salt

2 eggs
½ cup milk
½ tsp cinnamon
½ mace or nutmeg
½ cup chopped walnuts
½ cup raisons
3 tbsp candied lemon peel

Melt butter in sauce pan. Add sugar and molasses; stir to blend. In a large bowl sift flours, spices, soda, and salt. Stir in nuts and raisins. Beat eggs and milk and add to the bowl along with molasses mix. Stir to moisten all ingredients, then beat until well blended. Turn into a buttered 8 inch pan. Bake at 350° for 40 minutes. or until well done. Serve warm. Makes about 10 servings.

Sticky Buns (FM)

Betty was known far and wide for her delicious sticky buns. Ever since a leading lady from the Oriole Park Missionary Church, Natalie Polly, taught the younger ladies how to make these delicious works of kitchen art, she baked them wherever we lived (which was many places!). Folks always asked for more. Mrs. Polly indicated that she was doing this in obedience to Paul's admonition to Titus [2:4] to teach the older women to train the younger ones. That was back in the 1970s. These became a very popular item at the Three Hills Farmer's Market. A couple people came every Tuesday to pick up enough for the whole work crew at their shop. One lady said she would have been in serious trouble if she did not do this.

Start this recipe after supper. The dough rises over night and you bake the buns the next morning. First, make the syrup so it can cool before you use it.

In a large bowl dissolve 1½ cups sugar and 4 cups warm water. Add 1²/₃ cups milk, 3 beaten eggs, 2 tbsp salt, then 1 tbsp regular yeast (not instant). Stir, then right away add flour until you have a workable dough. Knead it until smooth and it does not stick to the mixing bowl. Let rise for one hour twice, punch down each time, then after a third hour put into pans and let it rise overnight.

For this much dough you need four 11 x 16 inch pans having sides of 2 or more inches high. First, slather margarine in bottom of pans. Then divide the *cooled* syrup between the 4 pans.

Syrup for buns: 1½ cups sugar, 1½ cups brown sugar, 3 cups hot water, and sprinkle of salt.

Divide dough in 2, then roll out in a large rectangle on a table about 10 x 20 inches. Smear lots of brown sugar and sprinkle on cinnamon. Roll up dough, divide each in half, then cut each half into 10 pieces. Arrange 10 pieces in a pan, leaving lots of room to rise. Let rise overnight. Then at about 8:00 AM, bake at 350° for about 15 to 18 minutes. Turn out on racks, bottom side up.

Swedish Tea Ring (A sweet dough always sold out at Christmas FM)

		Half Recipe
Milk, warm	1$^1/_3$ cup	¾ cup
Canola oil	$^2/_3$ cup	$^1/_3$ cup
Sugar	½ cup	¼ cup
Salt	2 tbsp	1 tbsp
Water	¾ cup	>½ cup
Eggs	2	1
Yeast	1$^1/_3$ tbsp	<½ tbsp
Flour, unbleached	4 to 5 cups	2 to 2½

Knead 9 minutes, let rise 3 times for 15 minutes. Roll out into 2 squares, spread with soft margarine, sugar, cinnamon and 1 cup glazed fruit. Form into 2 rolls, and let rise 60 minutes. Bake at 350° for 24 minutes. Turn in oven half way through. *Watch carefully!* Slather with almond flavoured icing. (Freezes well but do not ice until thawed.)

Waffles (whole wheat buttermilk)

3 eggs, separated
½ cup cooking oil
2 cups buttermilk
2 cups whole wheat flour

1 tbsp sugar
2 tbsp baking powder
1 tsp soda
1 tsp salt

Blend egg yolks, oil and buttermilk. Combine dry ingredients and sift into liquid mixture. Mix only until smooth. Beat egg whites till they peak and gently fold into batter.

Loaf, Cake, Muffins and Cookies

Zucchini Loaf (A favourite of Arnold's. The chocolate makes zucchini very edible!)

3 eggs, beaten	1 tsp salt
2 cups sugar	1 tsp soda
1 cup oil	2 cups grated zucchini
1 tsp vanilla	3 cups flour
3 tsp cinnamon	1 tsp baking powder
Optional: ½ cup walnuts, ½ cup dates	

Add cocoa for a chocolate flavour and a package of chocolate chips. Bake at 325° for 50 to 60 minutes. Yields two large loaves.

Crunchy Coffee Cake (Merle Holloway)

¼ cup sugar	¼ tsp nutmeg
2 cups flour	$^1/_3$ cup margarine
2 tsp baking powder	1 cup milk
1 tsp cinnamon	2 eggs

Topping:

$^2/_3$ cup brown sugar	2 tbsp butter or margarine
2 tbsp flour	1 cup walnuts

Make topping first. Combine brown sugar, flour, cut in butter to resemble corn meal. Add chopped nuts. Chill until ready to use. Mix together the first five ingredients. Add margarine and milk then beat a minute and a half (or 225 strokes) with electric mixer on low speed until ingredients are blended. Add eggs and beat another minute and a half. Pour one third of this batter into an 8 x 8 inch baking pan, with bottom greased. Sprinkle one third of topping over batter in pan, then cover with remaining batter. Sprinkle remaining topping. Bake in 350° for 35 to 40 minutes. Best served warm.

Morning Glory Muffins (One of Betty's and my favourites, very moist and tasty)

6 eggs	1 cup chopped nuts
2½ cups sugar	2 cups grated apples
2 cups oil	4 tsp soda
4 cups grated carrots	1 tsp salt
1 cup coconut	4 tsp cinnamon
1 cup raisins	4 cups flour

Mix all ingredients and bake for 20 minutes in a 375° oven. One quarter of recipe makes 6 muffins.

Pineapple Carrot Muffins (Lil Stauffer Nobert)

1 cup sugar	½ tsp salt
²/₃ cup oil	3 tsp cinnamon
2 large eggs, beaten	1 tsp vanilla
1½ cups flour	1 cup grated carrots
1 tsp baking powder	1 cup crushed pineapple (with juice)
1 tsp baking soda	

In a large bowl combine sugar, oil, beaten eggs. Mix in flour, baking powder and soda, salt and cinnamon. Add carrots, pineapple with juice, vanilla. Bake at 350° for 20 minutes. Serve with cheese. Makes about 18 muffins.

Rhubarb Cake (Merle Holloway)

½ cup cooking oil	1 cup brown sugar
2 eggs	1 tsp vanilla
½ tsp salt	1 cup milk
2 cups rhubarb, uncooked,	2 cups plus 1 tbsp flour
chopped fine	1 tsp baking soda

Cream oil and sugar. Beat in eggs and vanilla. Add dry ingredients alternately with milk. Add rhubarb last. Pour into 9 x 12 inch pan then frost – spread evenly – with uncooked mixture of 2 tbsp margarine, ½ cup brown sugar, 1 tsp cinnamon, 1 tsp, 1 tsp vanilla, ½ cup whole pecans. Bake at 350° for 45 minutes. Serve hot with vanilla ice cream.

Jumbo Raisin Cookies (Todd loved these)

Add 1 cup water to 2 cups raisins. Boil 5 minutes and cool.

Cream: 1 cup shortening (margarine) with 2 cups sugar. Add 3 eggs and 1 tsp vanilla. Beat well.

Add the following items to the first mixture.

4 cups flour	1½ tsp cinnamon
1 tsp baking powder	½ tsp nutmeg
1 tsp soda	¼ tsp allspice
2 tsp salt	

Add one cup of flour at a time. Mix other items in with first cup of flour. Drop on cookie sheet. Bake at 350° for about 12 minutes.

Pie Crust. (Another of Betty's specialties. She made the flakiest pie crust you could imagine!)

In a large bowl measure the following items and mix together until well blended. Add 1½ cups cold water. Mix thoroughly. Store in fridge or freeze as desired until use.

8 cups flour, 1 tbsp salt, 1 tbsp baking powder, 3 tbsp sugar, 1½ lbs margarine (room temperature), ½ lb lard

Candy and Apple Butter

Fudge ~ Chocolate (One of Betty's specialties)

1 cup white sugar	½ cup whipping cream
1 cup brown sugar	1 tsp vanilla
¼ cup Rogers Golden Syrup	2 tbsp butter
2 tbsp cocoa	

Mix sugar and cocoa well, squishing any lumps. Add syrup and cream. Mix, bring to a boil on medium heat. Boil to soft ball stage. Do NOT stir while doing so. Remove from heat, add butter; and vanilla. Beat with an electric mixer until fudge is creamy and loses it shine. Pour into buttered 7 x7 inch pan or a small pie plate. Cool and cut while still soft. If it is hard, you have either boiled or beaten it too long. Pretend there are only a few calories and enjoy!

Fudge ~ Maple Cream

This is an all-time Stauffer family favourite. Betty made it and the Chocolate Fudge every Christmas for almost 50 years.

2 cups brown sugar	1 tsp vanilla
¼ cup Rogers Golden Syrup	2 tbsp butter
½ cup whipping cream	pinch of salt

Mix sugar, syrup, cream and salt in heavy saucepan. Bring to a boil over medium heat to the soft ball stage. Do NOT stir. Remove from heat, add butter and vanilla. Beat until it is creamy and starts to hold its shape and loses its shine. Pour over buttered dish. Cool and cut while still a bit soft.

Betty's note: Good for those who do not enjoy chocolate as much as some of us.

Arnold's note: I like to put a chocolate and maple cream together – one on top of the other – and get a new taste sensation. My Mother used to put two fudges together and call it black and white fudge.

Apple Butter

4 quarts crab apples	¼ teaspoon cloves
2 ¾ cups sugar	$1/_8$ teaspoon salt
2 ¾ teaspoons cinnamon	

Quarter, core and remove stems and flower ends of crab apples. Cook in a minimum amount (½ to 1 cup) of water, until soft. Put through a colander used to make apple sauce. Put the applesauce with the rest of the ingredients in a crock pot. Cook on high for 3 hours, then on low for 5 to 8 hours until it is thick and dark. Stir occasionally. Seal in canning jars. NOTE: We have a large crab apple tree in our back yard with flavourful and sweet fruit that make very tasty butter.

Main Dish & Pie

Spinach Lasagna (no boil)

1 tbsp oil
1 medium onion chopped
1 clove garlic minced
1 lb ground beef
2 cans (14 ounce) tomato sauce
1 can (10 ounce) sliced mushrooms
½ cup water
1 tsp oregano
1 cup cottage cheese

1 10 ounce frozen chopped spinach, thawed
1 egg slightly beaten
2 tsp vegetable oil
1 tsp salt
6 ounce package sliced mozzarella cheese
375 g (half package) uncooked lasagna

Sauté onion and garlic in oil. Add beef and brown then remove excess fat. Add tomato sauce, mushrooms with liquid, water, and oregano, and bring to a boil. In bowl combine cottage cheese, Parmesan cheese, drained spinach, egg, oil and salt. Spoon one third of this sauce into 9 x 13 inch pan and cover with one third of the lasagna, spread $^1/_3$ of sauce then $^1/_3$ of lasagna. Add cheese/spinach mixture, then remaining lasagna and sauce. Top with cheese slices. Cover with foil and bake at 375° for 45 minutes. Uncover and bake another 15 minutes till cheese starts to brown.

Todd likes this recipe with only ½ pound beef and 2 layers of lasagna. We probably had this dish hundreds of times. Layer as shown here:

     mozzarella cheese
     rest of meat sauce
     noodles
     cottage cheese mixture
     noodles
     layer of meat sauce

Lemon Sour Cream Pie

1 cup sugar
¼ cup cornstarch
½ teaspoon salt
1 cup milk
3 egg yolks, beaten
¼ cup butter
¼ cup fresh lemon juice
1 teaspoon grated lemon peel
1 cup sour cream
1 pastry shell, 9 inch baked

Meringue

3 egg whites
½ teaspoon vanilla
¼ teaspoon cream of tartar

6 tablespoons sugar

In a saucepan, combine sugar, cornstarch and salt. Gradually stir in milk. Bring to a boil over medium heat, stirring constantly. Cook and stir 2 minutes. Blend a small amount into beaten egg yolks and mix well. Return all to pan. Mix well. Cook and stir 2 minutes. Remove from heat; add butter, lemon juice and peel. Mix well and set aside

Meringue. Beat egg whites with a clean beater until foamy. Add vanilla and cream of tartar. Add sugar one tablespoon at a time, beating until stiff peaks form. Set aside.

Fold sour cream into lemon mixture. Pour into pastry shell. Cover with meringue, sealing to edges of pastry. Bake at 350 degrees for 12 to 15 minutes, or until golden. Completely cool and store in fridge.

Appendix Three

Arnold & Gloria's Love Poems

G loria and I had so much fun and excitement writing these poems and notes to each other that we decided to share the fun with you. Sure, it's personal lovey-dove expressions of our love, but you can borrow them if they might forward your love relationship. Enjoy.

He is My New Love! I Weep for Happiness!
Facebook Messages, June 17
Gloria.
♥ OH ARNIE BABY I LOVE YOUR SWEET PROTECTIVE COVERING YOU PROVIDE FOR ME. THANK YOU FOR YOUR LOVE. CERTAINLY SENT FROM ABOVE. . .INTO EACH OTHER WE COMMIT OURSELVES WITHOUT REGRET. HAPPY FATHERS DAY TO THE MOST WONDERFUL MAN. . . if love does have wings then catch it and hold it to your heart, my sweet sweet man. ♥ your G.L.O.R.I.A.

Gloria. June 30. **You said**, "I desperately need a woman to keep me together. Will you by My Woman, Sweets? My Woman forever and ever? Do you have enough love to make that happen?"

I said, "Oh. . .YES!!! I am she!!! Hang on to your hat my love while we whirl thru space. Our love is a craft made for speed!! This poem is from my devotions this a.m.

Come My Love
 Your love calls to me,
 It fills my once empty heart.
 Becoming to my soul to "come take part."
 My soul answers, "yes!"
 I am here for you.
 Just the thought of you fulfills my secret desires.

I answer "I do."
My attention you have, no turning away
. . .drawing me. . .drawing me never to part.
Oh how I bask in the warmth of your love,
Cradling me to your bosom, our hearts beat as one.
Come my love, come!

My Man, My Love

Oh God. . .you promised to bring me a mate!
Longingly I've waited by my garden gate.
Oh suddenly swings open the gate to my heart!
There you are ~ my love! We shall never part!

My love is tall, like a cedar you stand.
Strong, protective a true man.
My heart yearns for my love's embrace,
He stepped forward touching my face.

My Gift, Just for You (Gloria)

Thank you my King!
You held out your scepter to bring love to me,
I bow before you on bended knees.

You my King remembered me
With my heartfelt prayers, my petitions.
You my King remembered my soulful renditions.

Never once did you turn away
When I approached into your Throne room.
It took great courage to stand before you.
Your love surrounded me boldly.

Yet, I held.
Yet, I stood.
You've had nothing but sweetness and grace from above.
You bid me to stand,
While you anointed me anew. . .you said,
"I have someone just for you."
"I've searched my kingdom to and fro. . .
Only one man stands out, he is made just for you."

Oh, I see him!!
He is my new love!!
I weep with happiness!
Thank you my King for such a man.

He is everything I could ever hope for,
Everything from your hand.

Arnold's Response: To Take, to Pick and to See

To
my house you brought a well of joy;
my heart you sparked alive my boy.
To
my ears the music of your laugh;
my bod your touch's more than enough.

Take
my love returned to you right now
my heart so full to you I allow

Pick
me every day from this point on
whatever's in my power you have won.

See!
our love will not grow old or stale.
our hearts entwined. Wow! What a tale!

Gloriaous, I woke this am thinking about you as I pretty much do 24/7 and these first four lines popped into my head. So I got up and opened my MacBook and wrote the rest. You have awakened something in my soul that methinks laid dormant for the past 70 years. I have attempted a few poems over the years but they have always been hard work. For you they just flow like fresh stream water over the falls. So I am sitting here with Emma drinking a cup of freshly brewed coffee, talking to you, 2,000 miles away. (Now don't get your shirt in a knot – Emma is our motor home. I call her Emma cuz she was purchased with my inheritance money from Mother.)

It is cold windy and raining, as it has been all evening and through the night. There is some concern that the river might rise up and flood the camp ground because of the rain and heavier than usual recent snow in the mountains. The run off from it could show up today. They did get some flooding here several years ago. Don't think I have to worry though, but those with tents may.

I sure did thoroughly enjoy our telephone conversation last evening, the talk of our "kindred spirits" – all the common interests we will explore in the hours and days and years ahead. In the kitchen, the living room, the dining room, and bedroom, the garden, on the walking path and park bench, in the Grand Caravan and with Emma, and in our woodart studio, we will create wonderful poetry of love and art to completely meld our hearts and lives together, and some to share with and inspire the whole world. Come to me My Love. Every room in my house, my studio and garden, my heart and every part of my soul and being eagerly awaits your arrival.

Lovingly longing to complete our love, your forever-yours Arnold.

Forever (Arnold)

I dream of you at night
And shiver with delight;
And even in the light
Though you are out of sight.

You bring to face a smile
And there it stays awhile.
I sure would walk a mile
To see your blue eyed smile.

Why in my heart you woke
A fire you know to stoke.
You love this Northern Bloke
In it he loves to soak!

And even when I'm tired
My 'drenaline is fired.
So soon my heart you mired
In deepest love desired.

I'm here for you forever.
To come and go wherever.
No thing will ever sever --
Our love will be forever.

Come My Love (Gloria, July 6)

My lover, my soul-mate
Come and dip your cup into the deepness
Of cool refreshing waters of my well.
You shall never leave with thirst,
No matter how often you visit and drink.
Drink deep my love, drink deep.

Love is effervescent,
Alive and bubbling over to the brim for you.
Come my love, come.
Drink deep and ever deeper.

A Love Beyond Compare (Arnold)

You say your love is deep as a well
But how could that be, I wonder,
Even as it makes my heart swell?
And then I also have to stop and ponder.

266

Why you also have to pause and ask,
How come that I can love you so.
Maybe we both have taken off our mask
So that we could be each other's beau.

We found in the other what we sought.
A deeply loving caring human being.
We both are wont to touch a lot;
A common loving language we're feeling.

So many things we dearly want to share;
We walk a path together that's the same
And want for each the other to be fair.
Always open, no secrets to name.

We've found in each other what we sought
So why should we wonder how this could be?
Let's just love and love and love a lot
And thank our Lord for his gift to you and me.

After all we asked the Lord in prayer
For a mate that was all that we want.
He gave us such a love beyond compare
A wondrous gift we never will recant.

This morning I think about how much I love you and of your passionate love for me. A magical mystery. It's a wonder, that places me in a continual state of wonderment, that your love for me is beyond compare – deep and full and bubbling over with compassion. To have such unusual love of a woman I count as an extraordinary privilege that seldom can be discovered on this planet. I revel in it moment by moment, every day. You have given me a precious gift that cannot be measured, that will not be weighed, which no one will ever count or assess. Because it's ensconced deep in my mind, enwrapping my soul and embedded in my body, where I and only I can experience and treasure its depth. Beyond measurement. Deep inside, yet it always bubbles over in my smiles, my chatter with others, and my shivers of delight when I dream you near and warm and snuggling, of holding you hand, kissing your lovely lips, of our love applied. Your desire for me has pushed me into an unpracticed level of deep joy and continuous excitement. You've flamed my soul, inspired my mind and energized my body. I love you, Gloriaous! Your lovely gift in me and before me and around me, I plan to invest the rest of my life slowly, with care and mutual enjoyment unwrap this precious treasure of yourself.

Email: June 17, 2012
Baby, this came to me while in prayer this morning. It was purposed for the Lord and then the thought came to me that it is meant for you too.

You help me to keep fresh and new;
you help me to keep my eyes lifted up looking at you;
How can I describe the way you bring such feelings of love?
Man cannot explain it. . .only you.

Your words are my life-blood, there is nothing else to
sustain me, but you.

When I have mis-spoken, my heart feels broken
until you hold me and have spoken
tender words soothing falling over me like sweet oil;

Peace shall reign in my soul forever,
my waiting finished when we're together.
💜 your gloria

Gloria to Arnie: September 4, 2012

Your tender expression
Your sweet embrace,
There could never be another place,
A place I would rather be
In your hand you hold the key
My heart was locked tightly it held,
Until one day when it fell,
Fell into the bottomless well of sweet love's calling. . .calling me ever still,
"Come, come, go away with me,
We will hold tightly as we go on this new destiny."
God's light is before us, the past behind,
Our two hearts forever entwined.
This journey's blessings unwrapping each new day, gifts from God above,
Kissed with his great love.

Appendix Four

Books to Help You Grieve Christianly

With comments adapted from the covers of each book

No author. 2010. *God Comforts You: Promises for Life*. Minneapolis: Summerside Press.

Warm, heartfelt expressions of wisdom and faith help give words to the prayers of your heart. Encouraging thoughts, accompanied by related Bible verses, share God's tender comfort and peace.

Bauman, Harold. 1999. *How do I Live Through Grief? Strength and Hope in Time of Loss*. Uhrichville, Ohio: Barbour Publishing, Inc.

Sooner or later grief comes to everyone. We can't really understand it until we walk through it ourselves. But grief has a common patter, and it helps if we know what to expect. As we make our way through the stages of grief, we will learn—with God's help—to live again. This practical, helpful book shares the special comfort and hope that the Christian faith has to offer, pointing the way to healing and new life.

Miller, James E. 2000. *Seasons of Grief and Healing: A Guide for Those Who Mourn*. Minneapolis: Augsburg.

A thoughtful, compassionate guide for anyone who has lost a loved one. Miller brings understanding and renewal to times of grief. It's a compa ssionate exploration of feelings and experiences, with inspiring reflections from the Bible, poetry and great literature. You will find simple, affirming activities to help you move through seasons of grief at their own pace and in their own way.

Mitsch, Raymond R. & Lynn Brookside. 1993. *Grieving the Loss of Someone You Love: Daily Meditations to Help You through the Grieving Process*. Ventura, California: Regal Books.

Few losses are as painful as the death of someone close. No valley is as vast as grief, no journey as personal and life-changing. The authors shine a light on the road through grief. They can help you endure the anguish; understand the stages of grief; sort through the emotions of anger, guilt, fear and depression; and face the God who allowed you to lose someone you love. A series of thoughtful daily devotions giving you wisdom, insight, and comfort that will help you through and beyond your grief.

AUTHOR'S NOTE: For me this book of 70 short meditations was by far the most helpful. Pithy, insightful, and to the point, they spoke to all of my issues, and helped me turn the pages to the next one. The writers answer your questions, not always the answer I was looking for, but they helped me move on.

Shepson, Charles W. 1996. *From My Grieving Heart to Yours*. Kearney, NE: Morris Publishing.

The devotionals in this book are designed to encourage and uplift the person who has lost a spouse or someone else dear to him or her. They were written during the period of deep grieving which followed the death of his dearly loved wife, Elaine. "He understands just how you feel," say those who have used these readings during their own trek through the valley of the Shadow of Death.

Other books to help you deal with trouble, pain and tragedy

Alcorn, Randy. 2009. *If God is Good: Faith in the Midst of Suffering and Evil*. New York: Multnomah Books.

Cymbala, Jim. 2001. *God's Grace from Ground Zero: Seeking God's Heart for the Future of our World*. Grand Rapids: Zondervan.

Lucado, Max. 1991. *In the Eye of the Storm: A day in the Life of Jesus*. Dallas: Word Publishing.

Lucado, Max. 1996. *In the Grip of Grace: You can't Fall Beyond his Love*. Dallas: Word Publishing.

Mann, Gerald. 1992. *When the Bad Times are over for Good: Transforming Trouble into Triumph*. Brentwood, Tennessee: Wolgemuth & Hyatt Publishers, Inc.

Martin, Catherine. 2007. *Walking with the God who Cares: Finding Hope When you Need it Most*. Eugene, Oregon: Harvest House Publishers.

McManus, Erwin Raphael. 2002. *Seizing your Divine Moment: Dare to Live a Life of Adventure*. Nashville: Thomas Nelson Publishers.

Stanley, Charles. 2001. *When Tragedy Strikes*. Nashville: Thomas Nelson, Inc.

Yancey, Phillip. 2000. *Reaching for the Invisible God: What can we expect to find?* Mandaluyong City, Metro Manila: OMF Literature Inc.

CPSIA information can be obtained at www.ICGtesting.com
Printed in the USA
LVOW02s1944030214

372140LV00001B/1/P